To Anne a;

May God bless you

and Keep you

and Keep you

forever!

[signature]

March 2012

MAKING GOD LAUGH

THE STORY OF MY LIFE

GREGORY
JOHN
ANDREWS

INFINITY
PUBLISHING

Copyright © 2011 by Gregory John Andrews

Front: Looking through Mesa Arch, Island in the Sky, Canyonlands National Park, Utah.
Back: Along the Steese Highway, northeast of Fairbanks, Alaska.
Title: Grand Teton National Park, Wyoming.

ISBN 0-7414-6485-3

Printed in the United States of America

Published March 2011

INFINITY PUBLISHING
1094 New DeHaven Street, Suite 100
West Conshohocken, PA 19428-2713
Toll-free (877) BUY BOOK
Local Phone (610) 941-9999
Fax (610) 941-9959
Info@buybooksontheweb.com
www.buybooksontheweb.com

CONTENTS

REVVING UP

If you want to make God laugh, tell him your plans.
That's the premise of this little book. It works every time.
I ought to know. Read on, you'll see what I mean.

Growing up I remember seeing the sign below. It made quite an impression on me because the sign painter obviously failed to heed his own advice. If you like to plan ahead, good for you. Good luck with that. In the long run, it doesn't really matter. Life is what happens when you're making other plans.

We all make God laugh once in a while. He's not laughing at us. He's just laughing, hoping we'll do the same. Better to laugh than to pout. Better to give God a good laugh than to make him cry. Laughing is good.

God's ways are not our ways. That's for sure. The Lord works in mysterious ways. Indeed he does. Man proposes but God disposes. My story proves that. Yours does too. Look at your life and you'll see. That's all the preaching you're going to get from me. So read on, and laugh a little.

Thanks to George Zeller, Vicki Wells-Bedard, and Mike Lydon for their constant encouragement and advice, and to Joshua Welsh for reviewing my work. This book is dedicated to my mother and father, Louann Ehret Andrews and Carroll Thomas Andrews. Without their love, there would be no story.

Gregory John Andrews   March 2011

I AT THE STARTING LINE

According to the IRS, I've reached the age where I can start taking money out of my IRA instead of just putting it in. What matters more to me, at sixty, is being able to say it's been a wonderful life – already. People who've loved me, of course, have been reason number one. Being able to go places has been another. For the most part, it's kept me sane. From the time I was a child, I've loved to travel. I always will. I'm told my first sentence was "Baby go bye-bye!" Ever seen a dog with its head stuck out a car window and a big smile on its face? That's me. Just thinking about going somewhere gets me excited. And I've gone places, as you'll see.

The first trip I ever took was home from Mercy Hospital. That was in Toledo in 1950. Being my parents' first child, I must have been something of a disappointment to them, coming into the world with my feet pointed in. Somehow they got me into plaster casts before I was a day old, so I'd be able to stumble through life like everyone else later on. I stayed that way for the first eight months of my life, wearing orthopedic shoes and braces for a year or so after that. In spite of this, in my mother's words, I was "good-natured, had a pleasant smile and fine sense of humor almost from birth, and was such a happy baby." Mom was a creative writer too. On my parents' first wedding anniversary, thirteen days old, I was baptized.

Mom and Dad met – where else? – at church. Having survived the attack on Pearl Harbor and led a dance band around Europe in the Army Air Corps during World War II, Dad was the organist at Sacred Heart Parish in east Toledo. He was also a staff composer at the Gregorian Institute of America – later GIA Publications – named, as I was, after Pope St. Gregory the Great.

The first trip I can barely remember, when I was three or four years old, was from Toledo to Milwaukee. This was more like a pilgrimage to visit the honorable ancestors, a

1

trip we made at least once a year to visit Grandma Andrews and her sisters. It was in a black 1950 Ford sedan, it was in winter, and it was cold. We were driving through Chicago in a blizzard when Dad hit a tree stump close to the curb, launching me into the windshield. My head trauma began there. In those early years, I had to have the bridge of my nose stitched up after hitting the headboard while jumping on my parents' bed. At some point I also fell out of my little red wagon in the garage while standing on it, trying to reach something I wasn't supposed to have. I still keep reaching for things I'm not supposed to have. My sister Julie was born when I was two.

We moved to west Toledo in 1955 where the first of my twenty-one years of Catholic education began. Ladyfield Kindergarten was run by the Sisters of Notre Dame. My mother's aunt and namesake, Sister Mary Louann Ehret, was secretary of the Toledo province. After I was born, those nuns prayed long and hard for me to then-Blessed Julie Billiart, their foundress and my sister's patron saint. On the first day of school, I'm told I asked: "Sister, what are we going to do with these kids?" Most five-year-olds haven't developed a take-charge attitude, but I had. I got to conduct the kindergarten orchestra. I learned how to read music and started taking piano lessons. That continued most of the way through grade school. Then Dad taught me how to play the organ – with two hands and two feet. My brother Mark was added to the family.

After kindergarten at Ladyfield, I spent the next eight years at Blessed Sacrament School, where the Adrian Dominican Sisters got their turn with me. My Dad, Carroll, was music director of the parish, and Mom was school secretary. We lived in a parish house. What can I say? My life, like my parents' lives, revolved around the Catholic Church. Dad's being a prominent composer of church music brought me into contact with even more priests and sisters, many of whom came to our home. As a kid, I got to know the parish priests and nuns better than most. I still remember their names and faces. A few fell by the wayside even in those days, so I knew they were human, but they were still larger than life. My parents held them in esteem, so I did too. Besides, they liked me. I sometimes think I could do no wrong in their sight. I liked the attention. I knew I had an inside track. I learned later that this did not particularly endear me to my younger siblings or to my classmates. I also learned that when you're regarded as the perfect child by your elders, you start behaving as though you are, and then you have to keep it up.

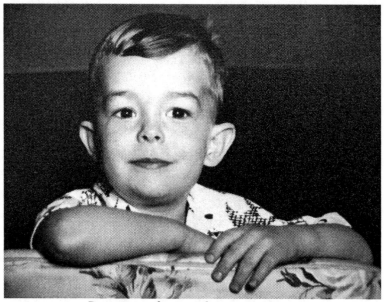

Dreaming of going places at age two.

Two childhood traumas come to mind. Always eager to please, I had done something helpful for my second grade teacher, Miss Beneteau. She promised to take me out for a spaghetti dinner – still my favorite food – as a reward. I was all excited and ready to go. She cancelled. It broke my heart. I cried and cried. I couldn't understand how a promise could be broken. I guess it had never happened to me before. As it turned out, I discovered life could go on. When I was about ten, I rode my bike up to the neighborhood market to get something. A group of boys, bullies, came along and started taunting me. They threatened to 'pants' me – take my pants – and steal my bike. Again, I cried. They were pleased. Nothing actually happened, but I recall being terrified at the threat. I always felt safe at home. I can't imagine what it must be like not to.

So many memories of grade school I treasure to this day. I fell off a ladder trying to put an angel on top of the Christmas tree in first grade. On my way to church to 'marry' my second-grade girlfriend, MaryAnn Overcamp, Richard Dudley gave her a bloody nose with a snowball. For five dollars, the Holy Childhood Association let me ransom my very own 'pagan baby' and name him. Playing Juan Diego in a fifth-grade version of the miracle of Guadalupe, I got to pick roses in the snow. My writing career began editing the school newspaper with three girls in my eighth grade class, and my science project on optical illusions ended up on display in the Toledo Zoological Museum. I loved Cub Scouts, and reading library books all summer long. To this day I'm in touch with my fifth grade teacher and my second-grade betrothed.

Growing up in Toledo wasn't hard for me. I was brought into the world by two devoted and affectionate parents of German ancestry, and blessed with three younger siblings I teased a lot. Mom was an only child. Dad, now ninety-two, came from a broken home. Consequently, I hardly ever saw my only uncle or my cousins. I never knew my grandfathers since they both died young, but my grandmothers made up for it. I remember the excitement of going down to pick Grandma Andrews up at the train station. I used to ride my bike to Grandma Ehret's bungalow to mow the lawn. I even remember my great grandmother we called "Little Grandma." These three devout women played a big part in my early life. My parents undoubtedly made a lot of sacrifices to have and to raise four kids. Family life was good. We weren't the Holy Family by any means, but we were about as Catholic as you could get. Though my siblings and I were occasionally at each other's throats as brothers and sisters are wont to do, Mom and Dad never were. For sure, Dad never failed to let us know exactly what he felt and thought. The apple didn't fall far from the tree in this regard. Mom always provided the moderating influence our family needed.

The house I grew up in I remember well. Dad wired every room in it for hi-fi sound. I can still smell the chemicals he used to develop film and print black-and-white photos in the makeshift darkroom in the basement. A case of Stroh's beer was a fixture, and whenever Dad had a bottle, I would get a shot glass. I can still smell the cabbage we fermented in crocks to make sauerkraut. We all had to help clean the house on Saturday. Dad baked bread every week. He still does today, though not as often. My sisters still make the Christmas cookies Mom made. Observing my parents from the time I could see over the kitchen counter is how I learned to cook. Spaghetti with meat sauce is my signature dish. Many nights we'd cook out on the fireplace Dad built in the back yard, and say prayers at the shrine he made for Mary. We passed endless hours on the swings and teeter-totters and climbing the monkey bars at Close Park a block away. Neighbors visited each other in those days, and parents didn't have to watch their kids like hawks. Mom and Dad enjoyed sixty years together, watching the family they started grow well into adulthood.

As for the car trips we took, most were to family re-unions in Sandusky and Shelby, Ohio, and to lakeside beaches and parks in Michigan and Ohio. As a child I was traumatized by a crawfish that pinched me, and for a while – after being forced to jump into the deep end of a pool – I was afraid of water over my head. I'll never forget seeing Niagara Falls for the first time, or visiting Mammoth Cave or the Luray Caverns in Virginia. Riding the roller coasters at Cedar Point, driving antique cars at Greenfield Village, catching perch in Lake Erie, crossing the Mackinaw Bridge and going through the locks at Sault Sainte Marie, visiting the Benedictine abbeys at Collegeville, Minnesota, and Latrobe, Pennsylvania, touring the breweries and the zoo in Milwaukee, boating on the Wisconsin Dells, and climbing the steeple at Holy Hill were all childhood thrills. When I was twelve, I flew with my friend Mark Lazar in his dad's small plane to Cleveland where we saw Roger Maris and the New York Yankees play baseball into the night. A bobble-headed Cleveland Indian doll came home with me. I was a happy kid.

Closer to home I loved taking the bus downtown on Saturday mornings to the Toledo Museum of Art where children from all over the city gathered. We explored every part of it, guided by local artists who then helped us learn how to work with the particular medium we had examined – clay, oil, metal, wood, chalk, and then some. I kept this up for five years, so much did I enjoy it. My sister Julie came too and now paints in watercolors. It took another forty years before I started painting in acrylics, but that's another story. The last couple of years we lived in Toledo, our family spent much of the summer around the Olympic-sized pool at a swim Club where I improved my water skills.

On Sunday afternoons we'd often visit relatives or the nuns or family graves at the cemetery, careful to steer clear of mausoleums – 'spook houses' we called them – and stopping for frozen custard on the way back. As a boy, I can recall the smell of printer's ink and the thunder of the presses where Dad worked, going with him to pipe organ concerts, and when I was old enough, turning pages for him when he played graduations at Bowling Green State University. Building snow forts and flooding the backyard to make a skating rink provided tireless winter fun. Growing up up north, who can forget snowball fights and acorn fights? We couldn't wait for summer to put cardboard wings on our bikes. I could jump on a pogo stick for half an hour without falling off. I'll never live down breaking four windows at the neighbor's house next door in one fell swoop on a pair of stilts. When I was ten, I ran up and down Grantwood Drive to tell the neighbors I had a new baby sister, Beth. You could get a hamburger at McDonald's for fifteen cents. My family had to run for cover in the basement when the Palm Sunday tornados tore up our neighborhood in 1965. Dad was away the day President Kennedy was shot, so I had to toll the church bell from the organ console. By eighth grade I had begun playing the organ, even singing the propers in Latin, at Mass on weekdays. Already a choir boy and an altar boy, I became a commentator at Sunday Mass when changes in the liturgy were introduced in 1964. By then I had become a full-fledged church brat.

Possessing a fair degree of native intelligence, I was for the most part a nerd in high school. I certainly looked the part, getting braces at thirteen and glasses at fourteen. Apparently I acted the part as well, chipping my front tooth on the gatepost in the backyard, and cutting the back of my head open going down a waterslide on my knees. Nevertheless, I survived my first year of high school at St. Francis de Sales, run by the Oblates, in Toledo. My public education was limited to a typing course at Start High School in Toledo, and later, driver's education at Dixie Hollins High School in St. Petersburg. During the summer of 1967, I spent two weeks studying photo journalism at the University of Florida in Gainesville – making me an honorary 'Gator' – before becoming editor of Bishop Barry's yearbook. That took up most of my senior year, though I played the organ on Sundays at Sacred Heart Parish in Pinellas Park. As graduation approached, I had to make a decision. Studying engineering was popular in those days but didn't appeal to me. Almost by default – and because I knew it would make a lot of people happy – the seminary did.

Did I mention that my family moved to Florida when I was fifteen? Dad's signing on as Director of Music for the Diocese of St. Augustine affected all our futures. The Catholic Church has never stopped affecting mine. I once got to meet the legendary Archbishop of St. Augustine, Joseph P. Hurley. Small in stature, this pioneering hierarch possessed great foresight for the Church in Florida, but was regarded as impulsive and autocratic by most priests and hence feared. When he asked me what grade I was in, I said, "I'm a sophomore." Then he said, "Well, don't be!" The dictionary later yielded the true meaning of 'sophomore' –

foolish, silly, conceited, overconfident. That advice made a lasting impression.

Leaving all things familiar behind wasn't my idea, but I must admit being intrigued by the mystique of Florida. Mom had to make the biggest sacrifice of all, leaving the place she had spent all forty years of her life. On the trip south, I remember eating grits for the first time in Macon, Georgia, and not understanding why there were separate bathrooms for blacks and whites at a gas station where Interstate 75 ended at Floral City. Moving into a new model home, we discovered our back yard was a giant sand lot. It was June, so it was hot, but the beaches were gorgeous, and I've loved them ever since. Fort Desoto was our favorite. We made a few trips as a family back to Toledo after that, but Florida quickly came to be home. I missed a few friends, especially a girl from eighth grade, Eileen Wagner, with whom I had begun to enjoy sharing time, music and art.

More often than not, I rode my bike to my new high school in St. Petersburg. It's safe to say a jock I was not, nor was I a fighter. Only once do I remember getting punched and seeing stars. Nor was I much of a ladies' man. Going to two all-boys high schools clearly retarded my social life. I hated to dance, and I'm still no good at it. Nevertheless, Mom fixed me up on a few dates and pushed me out the door. Not yet having developed a rebellious attitude, I can only recall skipping a single day of high school for a road trip in my friend's Barracuda to Daytona where we rented mopeds to drive on the beach. Dad taught music appreciation at Bishop Barry. My sketching ability won me a fifty dollar savings bond. French club was my favorite activity. I also enjoyed debating, chess, and occasionally smoking a pipe with my friends. I remember a ride around town with my art history teacher, Sam Burton Rosevear, and his wife in his tiny MG. A local artist, Sam had also come from Toledo. An adult I could easily talk to, he considered me his seventh son. We stayed friends for many years, warming a few bar stools and smoking a few cigars along the way. I still treasure the native Florida scenes he painted and gave me.

I also recall trying to solve the mystery of where my English teacher lived. Always impeccably dressed, this little man wore lifts in his shoes to make himself look taller. Once while working on the yearbook, he pulled a *Playboy* magazine out of his desk and tried to get me to look at it. I have no idea why he did, but it made me uncomfortable. I remember ninth grade, before moving to Florida, best – learning how to wrestle, riding to school in the rear-facing seat of a Vista Cruiser listening to the Beatles on the radio, the bass drum of the school band pounding in my chest, having to wear a freshman beanie and getting bopped on the head by upperclassmen. Academically, I did very well in high school. But looking back, I spent too much time on studies. I wish I had made more friends, and I didn't have much fun.

After graduating from high school in 1968, I spent the next two summers as a counselor at Our Lady of Good Counsel Camp in Floral City. It was a blast. Basically a big brother to the ten-year-old boys in my cabin, I was in charge of the handicraft lodge. Drinking bug juice, paddling war canoes on Lake Tsala Apopka, weaving lanyards, and night stalking the elusive snipe are cherished memories. I've loved the outdoors ever since, and revisited Tomahawk Lodge on the Rainbow River many times. After the kids were asleep, the counselors came out to play. We had so much fun playing practical jokes, like putting water balloons under mattresses, and transporting a counselor asleep in his bed out into a field in the middle of the night. Putting cow pies under the concrete deer in front of the caretaker's cottage was the best.

Camp was also where I started drinking. A six-pack of Busch beer cost eighty-nine cents in those days, and the camp nurse kept eighty-six proof 'medicine' in the infirmary. I picked up another hobby as well – climbing abandoned telegraph poles around Citrus County to collect antique glass insulators. Dad still has three of them. But the best thing I've kept from Good Counsel is my friendship with Monsignor George Cummings, one of the great pioneering priests of Florida and one of my heroes. While I was recently taking care of the parish he started in Citrus Springs the year I was ordained, he gave me one of his prized hunting trophies – a deer head he also stuffed and mounted. Of course I named it 'George' – to remember my good friend by, and my wonderful days at camp.

At eighteen, I took my first trip out of the country, flying home with my friend from camp, Jaime Mailla, to Santo Domingo, Dominican Republic. That's where I learned my first Spanish words – including his address in case I got lost – and how to dance the *merengue* before we went to a *quinceanos* party and drank *Cuba libres*. The sight of heavily armed soldiers on every street corner shortly after the revolution in that island nation has never left me. For years I treasured the model sailing ship made from cow's horn I brought home. That summer was also my first visit to New Orleans and my family's last vacation together. I remember proudly sipping my first legal beer as we walked down Bourbon Street together, staring in amazement.

Little sister Julie, big brother Greg, little brother Mark.

II   A LONG HAUL

The next eight years still seem surreal to me. The Vietnam War dragged on, and society was shrouded in a drug-induced haze. Everything changed when the Diocese of St. Petersburg was created in 1968. You could say I got in on the ground floor. Mom and Dad worked closely with Father James Gloekler, the priest who had brought my family to Florida three years earlier, getting a residence ready for the new bishop – a house on Bogie Avenue off Park Street – and setting up offices at 5201 Central Avenue to serve as the first chancery. Father Gloekler quietly introduced me to the man who ordained me eight years later – and my dad's new boss – before the announcement of his appointment as bishop was made. Charles B. McLaughlin, a gruff but simple, zealous man, welcomed me with open arms as the first seminarian of his new diocese, describing the priesthood in glowing terms as "the greatest adventure in the world." I had a great relationship with Bishop McLaughlin until his sudden death ten years later. He and Father Gloekler have permanent places in my ecclesiastical hall of fame.

Timing is everything, and something else happened that affected the next eight years of my life. I learned that I wouldn't have to go back up north to go to the seminary, as I had been slated to attend the Pontifical College Josephinum near Columbus, Ohio. For the first time, the seminaries in Florida began accepting students from outside the diocese of Miami. So that fall, my whole family drove down to Miami to drop me off at St. John Vianney. Called a minor seminary in those days, St. John was a liberal arts junior college – with an adjunct ninth through twelfth grade boarding school on campus – oriented toward priestly formation. Being the first bird to fly out of the nest, I was homesick for a few weeks, but the Vincentians who ran the seminary were fatherly and fair. Far from the prison-like priest mills of bygone days, St. John gently led young men into the brave, new post-Vatican II world.

11

Nevertheless, I felt compelled to sneak out a few times. Once, I snuck out with two girls from Madonna Academy, Pat and Estelle. Without a car, they picked me up outside the fence. We met when they were 'imported' to appear in the seminary's 1969 production of Agatha Christie's *Ten Little Indians*, in which I had my first serious dramatic role. For this I had to feign a British accent. I also had to writhe on stage and die convincingly. That proved more difficult. We didn't really need cars at St. John, and I could fly home on TWA in half an hour for nineteen dollars in those days. It was only a five minute walk across campus to St. Brendan Parish where I taught C.C.D. Some of the kids from my cabin at Good Counsel Camp lived in Miami. I spent quite a few weekends having fun with them, just hanging out with their families at home. We all had chores to do for the 'house' – I got to go shopping, take guys to the doctor, and run errands. I loved driving that big old Ford Country Squire station wagon all over Miami. One of my two roommates that first year, Tom Wenski, is now Archbishop of Miami.

Donna Milliken was a friend and fellow counselor from camp who lived across from St. Paul Parish in St. Pete. She and I decided to spend a day at an abandoned limestone quarry in Citrus County not far from Good Counsel where we used to take our campers – a great place for swimming and jumping off a cliff. We invited the young assistant pastor newly arrived from Ireland to go with us. He did. We took a parish car, and the three of us had a blast. His name was Brendan Muldoon. Brendan went on to spend twenty years in service to the Diocese as Chancellor, Vicar General, and even Apostolic Administrator while we were waiting for a new bishop. A great listener and a wise pastor, Brendan is a 'priest's priest.' There was only one problem on our little outing. After we got there, I tossed the keys on the dashboard, and they promptly disappeared down the defroster vent. Mom and Dad came to the rescue, picking up a spare set of keys at St. Paul's and driving them ninety miles up to us. That's the kind of parents I had.

After another summer at Good Counsel, I started working as a busboy at The Careless Navigator, an upscale restaurant on Treasure Island beach. Working with adults in serving the general public was revealing, and earning money for the first time was fun. Life was becoming more structured, but even in the seminary, I never found it oppressive. White shirt, black pants, shoes and tie were the order of the day, with cassock and surplice for Mass. That's about as regimented as things got. The heart of the seminary was its monumental chapel. Built with the Maytag fortune, its resemblance to a giant winged washing machine did not go unnoticed. Singing in the *schola cantorum* at the cathedral in Miami, I remember the old archbishop thundering, "There's no vacation from a vocation!" Unfortunately, I started smoking at St. John. Twenty-one of us got our Associate of Arts degree in 1970.

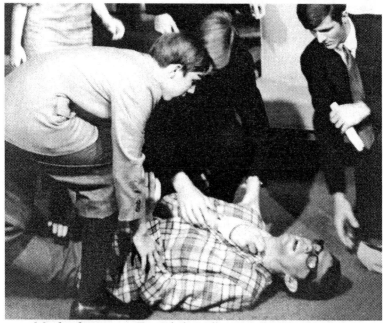

My death scene in Ten Little Indians *at St. John Vianney.*

Since I didn't yet have a car of my own, Father Gloekler always found one for me to drive when I was home. I remember putting a dent in a classic '57 Chevy, a car owned by the parish where he was pastor. That was my first fender-bender – in Crossroads Shopping Center parking lot, going to pick up a pizza for dinner. I also remember tearing up Interstate 4 in his own brand new '68 Grand Prix. Gas in those days was cheap, hitting a low of nineteen cents a gallon at the Gulf station on Fourth Street. Later on I had great fun trying to teach an otherwise brilliant and jovial Dominican priest how to drive. Father Joseph Grech was a native of Malta with an infectious laugh. I hauled him all over Florida, showing him the sights and looking up friends. I learned a lot from this professor of theology, and years later, I stopped to visit him in Rome. I also took a trip of several days and nights with three friends from the seminary in a twenty-one foot boat on the St. Johns River, from its source in Lake Sanford all the way to downtown Jacksonville. Less than intrepid adventurers, we found ourselves fighting off ferocious mosquitoes, losing sight of the horizon during a furious thunderstorm on Lake George, dodging submerged tree trunks in the Rodman reservoir, and squeezing through the locks of the never-completed Cross Florida Barge Canal.

When Father Gloekler became pastor of St. Mary Parish in downtown St. Petersburg, my parents and I did everything we could to help him. Being Chancellor of the Diocese as well, he hosted a Christmas party for the fledgling Chancery staff at St. Mary. Still a teenager, I really had no experience with hard liquor at that point. I'm sure I embarrassed my parents when I threw up in the hallway of the old rectory before I knew what was happening and could get out the door. I also embarrassed myself, of course. Like a lot of priests, Father Gloekler struggled with alcohol his whole life. But he also had a place in his heart for his fellow sufferers. He took in a number of priests no one else wanted – in and out of recovery – and gave them a home. One of those priests asked me to drive him up to Milwaukee for a few days that summer. I was only too glad to oblige, as I liked him and I liked to drive. He could have driven himself, but the poor guy would never have been able to sip his jug of wine all the way up and back by himself. He insisted on taking me with him to a gay bar in Milwaukee – a quiet, pleasant place he knew to get a drink. I really don't know what he was hoping to accomplish, though he did get a little too friendly later that evening. I'm sure it was the wine talking. That was the end of that. All this was part of my introduction to the priesthood.

Was this priest gay? I suppose he was, but I didn't see this as a reason to refuse his friendship and support. Quite a few priests are gay. So are some bishops. The priesthood has always attracted a lot of gay men. So what? Being gay or straight has nothing to do with being a good priest or a good bishop. The vast majority of priests who are gay are celibate, just as the vast majority of priests who are straight are celibate. Being gay or straight has nothing to do with pedophilia, a psychological disorder with no correlation to sexual orientation. Homosexuality did not cause the clergy sex abuse scandal. Human beings do not choose their sexual preference any more than they choose their gender or the color of their skin. They are born one way or the other. All human beings – straight and gay – are created by the same loving God.

Sexual preference does not change. What priests do choose is to be celibate – to the best of their ability. But priests are only human. Like everyone else at times, straight or gay, priests struggle to remain faithful to the promises they make. It amazes me how many people in general and Catholics in particular do not understand or refuse to accept these basic facts. To maintain that a man should not be admitted to the seminary or ordained solely because he happens to be gay reflects deliberate ignorance. Like other minorities, gays have been misunderstood, misjudged, and mistreated from time immemorial. Somewhat ironically, homophobia is no stranger to the Church. At a time when our armed forces are abandoning the 'don't ask, don't tell' policy, it seems the Church is holding on to it more firmly than ever. We live in an imperfect world.

It's hard to believe I spent the next six years of my life at St. Vincent de Paul, the major seminary in Boynton Beach. These years were confusing and downright crazy at times, but I managed to survive and have some fun along the way. I took a trip with a classmate, Mark Fontaine, to Stone Mountain near Atlanta. We stayed overnight at a state park in Georgia, thinking how cool it was to be drinking beer in our tent. I remember my little Corvair being no match for a semi that tried to run us off the road on Interstate 75.

At Boynton Beach, the first two years were largely devoted to the study of philosophy, the final four to theology. The seminary underwent traumatic change in those years. My first year was the last for the Vincentian community that owned and staffed the seminary, and it showed. The faculty was coming apart. A casual atmosphere of 'anything goes' prevailed, a bizarre change from the previous two years at St. John in Miami. A fight with the Archbishop of Miami over the future ownership of the seminary ensued. Caught in the crossfire, the seminarians were bewildered by the turmoil, but equally dismayed by the harsh reaction when the Archdiocese took over. This prompted a "Statement of Student Concern" that was all but ignored, making morale worse. Half the priests on staff dropped out. A third of my class succumbed over the summer of 1971. Others of us applied to study at Louvain University in Belgium in the fall. I was accepted but never went.

The new faculty hastily assembled that summer left much to be desired. My second year of philosophy became an endurance test, and Boynton Beach was not a happy place. There was a great deal of unresolved tension. I can remember gathering on break with my classmates at Camp San Pedro near Orlando to blow off steam. We had too much to drink and ran around outside dodging lightning bolts before a thunderstorm. I lost my taste for rum after that. Only six of us made it to graduation. I gave a ponderous speech. Instead of writing my thesis on the philosophy of Aristotle or Thomas Aquinas, I dove into the existentialism of Jean Paul Sartre – more reflective of the times – earning my Bachelor of Arts Degree with highest honors in 1972. After four years in an all-boys high school, I spent four more years in an all-male environment in the seminary, with four years to go. I was feeling the strain.

I've never met a priest who said he liked the seminary. We spend an ungodly long time there in a closed, pressurized environment lacking any feminine dimension. It's just the way the system's always been. The food was palatable but bland. Institutional cooking always is. That's one reason I like to cook so much today. We had a rather intimidating chef from Germany named Max. He'd have done well on *Hell's Kitchen*. We used to say the food at the seminary was what the Book of Revelation says about Jesus – the same yesterday, today, and tomorrow. Some of the relationships I formed in the seminary proved to be healthy, some not. There was always plenty of drama. But that's true of life in general, too. Most of us came to see the seminary as a necessary means to a desirable end. It's amazing how much a person will put up with to secure a goal, and for how long. In this case, the prize was priesthood, a noble calling to be sure. But while the commitment is made for a lifetime, I've come to realize that the call can only be answered a day at a time.

There were some bright spots along the way. I had the distinct pleasure of spending a little time with Henri Nouwen, a Dutch theologian and psychologist who gained great prominence as a spiritual writer. His telling description of the priest as a "wounded healer" met with universal acclaim. Driving him to a speaking engagement at the seminary from the airport in West Palm Beach, he graciously accepted my invitation to hang out with a small group of students rather than faculty that evening over a few beers in my room. It proved to be one of the most engaging exchanges of ideas, stories, and humor I can remember. Then there was what turned out to be a consolation rather than a victory party I hosted the night of George McGovern's loss to Richard Nixon in the presidential election of 1972. If ever there were a turning point in American politics, that was one.

Unlike the stuffy, winterized corridors of northern seminaries, the ground floor was the only floor at Boynton Beach. Every door around St. Vincent's four sprawling courtyards opened onto the great outdoors. Walk out the door of your room and you were outside. You never knew what was waiting for you, especially in the middle of the night. The worst kept secret in the world was that the sinks in the rooms were used for more than washing hands, especially when it was cold. The seminary was surrounded by cow pastures in those days, and the noise of cows doing in the fields what comes naturally to them often punctuated the stillness of the night. A multitude of winged creatures fly through the night skies of southern Florida, but the occasional pygmy rattlesnake coiled on a sidewalk posed a greater threat. Then there were the walking catfish that appeared *en masse* whenever torrential rains flooded the lake on campus. I'd heard of flying fish before, but these air breathers – propped up on their pectoral fins wriggling back to the water – I had to see to believe, and I did.

The seminaries I attended were pleasant enough places, and I never felt confined – something I cannot stand. No one has ever had to tell me to 'get a life' because I've always had one – before and beyond the seminary and the rectory – and held on to it. This is just another way of saying that I've never been afraid to be myself. With me, what you see is what you get. Though it may not sound like it, from the beginning of the eight long years I spent in the seminary to their end, I took everything – including myself – very seriously, too seriously at times. From day one I was regarded as having an excellent attitude and my academic performance was considered superior. I was fortunate not to have to work as hard as some.

I cannot speak for the seminary experience today. Smoking is certainly not as common as it was thirty-some

18

years ago. But the seminary experience, for me and surely for others, provided fertile ground for addictive personalities to thrive and for addictive behaviors to grow. My use of alcohol would prove to be problematic as time went on. That drinking was commonplace should hardly come as a surprise. Boynton was a Catholic seminary, not a Baptist or a Methodist one. Drinking helped pass the time. I did not find the seminary environment conducive to the attainment of sexual maturity. Life, thank God, has a way of smoothing out the rough spots everyone experiences growing up – in my case, through the tedious process of priestly formation. It was what it was – an imperfect means to an end.

In any case, my new summer job provided comic relief from the tension of those years. Turning twenty-one, I was hired as a toll collector on the old two-lane Sunshine Skyway Bridge across the mouth of Tampa Bay before it was knocked down by a ship in 1980 and rebuilt. Since I was to handle money, I had to be fingerprinted. Filling in for vacationing full-time employees, I worked every shift around the clock, on both ends of the Bridge. The sand gnats by the tidal waters near the Skyway were awful at dawn and dusk. Other than that, dealing with the general public was an education in itself. Off peak hours, I shot the bull with two Highway Patrol officers, 'good old boys' assigned to the Bridge full-time in those days. Once during the middle of the night, one of them called me up at work pretending to be a robber on his way. In a panic, I called the Highway Patrol on the radio in the toll booth. They all had a good laugh over that little joke, and so did I. Once in a while someone would jump from the Skyway or nearly run me down. Some motorists were friendly, some weren't. One left a watermelon instead of paying the toll. Others who didn't have the fifty cent toll offered me their empty wallet or their watch. At times my toll booth looked like a pawn shop. Bishop McLaughlin, having to drive south frequently to the lower part of his diocese at that time, always got a kick out of seeing me. With nary a dull moment, I found it all great fun. I even penned an ode extolling the merits of my summer profession that was published statewide. Ten years later I received a standing ovation, reciting it as I gave an invocation at the convention of the International Bridge, Tunnel, and Turnpike Association.

A girl I knew from grade school, Barbara Blank, came down from Toledo for a visit. I enjoyed taking her to hear the carillon at Bok Tower in Lake Wales, to see the Southern belles and the water ski show at Cypress Gardens, and the newly renamed Kennedy Space Center at Cape Canaveral on the east coast. Then it was back to school. Boynton Beach is happily the place I met the person who was to become my best friend, a seminarian from St. Petersburg named Mike Lydon. Three years older and two years ahead of me, Mike was like an older brother to me from the start. The oldest children in our families, we both attended Bishop Barry and came from St. Jude. Though our paths hadn't crossed before, our siblings' had. We got to know each other driving home from the seminary and revisiting Good Counsel Camp where we had both been counselors.

I'll never forget the wild night Mike and I had shortly after I graduated from college when we hooked up with Dick Allen who had preceded us at Boynton Beach. We started out at Woody Riley's Warehouse, a Dixieland jazz beer club in downtown Clearwater, and ended up smoking pot in Clearwater Central Catholic High School's old school bus in Dick's back yard. Mike and I were never into this, but having drunk all the beer we could, we thought it would be fun. When you're young you do stupid things and even more stupid things when you're drunk. I didn't want my parents to see me like this, so Mike drove me – ignominiously slumped out the window of my own car – to his parents' house, briefly attracting the attention of a passing patrol car on Drew Street. I ended up stretched out in his front yard. Coming out to water her dogs at dawn, Mike's mom at first took me for a dead body before recognition set in and she kindly threw a blanket over me. I must have gotten whatever it was out of my system, as things calmed down after that. In the winter of 1973 we took the first of many camping trips together to Hot Springs, Arkansas, driving atop levees along the Mississippi River and nearly freezing in our tent.

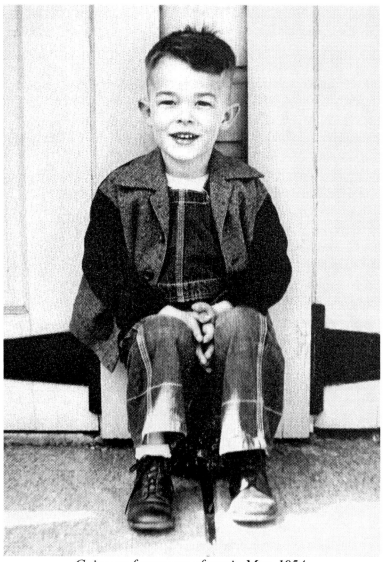

Going on four years of age in May, 1954.

III THRILLS AND SPILLS

The worst thing that ever happened to me also happened at Boynton Beach. A priest on the faculty of the seminary took a liking to me. He praised me up and down every time he saw me. Frankly, I enjoyed the attention and spending time with him, smoking his cigarettes and drinking his booze. He knew quite a few famous and wealthy people, so he had plenty of money – to spend on me. No doubt about it, he was slick. First he took me on a cruise. He ingratiated himself with my parents, who invited him to preside at my sister's wedding. He commissioned my father to compose a new Mass setting. My parents thought the sun rose and set on him. After all, he was a priest.

After a while I began to feel uncomfortable with him and I realized what was going on. At twenty-two, I was naïve, immature, and confused about a lot of things. When he took me on a trip to Europe the following summer, his true intentions became clear. I was trapped, or so I thought. He couldn't keep his hands off me, and sooner or later I'd pacify him in some way, just to get him to leave me alone. Only a person who has been in this situation – and sadly there are many – can understand the distress one feels. I put up with this harassment for three long years.

This priest used his position of authority over me to gain access. He violated the trust my family and I placed in him because he was a priest. I knew that once I was ordained, I would be free of him for good. I hated him by then. I regretted ever having known him. I only saw him once after I was ordained. He knew how I felt by then, but that didn't stop him from coming to my parents' thirtieth wedding anniversary three years later. Like all abusers, he counted on me keeping my mouth shut. I did, for another twenty-five years.

That priest is long since dead. I still wonder how many others there were like me. Like most victims, I never told anyone about this until a few years ago. I never fully came to grips with what happened to me until then. For years I was unaware of what he had done to my younger brother, a teenager, around the same time. Even when my brother told me, I was unable to deal with it. This caused a rift between us that is still healing. Nothing can describe the reaction of my parents and my sisters when we finally told them a few years ago. One never quite recovers from this, but Mark and I are both on the mend.

Nevertheless, my first trip to Europe during the summer of 1973 was unforgettable. London, Paris, Brussels, Rome, Florence, Venice, Milan, Munich, Zurich, Amsterdam, Copenhagen, Salzburg, Vienna, Madrid, and Toledo – first class all the way. In Vienna I attended the European premier of Leonard Bernstein's *Mass* – an elaborate theatre piece featuring the Vienna Choir Boys (I had seen them before as a child). Needless to say, I enjoyed getting away from my captor every chance I got and going off by myself. I took a trip to Mont St. Michel, the famous abbey on the coast of France rising out of the sea, and a trip to Sweden on a hydrofoil. Dining out was an experience in itself, late at night by American standards, especially in Spain where there was more tableware than I could count. Drinks came with one ice cube, if that. An Indonesian "rusttafel" in Amsterdam was my most unusual culinary adventure – dozens of highly seasoned meat and vegetable side dishes surrounding a mountain of rice. We stayed at Cardinal Wright's private villa in Rome – quite a cozy crib. A private audience with Pope Paul VI had been set up for me to deliver a leather-bound copy of Dad's new composition – *A Mass for All Seasons* – dedicated to the Pope on the occasion of his tenth anniversary. Unfortunately, it didn't arrive from the publisher in time. Instead, I had to settle for a front-row seat at a Papal Mass in the Basilica on the feast of Peter and Paul.

Mike was a deacon at my sister Julie's wedding to Bill Welsh at St. John Parish on St. Pete Beach that August. After that, it was back to school for my final two years of theology. Though I was able to get home every other month or so, I always looked forward to a visit from Mom and Dad.

Once they even hauled my sisters and Grandma Andrews across the state to visit me at the seminary. Various priests from the Diocese came to visit, including Keith Symons, always a friend to my family. A couple of short stories I wrote were published in the seminary's literary magazine. I went to my first and only football game at the Orange Bowl in Miami, only to witness the slaughter of the Dolphins by the Patriots. That cost six dollars. I learned something from working weekends at several east coast parishes, including St. Helen in Ft. Lauderdale, where I organized a new adult choir, and Sacred Heart in Lake Worth, where I taught C.C.D. I recall obediently if not licitly blessing throats on the feast of St. Blaise at Ascension in Boca Raton. At St. Vincent in Margate, every Sunday afternoon over Whoppers from Burger King, I would count the collection with the pastor, his secretary, and his 'girls' – two female schnauzers, Trixie and Tinkerbelle. While not officially members of the parish staff, they might as well have been. During the summer of 1974, I worked at a nursing home, Cor Jesu, in Tampa while living at Christ the King. I even taught remedial reading to the children of migrant farm workers in Palm Beach County. All this was my field work for becoming a priest.

On one occasion I had the thrill of sitting at the table with Abigail Van Buren for lunch. While I didn't ask "Dear Abby" for advice, I did get her autograph. She also gave me a big kiss. You don't get to meet a lot of famous people in life, so I've kept the imprint of her lipstick on my cheek to this day. I needed my own car by then, so I got a used two-tone '66 Corvair, one of the slowest cars on earth. I repainted it canary yellow, adding a black racing stripe in the hope it might go faster. It didn't. It had an air-cooled engine in back, the trunk in front, and if you believed Ralph Nader, a killer heater. That may have affected my brain. I learned a valuable lesson when I loaned it to another seminarian who promptly cracked it up but never paid me for the damage. When I could afford to make car payments, I bought a fire-engine red '74 Mazda from my new brother-in-law who was selling cars at the time. It had a turbo-boosted rotary engine that deserved the white racing stripe I put on it. Not quite *Fast and Furious* material, but it was close – better than the silver Vega and the green Nova I got to drive at home. I don't know much about cars, but I've always liked driving them.

During my second year of theology, I took on a major project – directing a play. Actually, I had to supervise the entire production. This took months of preparation and involved at least half the student body. We melted a lot of dry ice in boiling water learning how to create a celestial scene. I won't pretend I didn't enjoy bossing so many people around – that's what a director does. My temperamental nature suited me perfectly for the job. The play – *The Devil He Did* – was a plodding, philosophical drama, but a little creativity and imagination made for an excellent result. I learned a lot about theatre and public relations. Music also remained an interest. From time to time I played the organ for Mass in the seminary chapel. For a formal evening of music, I performed a simple piece by Handel. I even trained and accompanied a choir to record a demo of Dad's new Mass for GIA Publications. Back home, Mike and I went to a deafening rock opera concert of *Jesus Christ Superstar* at Bayfront Center.

In 1973, Bishop McLaughlin formally accepted me as a candidate for priesthood in a ceremony at Boynton Beach. I was also formally installed as an acolyte, allowing me to distribute communion for the first time. Since lay eucharistic ministers were not yet in use, that made me very useful. My journey through the seminary had taken five years thus far. There were three years to go. I was steadily getting closer to my goal – being ordained a priest.

Over Christmas break the following year, four of us took an overly ambitious trip out West – the first for all of us, but certainly not the last for me. Four guys in one car for two weeks trying to cover too much ground resulted in some frayed nerves. In Flagstaff on New Year's Eve, I was the only one who wanted to party. None of us will ever forget laying eyes on the Grand Canyon for the first time. I remember timidly driving along the snowy rim on patches of ice when no one else would. Out of curiosity, we also went to Death Valley, Tijuana, and Las Vegas. I didn't care for these places and have never returned. Not used to twisting mountain roads, crossing the Sierra Nevadas was a hair-raising experience for us all. The coldness of the Pacific Ocean surprised me. However briefly we visited the deserts and meadows, canyons and caves along our route, the newfound scenery stunned us. My desire to explore the country was ignited, and my love affair with our national parks began.

My Ordination to the Priesthood on May 8, 1976.

I also jumped in a car with three other guys to attend an ordination in Nashville. The seminary had not recommended Andy, but his bishop was ready to ordain him. We were advised not to go, but because he was our friend, we did. On the way back, we stopped in Lynchburg, Tennessee, to tour the Jack Daniel Distillery, ironically located in a dry county. As time went on, I got to know Jack a little too well for my own good. College boys also drink a lot of beer, and seminarians are no exception. Many late evenings were spent at the Dutch Mill in town, discussing everything under the sun with a rowdy group of friends and our church history professor. These were the not-so-halcyon days of Watergate and the nation's first energy crisis. With gas in short supply everywhere, long lines formed at the pump. People paid through the nose for gas, when they could get it. That made it difficult to travel very far or very long. Even getting home was a chore for a while, but whenever I did, going out on my folks' boat was what I loved to do, and what we did as a family whenever we could.

One more thing I did at Boynton Beach that was highly unusual for a seminarian was to drive Mrs. Hardy. It wasn't *Driving Miss Daisy* but it was close. We weren't allowed to have jobs, but Mr. Hardy – a retired president of U.S. Steel – convinced the rector to let a respectable young man chauffeur his wife around a couple of afternoons a week. I was one of the chosen few. Actually, I 'inherited' this sweet little deal from my good friend Mike, making fifteen dollars at a time. The only other source of income we had in the seminary was selling our blood to the blood bank. That was worth thirty dollars a pint. Of course, we did this dutifully every six weeks. One does what one has to do. The Hardys lived in Ocean Ridge, an enclave of wealthy folk on the Atlantic ten minutes away. Mr. Hardy played golf, and Mrs. Hardy went shopping – in the new Cadillac her husband bought her every year. That was their life. And I was part of it, for a year or two. Usually we went to the shops of Palm Beach or Boca Raton. Now and then she'd treat me to lunch at the Club or buy me ice cream. Once I drove Mrs. "Doonesbury" – Gary Trudeau's mom, a friend of Mrs. Hardy – to a posh party. The Hardys weren't Catholic, they were just lovely people. For a time, this was my great escape.

Mike was ordained a priest in May of 1974. Being involved in his ordination at the Cathedral in St. Petersburg with the other seminarians from our Diocese was a dress rehearsal of sorts for my own two years later. A year later, at the end of my third year of theology, I was awarded a Master of Divinity degree, again with highest honors. Again there were six of us, and again I got to give a speech. A week later, on May 24, 1975, I was ordained a deacon by Bishop McLaughlin at St. Jude. I was twenty-four years old.

It was at St. Cecelia Parish in Clearwater, where I was assigned to work that summer, that I really got my feet wet, so to speak. Deacons can do everything a priest does except celebrate the Eucharist and the Sacrament of Reconciliation. I didn't marry anyone, but I did preach for the first time, visit the sick in hospitals, and baptize babies. About the only practical thing we ever did in the seminary was to pretend we were baptizing a doll. Everything was new to me at this point, and fun. The priests and nuns I worked with, though old enough to be my parents and then some, were kind to me. Much of my time was spent taking a door-to-door census of Island Estates – between Clearwater Beach and the mainland – to determine if a new parish was needed in that area. I was welcomed warmly by most of the people who opened their doors to me, including Art and Pat Deegan, who remain friends to this day. That summer I also helped stage a COR weekend retreat for teenagers, and a day camp for pre-schoolers called 'Tiny Tots.'

Mike's pastor was an Irishman named Tom Earner. Tom must have been raised by leprechauns because he was so full of blarney. He loved to play practical jokes on anyone he could, including Mike and me. It was time for payback. One Sunday I was home from school and helping at St. Patrick in Tampa. Father Earner gave me the collection bag to bring back to the rectory and put in the safe.

Mike and I had a plan to make it look like a robbery had taken place. Leaving the safe and the front door wide open, I threw some of the money on the floor and splattered ketchup on myself. Then I lay down on the floor and waited. It wasn't long before the pastor came in the back door. Mike was on his heels since he didn't want to miss his boss' reaction. For one brief shining moment, Tom Earner stood motionless. Struck dumb at the scene before him, the expression on his face was priceless. We got his goat, he got a taste of his own medicine, and an urban legend was born.

In August of 1975, Mike and I took the first of our many camping trips out West together. The two boys we brought along made it all the more fun. Tom Reilly was a younger brother of the music director at Mike's parish. We got to know the entire Reilly clan, making several trips to visit them in Garden City Park on Long Island. When they came to Florida, we took them to Disney World and out on our boat. Still in our twenties, Mike and I partied hearty in those days, and the Big Apple was a fun place to go. Broadway shows only cost an arm or a leg in those days, not both. You always hope to spot a celebrity when you're out on the town, and one night – after seeing *The Best Little Whorehouse in Texas* – we did. There we were, sitting in Ted Hook's *Backstage*, New York's most theatrical restaurant, when Phyllis Diller came along. Never one to shy away from the attention of young men, with her trademark raucous laugh, she plopped herself down at our table, right in my lap.

Dave DeFreitas was the other boy on this trip. Intense and moody at times like me, David was also very affectionate. As a boy he used to come over to my house to take organ lessons from Dad. Now he was thinking about entering the seminary. He later did but sadly died before being ordained a priest. Only a couple of years younger than Mike and me, Tom and Dave were just as excited as we were to visit the Grand Canyon, Hoover Dam, Lake Mead and Nevada's Valley of Fire State Park, Bryce and Zion National Parks in Utah, the Painted Desert and the Petrified Forest.

We were also excited about being able to drink Coors beer, at that time available only west of the Mississippi – the plot line of the *Smokey and the Bandit* films.

Having arrived at the campground on the floor of Zion Canyon after dark, we unzipped the door of our tent to the cool fresh air of morning only to be startled by the fiery orange light of day on the towering sandstone cliffs all around. The medley of wildflowers at Hannagan Meadow and the open-pit copper mine at Morenci in southeast Arizona were also sights that thrilled us. These places are along what is now U.S. 191 but at that time was U.S. 666 – until the route was renumbered in response to complaints from the public about its diabolical symbolism. This cross-country marathon also took us through the Badlands of South Dakota to Mt. Rushmore, through Denver to visit my godmother Kate Harris on the Fourth of July, to the Wisconsin Dells, all the way to New York, and down the length of the Jersey shore.

Mike's car was never the same after putting on all those miles. A few times we got into campgrounds late at night or weren't able to find one at all. Then campgrounds started taking reservations – and charging more money. I began to do a little more advance planning. Picking up the phone took the guesswork out of finding a place to stay. Today it's as simple as clicking your mouse. Denver became the jumping-off point for most of our subsequent trips. Spending a night at my godmother's house or at my brother's when Mark settled there became almost a ritual of summer.

During my last year at Boynton Beach, Dad came to give an organ recital in the lofty seminary chapel for the parishioners of St. Thomas More. I was assigned to spend most weekends at St. Hugh Parish in Coconut Grove, the artsy section of Miami – home to the famous Playhouse. Of course we went to see the original version of *Hair* there, when nudity on stage was still avant-garde. At St. Hugh, I successfully baptized my first baby – in Spanish no less. Taking a liking to me, the pastor, John Glorie, gave me an ornate gold stole – the symbol of spiritual authority a priest wears over his shoulders – as an early ordination present. All these years later, I still think of him when I put it on at wakes and gravesides. The other priest at St. Hugh, Jay Huck, gave me a gerbil – a gift he was probably 'recycling.' That lovable little rodent was my first real pet, and his descendants were as numerous as Abraham's. Watching him run around furiously on the wheel in his cage reminded me of me the first few years I was ordained. Back at school, I completed the work needed to secure a Master of Theology degree – with highest honors once more. Commencement was the day of my First Mass, so the seminary mailed me my diploma. The week before ordination, the six of us in my class went on the customary retreat at the Passionist Monastery in North Palm Beach. We chose one of our theology professors, Felipe Estevez, now auxiliary bishop of Miami, to be our guide. Any pre-ordination jitters were dispelled by riding the go-carts at the track across the street. It hardly seemed possible, but at last – after eight long years – I left the seminary to come home for good.

At home with Mom and Dad after Ordination.

IV CHANGING GEARS

On the way home, I bumped into the back of a car stopped in front of me on the railroad tracks in Gulfport. There was no damage, but that didn't stop a nuisance lawsuit from being filed. I never heard any more about it. I remember it only because a uniformed bailiff brought a summons to the door of my parents' house a few days later, just as I was about to celebrate my first home Mass. I caught a cold the day before I was ordained, but after waiting so long, I'd have crawled up the aisle if I'd had to.

The ordination of a Catholic priest is an impressive ceremony by any standard, and mine was no exception. I had served early Sunday morning Mass during high school in the same church where I was ordained. St. Jude in St. Petersburg had become the Cathedral. While the Diocese was twice its current size in territory, it had half the Catholic population thirty years ago. The presbyterate I was joining was more closely knit then than now. There was a greater sense of belonging and common purpose. The Church had not been rocked by scandal, and there was an enthusiasm about moving forward with the times that no longer exists. From my perspective, we've lost a lot as Catholics. No wonder no one is lining up for my job.

Celebrating my First Mass on Mother's Day.

32

Only one other young man was ordained with me – a native of Italy also transplanted from Ohio – Vince Clemente. Vince and I wanted *Amazing Grace* sung at our ordination, but someone put the kibosh on that – we never knew who. While the litany of the saints is sung, those to be ordained lie down on the floor in front of the altar as a gesture of submission. It's the traditional photo op, as well as when the bishop – followed by all the priests present – lays hands on your head and gives you a hug. You also have to promise to obey him and his successors. The promise to remain celibate was actually made when I was ordained a deacon the year before. Another common misconception is that priests take vows, but diocesan priests do not. Finally, someone dresses you up, literally. For the first time, you get to wear what everyone else is wearing – a chasuble and stole. Now you're ready to concelebrate the rest of the ordination Mass. So your 'First Mass' – when you 'solo' at the altar, usually the next day – is a misnomer for at least two reasons. You always invite your friends to concelebrate, so you're not alone at the altar, and it's really your second Mass, not your first. No wonder people have such trouble understanding church-speak – and that just describes the first two days of a new priest's life.

All four of our parents brought up the gifts of bread and wine to be used at Mass. They were in fact also handing over their firstborn sons, just as the Bible describes. Standing at the altar beside the bishop surrounded by dozens of priests, one experiences a palpable sense of solidarity. To be asked by hundreds of people for your blessing – as well as to have your bishop kneel before you to receive it at the end of Mass – can only be described as humbling. While I always say Bishop Favalora was my favorite of the four bishops I've had because he made me a pastor, I think Bishop McLaughlin really was. He had a way of letting you know when he was pleased – and when he wasn't. On the day of my ordination he obviously was, and everyone including me knew it.

At the reception that followed, I got my first assignment. Actually it had been leaked to me. Being appointed assistant pastor of St. Cecelia in Clearwater would hardly have come as a surprise in any case. I had spent the previous summer there as a deacon. I must have done something right that Monsignor Larkin wanted me back. I was also supposed to spend one day a week teaching at Clearwater Central Catholic High School. I wasn't keen on that part of my assignment, but I made a showing now and then – though I always tried to arrange a funeral on those days. Simply because I was a young priest, I was thrown in a room with sixty fifteen-year-olds and told to teach them morality. I might as well have been thrown to lions.

Following the formalities of the reception, Vince and I adjourned with our families and friends to a smorgasbord at the Sweden House restaurant. To avoid competition, we decided to share this event. It was a good move. An ordination is a lot like a wedding. It's supposed to be the biggest day of your life and last forever. My marriage, of course, is to the Church, and like most marriages, it's less than perfect. There are days I can't live with 'her' and days I can't live without 'her,' days I wish I never knew 'her' and days I'm awfully glad I do. Like a newlywed, I received a ton of cards and gifts – none more beautiful than the hammered gold chalice and paten from Spain given to me, in keeping with tradition, by my parents. To this day I also treasure the set of four stoles handmade for me by Mike's mom, Ginny.

I used that chalice for the very first time at my First Mass at St. Jude the next day. Ten priests joined me around the altar, two of whom later became bishops. Two of my classmates not yet ordained in Miami served as deacons, and half a dozen seminarians, later ordained in front of the same altar, as acolytes. I remember little else except for being nervous as one might expect, being surrounded by family and friends, and that it was Mother's Day – a fact that made this event even more special. I had a second First Mass at St. John Vianney, the stately church on St. Pete Beach where

Dad was music director, with equally glorious choral music the following Sunday.

After eight years in the seminary and all the pomp and circumstance surrounding ordination, it was time for a real vacation. Flush with cash and a first-class Eurail Pass, I was off to Europe with my classmate Vince and two other friends from school, Bill Zandri and John McGraw. While this was my second trip, it was ironically the first for Vince who had been born in Italy – one of our major destinations.

We flew into Luxembourg, a tiny country the size of a city filled with quaint gardens, Old World charm, and an immense Gothic cathedral. A letter of introduction from the Chancery and my high-school French enabled us to celebrate Mass at the main altar – not without some trepidation. From there we began our three-week train trek criss-crossing the continent. In Paris we saw the glass-encased remains of St. Vincent de Paul beneath an altar, gargoyles on the roof of Notre Dame, and the famous stained-glass windows of the cathedral at Chartres. After a day drinking dry German wine, the boat trip down the Rhine was a bit hazy. We hoisted a few steins of *Kronenburg* over schnitzel and kraut at a rathskeller or two in Germany. In Rome we concele-brated Mass in St. Peter's Basilica – obviously not on the main altar this time – and visited my old friend Father Grech at the Gregorian University. In little rowboats we ducked into the luminous Blue Grotto on the Isle of Capri off the coast of Naples. Some ladies of the evening approached us one night, only to be succinctly rebuffed by Vince's coy *"Buona notte!"* Genoa proved to be a rough and musty old port town. We toted heavy magnums of cheap Lambrusco around on the street at night in case we were mugged.

By far the highlight of this trip was revisiting Vince's roots in the tiny town of Rocca Pia high in the mountains, in the L'Aquila province of the Abruzzo region of central Italy. I don't think we'd ever have found Rocca Pia were it not for the smiling little priest who found us at the train station in Sulmona and piled us all into his tiny car. In polyester leisure suits, we looked like giants next to him and his Fiat.

Our combined weight is about the only thing that kept us on the road around the curves and along the cliffs on the wild ride home. Coming from Florida, we were amazed to find snow on the ground here and there – in May. That was only the beginning of a week like no other.

Vince and I were shocked to see our names in Italian – Don Gregorio and Don Vincenzo – on neon-colored posters plastered all over town on the ancient stone walls. To be greeted with the honorific title *don* meant we had finally arrived – literally and figuratively. It might have been a scene out of the *Godfather* except that, in our case, *don* referred to our newly-minted status as 'Fathers' – godly or otherwise. "Long live the Pope! Long live the Bishop! Long live Father Greg! Long live Father Vince!" the posters exclaimed in Italian. I've never had another welcome like that. The respect these people had for us as new priests knew no bounds. The reverence they had for what we stood for astounded and humbled us. Bill and John shared our joy as well. The return of a newly-ordained native son was an occasion that merited celebration by the whole town.

It was exhilarating to celebrate yet another 'First Mass,' this time with the local bishop, for the townspeople of Rocca Pia. Many of them were Vince's relatives, some of whom remembered the bombing of their village by Allied forces in World War II. During Mass, the doors of the church remained open. Dogs, cats, and chickens came to pay their respects as well. Dressed in black with their heads covered, all the women sat on benches on one side of the church, and in their wool suits, all the men on the other. At this altitude it was freezing in the morning, requiring heavy clothes and covers to sleep at night. However crudely we made signs with our hands, Vince's relatives attended to our every need. Herds of sheep and goats roamed the narrow, cobbled streets. The dinner that followed Mass lasted for hours and had more courses and more toasts than I could count. As I wrote on a postcard to my parents, none of us ever ate or drank so much as we did that week, because with those people, we had no choice. Their hospitality knew no bounds. After all the pasta, the meat, the fruit, the cheese, and the wine, the men adjourned to a place by themselves – taking the four of us with them – where they started pouring shots of grappa. They distill this potent, colorless liqueur from the stems of grapes. It tastes like turpentine but it keeps you warm while it knocks you out. Sleep came effortlessly after a few shots around the fire with the guys.

After being treated like royalty for days, we were surely sorry to leave Italy. Before we did, the bishop of Sulmona graciously invited us to his home for lunch. Then we rode the rails to northeastern Italy to visit other relatives of Vince near Bolzano in the shadow of the Alps. The date we were to begin our first assignments was rapidly approaching. The names of other places we visited on this trip escape me, but the memories collected do not.

Getting the feel of a barrel cactus in Arizona.

V   ON THE ROAD AGAIN

Finally it was time to get to work. A priest's first assignment must be chosen carefully as it sets the tone for his entire ministry. His pastor effectively becomes his 'handler' and has to be a sensitive man. Mine surely was. I also had the advantage of having spent two months at St. Cecelia as a deacon the previous summer. So becoming the newest 'assistant,' as parochial vicars were called in those days, was a homecoming of sorts for me. St. Cecelia had the worst possible combination of living quarters and offices – in the same fortress-like building. There's no privacy, no peace and quiet, in a setting like that. I was fortunate however to live in a separate frame shack on concrete blocks elsewhere on the property – almost like my own little house. I could see the ground through a hole in the floor of my tiny closet, and the furniture was shabby, but I thought it was great. I did my best to spruce the place up, covering everything I could with wood-grain contact paper – even the toilet seat.

Another young priest lived in the back of the house, and for a time a third priest stayed in the bedroom between us. Eventually they both flew the coop. The five priests who lived in the big house are all dead. I guess that makes me the sole survivor. The Church had priests coming out of her ears in those days. Not so any more. One person is still at St. Cecelia. As parish secretary, Cathy Kaiser gave me my basic training thirty-five years ago. Today she manages the parish. To say she's an institution doesn't do her justice. She's more like St. Cecelia's heart.

With so many priests in residence, the parish had a full-time housekeeper and cook, and a woman who came in just to do laundry. I went over to the rectory to eat. I wasn't used to being waited on. I was used to carrying my dishes back to the kitchen after meals, so that's what I did. I know I didn't need to, but after watching me a while, the others took the hint and followed suit. The housekeeper never knew what happened. Few parishes have more than one priest today. Even those that do can't afford a full time house-keeper or cook. I've been doing my laundry, cooking my meals, and cleaning my house for twenty-some years. It hasn't hurt me a bit.

Each parish has its own unique personality, determined in part by the pastor himself – especially if he's been there a long time. Some parishes, for example, are friendly, some are not. Some think they do a better job than anyone else. A few are notorious for chewing up priests and spitting them out. A priest's first parish is like his first love – he usually retains a fondness for it even after many years. Tom Larkin, my first pastor, was a good man. A bit aloof, perhaps, and a very private person, he bore a great deal of responsibility beyond the parish as Vicar General of the Diocese and head of the Tribunal. Until recently an outpost of the Chancery, this office handles all matters governed by Church law – especially pertaining to marriage and declarations of nullity. With the Tribunal located next to St. Cecelia, I learned quite a bit about its operation. Over the years, I was able to help hundreds of people obtain annulments so they could remarry with the Church's blessing. Since then, the process for doing so has become more cumbersome.

Monsignor Larkin was ahead of his time in at least two ways. He was the first pastor in the Diocese to hire a lay person full-time as parish manager. I'm sure he raised some eyebrows when he let all the Lutheran congregations in the county celebrate Reformation Sunday in St. Cecelia Church. I remember giving him a hug when he came down the stairs after his mother had died. I figured he needed it. Early one morning at low tide, I went clamming with him and his sister Clarice near Sand Key. With a couple of hundred clams and a little melted butter, we enjoyed a steamy feast.

The only thing Tom Larkin did that I objected to was to allow two separate First Communion Masses to be celebrated – one for the parish school and one for C.C.D. – rather than one. Because the Eucharist is supposed to be the sign of unity for the Church, I didn't think this was right.

Instead of insisting that the nun who was principal of the school and the ex-nun who was director of religious education work together, he gave in and let them work apart. These two women gave him more headaches as pastor than everyone else put together. They couldn't stand each other and refused to communicate – and everyone knew it. They should have been ashamed of themselves. There's no place for mortal combat in the Church.

With three hospitals and at least a half dozen nursing homes in the parish to care for, a lot of my first two years were taken up with visiting the sick. This wasn't so much a social call as it was to anoint the elderly and seriously ill with oil specially blessed for this purpose – something only a priest can do. One priest at the parish used to refer to this as "oilin' 'em up" with "the fastest thumb in the South." Commonly referred to as 'last rites' even today by uninformed Catholics, the Sacrament of the Sick uniquely mediates healing grace, forgiveness of sin, and peace of mind to those in a life-threatening condition due to age, illness, or injury. Emergency calls at any hour of the day or night were common at St. Cecelia. I'll never forget the first time I was called to the emergency room where a dozen medical staffers were trying to save the life of a teenager critically injured in a car crash. I can still feel the intensity of the scene I entered as a newly ordained priest. The importance of this graced moment in the eyes of a victim's loved ones cannot be overestimated. It is never forgotten. Recently, more than thirty years after the fact, this dying boy's sister – remembering my name all this time as I remembered his – recognized me in church. She had to thank me again for what I had done for her brother so long ago. For me, this was a humbling reminder of the treasure I have been given to carry as a priest in this earthen vessel.

When I was first ordained, priests were still the only ones permitted to handle the Eucharist. That meant I did a lot of running around bringing communion to the sick, especially on the first Friday of the month, according to popular devotion in those days. That also meant I had to be present in time to help with the distribution of communion at every Mass on Sundays and holy days. Back then, almost as many people went to Mass on holy days as on Sunday. A lot more people went to Mass on Sunday in those days than they do today, because they were led to believe with real trepidation that they'd go to hell if they missed Mass even once. In other words, priests, including me, spent a whole lot of time doing things we no longer do today – either because there are fewer of us, or because others now can do these things. For example, lay women and men have assumed far more of the responsibility that is rightly theirs by baptism for such things as parish administration, visitation of the sick, religious education, and sacramental preparation. Far more, however, have yet to step up to the plate.

We also used to spend a lot more time celebrating the Sacrament of Reconciliation, or 'hearing confessions' as some still crudely refer to it. Long lines of penitents and multiple confessors were standard fare on Saturday afternoons. Communal penance services during Advent and Lent that today draw great crowds had not yet been introduced. In terms of the renewal envisioned by the Second Vatican Council for all the sacraments, Reconciliation seems to have fared the worst – at least as far the rite for the reconciliation of individual pentitents is concerned. In practice, almost nothing has changed since the *Rite of Penance* was published in 1975. As a rule, people still rattle off a long list of petty offenses. For some the list has changed little since they were children. It seems safer for them that way, just in case God is not really going to forgive them but punish the hell out of them. This is especially true when it comes to the sixth and ninth commandments – for many the only two that count, and for some the only two that exist. Whether it's a thought, a word, or a deed, if it has anything to do with sex, it's got to be bad.

Is the Church still hung up on sex? From my experience 'hearing confessions,' a lot of Catholics sure seem to be. People just don't seem willing to do the work of looking deeply into their hearts to see what God sees. It's as though they see no connection between their lives and the Word of God they hear proclaimed and preached on Sunday. That the quality of preaching still leaves something to be desired is well known. But no one seems willing to admit that an unhealthy and increasingly neurotic tone has crept into the contrition of a lot of Catholics. There seems to be little interest in a true change of heart – real conversion – without which no change in behavior can occur. It's no wonder they keep confessing the same old 'sins' – trivial matters for the most part. This is not what the Sacrament of Reconciliation is supposed to be about. How wonderful it is when once in a blue moon a person genuinely in need of repentance seeks it wholeheartedly, and I have the awesome privilege of mediating it. It's like coming upon an oasis in the middle of a desert of drivel. If you've ever wondered what 'hearing confessions' is like, now you have a better idea.

My first experience of prison ministry occurred while I was at St. Cecelia. In those days, the 'good old boy' network – not particularly friendly to Catholics – still prevailed in Florida politics, including the governance of its correctional system. Before new prisons were built on the other side of the county, I went to visit inmates housed at the jail in the old courthouse in downtown Clearwater. I have to admit being a bit wary, not knowing what to expect. But behind bars, I found what seemed to be genuine remorse, even on the part of 'hardened' criminals – people who committed murder and rape. Perhaps taken aback by my youthful appearance, they impressed me as being like lambs – some of them undoubtedly waiting to be led to the slaughter.

What a priest brings to a person who is seriously ill or in prison differs from what a friend or relative brings. For example, people who know how ill they are may share thoughts and feelings with a priest they share with no one else. They hear plenty of pious platitudes from well-intentioned people who don't know what else to say. The presence of a priest, on the other hand, before he ever says a word, somehow brings peace and speaks of life – far more so than in times past when the presence of a priest, summoned at the last minute for the 'last rites,' signaled only the imminence of death. For the most part, changing the understanding of the Sacrament of the Sick – unlike the Sacrament of Reconciliation – has been successful for the Church. To the person who is seriously ill, a priest brings neither judgment nor expectation but a respite that gives lingering comfort to the soul – often to the amazement of onlookers. Who but a priest can discuss death openly with one who is dying without fear? A small defeat for death at work, a firm new hold on life, and the forgiveness of all sin – such is the gift that is mine to give as a priest.

As with everything in life, there is a lighter side to death, and my association with funeral directors over the years has proven therapeutic in that regard. With the large elderly population in Florida, we have an awful lot of funerals – so many in fact that parishes in Pasco County have long engaged in good-natured competition for the proverbial 'Golden Casket Award.' Stipends from funerals form a considerable portion of a priest's compensation. I like funerals not only for the money, but because they provide a 'teachable moment' – a rare window of opportunity to touch the hearts of people otherwise unavailable to us. People never forget what a priest says and does at a funeral. Most of the time they're deeply grateful. While celebrating a funeral for a friend or relative is tough, it is a gift I am uniquely privileged to be able to give. Celebrating my mother's funeral was difficult, but I did not find myself overcome with grief. People wonder how a priest can do that, but who better to? While I do not look forward to dying, I can honestly say I am not afraid to die. If I am a believer, why should I be? Why should you?

Weddings are another story. I don't like weddings and will do almost anything to avoid one. Most priests – and according to Ann Landers, clergy across denominational lines – feel the same way. I'll take a funeral over a wedding any day. I have great respect for the Sacrament of Matrimony, but again, like most priests, I wonder why the Church is in the marriage business to begin with. Good marriage preparation is important, but in my experience it has little to do with how, if, and when a marriage ever reaches the level of sacrament. In our culture, the dignity of marriage has largely been lost. Perhaps the Church could recapture it by celebrating marriage as a sacrament only when it becomes appropriate to do so, rather than every time a person merely baptized in the Catholic Church is involved. The fact is that many priests do not encourage couples living together – by far the norm today rather than the exception – to get married in the Church, at least not right away. If their union succeeds – at least half will not – and when their commitment to one another and to the Church is certain, then they are ready. For many that will take years, for some it will never happen. Only when a couple has reached that point do we in fact have a union than can then be declared indissoluble, a marriage than has in fact become a sacrament and deserves to be celebrated as such. It has been asked, if the Church requires eight years of preparation for Holy Orders, why does Matrimony require only six months?

In 1975, I wrote my thesis for the Master of Theology degree on *The Pastoral Care of Divorced and Remarried Catholics*. This opens up a can of worms for a lot of people. The title itself is something of an oxymoron. How does the Church care for people it has excluded from its purview? In fact, it doesn't. To my knowledge, nothing in the official discipline of the Church barring remarried Catholics from the sacraments has changed since I wrote that. What has changed is the attitude of those who want to remain actively involved in the life of their Church, including its sacraments. Acting in good faith, they see no harm in doing so without official sanction. The attitude of quite a few priests has changed along these lines as well. Many desirous couples have been helped to resolve their dilemma conscientiously through the use of the 'internal forum' – especially where petitions for a declaration of nullity have been unavailable or proven too arduous. People in this situation usually do not advertise their status or make a point of telling their parish priest. The number of people in 'irregular' unions of one kind or another in every parish is enormous – gay couples, unmarried couples, as well as divorced and remarried couples. Some still feel they need the Church and are part of it, even if the institution doesn't regard them as such.

St. Cecelia afforded me plenty of other opportunities to spread my wings for the first time. I worked on social justice issues – trying to raise people's consciousness of their responsibility for the plight of migrant farm workers, the right to life, and world hunger. I ran a fifteen-week open faith-sharing seminar focused on the still-fresh teachings of the Second Vatican Council. These served the same purpose that RCIA does today. I wanted to put potential converts at ease by creating a more casual setting for instruction and conversation than the traditional classroom. Every week I set up comfy chairs, cozy coffee tables, and soft lamps – satisfying my own need to 'rearrange the furniture' in the process. This is something I still delight in doing – at home, in worship spaces, and in other people's houses if they'll let me. Along with the documents of Vatican II, we used *Christ Among Us* as a weekly text – at that time a wonderfully modern presentation of the Catholic Faith by Anthony Wilhelm. Sadly, this book was subsequently viewed by Rome as too liberal and banned. The people who did that would probably have liked to ban the documents of Vatican II as well, but that would have been a little above their pay grade. Liberal or not, it's the best resource I've ever found for people interested in becoming Catholic.

One of the things I enjoyed most at St. Cecelia was teaching twice a week at the parish school, located a couple of miles away. I really got to know a lot of kids in the parish that way and they got to know me. I tried to make it fun, for my sake as well as theirs. I know I could never have taught school full-time, but this proved to be a learning experience for me as well as for the kids. I caused a ruckus when I said – without thinking of my audience first – that pets don't go to heaven. I managed to redeem myself later. I literally fell down on the job altogether when I went roller skating on St. Patrick's Day in 1977. I'm actually a good skater, but I tripped over some little kids in front of me, going down on my wrist and creating a pile-up on top of me. After a trip to the emergency room, I thought I had better tell my boss. I was anxious about how he would react when he saw the cast on my arm. Never having been to the third floor of the rectory where the pastor lived, I summoned the courage to climb the stairs – like Dorothy in *The Wizard of* Oz. Gently rapping on his chamber door, I waited. At the sight of me, he laughed. My fears were relieved. God probably laughed too. I had to give left-handed blessings for a while, but life went on.

Monsignor Larkin never gave me a hard time. Only once did he ask me not to do something – not to turn off the lights for morning Mass in the old wing of the church where a few die-hards sat in silence while everyone else actively participated – the way we were all supposed to. St. Cecilia had to add a wing that turned out to be larger than the original church, resulting in an L-shaped building with a cock-eyed sanctuary – a dreadful arrangement for liturgical celebrations because people on one side couldn't see or hear those on the other. In my naïveté, I thought I could get these recalcitrant souls to move. I'm now convinced that no power on earth could have accomplished this. Had an earthquake occurred in the old wing, they would have remained sitting in the rubble. I've slowly learned to leave these people alone, because you can not win. The physical arrangement of St. Cecilia church has not changed to this day. For me, it accurately represents the Church at large today – with a 'new' wing much larger than the 'old' to which some still cling, lifelessly. If people on one side will not recognize and welcome those on the other, trying to get them 'on the same page' will not work. In a situation like this, everyone loses and nobody wins.

One of the reasons I enjoyed my time at St. Cecilia was being surrounded by fun-loving people. Harvey Toonen, a Norbertine from Minnesota, was a happy-go-lucky priest I could talk to about anything. Like me, he loved the beach and being out on the water. Harvey really knew how to enjoy life. Margaret Vandenberg, a British lady older than God with a wry sense of humor, was the quintessential sacristan. Her nephew Simon, a magician, once hypnotized me at a party and got us all to do some crazy stunts. Then there was the time Michael Rhodes, a young man in the parish, and I tried to flock the Christmas trees for the church with fake snow using a vacuum cleaner. It was great fun but it got a bit messy. I discovered that the music director, Tom Carey, though good at keeping a straight face, had an impish side as well. I'll never forget the time I talked Tom into having a drink with me in the sacristy while the priest went to town giving his sermon at the last Mass on Easter Sunday. There we were when the pastor walked in. The expression on Tom's usually impassive face was priceless. Rather than cop to any impropriety, I simply raised my glass and proposed a toast. Monsignor Larkin just smiled, knowing something was up but not quite what.

With this crew, plastic bugs and rubber snakes had a way of turning up in some strange places. To this day, Tom Carey and I still enjoy seeing each other when we both happen to be booked at the same church for the same Mass on the same day – one of us at the altar, the other at the organ. At this point we could probably trade places and no one would be the wiser. Everyone knows church musicians have a reputation for being tempermental. So do I. That's always made it easy for me to bond with them. All this may sound slightly irreverent. But ask anyone who works for the Catholic Church – especially these days – and they'll tell you how valuable a sense of humor is. It takes some of the heaviness out of what we sometimes have to do. I've learned that taking things too seriously is definitely worse than not taking them seriously enough.

Re-introducing communion in the hand in 1977.

VI ALONG FOR THE RIDE

A young priest has a way of becoming part of a number of families in every parish he's assigned to. It didn't take long for me to become a fixture at the Sikorras. The mother of eight, Mary Sikorra was in constant motion. Exuberant is the only word to describe her. Her energy level was phenomenal. The Sikorras' big house in Belleair was the center of activity for the whole neighborhood, the place everyone – including Harvey Toonen, Mike Lydon, and I – liked to hang out. One of the things we all did together was ride mopeds. We got a great deal on six black-and-white Pacers. Mary and Harvey, Pat Deegan, Mike, his mom, and I rode all around Pinellas County on them. One day I found a photo of myself in the newspaper, taken from behind, riding solo through South Pasadena. Teaching at St. Cecelia School, I got to know Joe and John, Mary's youngest two kids, quite well. With the same effervescent personality as their mother, they were just as much fun to be around.

During the summer of 1977, Mike and I borrowed a Coleman pop-up tent trailer from a parishioner, hitched it to Mike's car, and headed northwest with Joe and John, going into eighth and ninth grade, along for the ride. And what a ride it was – first to Rocky Mountain National Park in Colorado, then to the Grand Tetons and Yellowstone in Wyoming, Glacier National Park in Montana and Waterton Lakes in Alberta across the border, and the spectacular scenery between Banff and Jasper in the Canadian Rockies. With wildflowers at their peak on Mount Revelstoke, the hillsides were bursting with color. Seeing Old Faithful erupt, beholding the icy blue splendor of Lake Louise, and walking up on Athabasca Glacier were exciting new experiences for all four of us. Our best or worst adventure – depending on your point of view – was paddling past towering snow-clad peaks in our inflatable Florida raft down the strong and swift Bow River in Canada. John and I went first, intrepidly floating through the alpine scenery without incident, till we spotted Mike and Joe parked downstream an hour later. Then it was their turn. They weren't as lucky. Caught by a felled tree across the river, their small craft was quickly flipped by the current. They themselves were submerged in near-freezing water till they could get to shore. John and I didn't know what had happened when we finally caught sight of them. Dried out by then, they had begun turning blue from the cold. To add insult to injury, it began to snow. A few hours around the campfire finally thawed them out, and they were good as new.

Mary was waiting for us in Minnesota, where her older kids lived, as we made our way back across the northern Great Plains. After giving her back her boys, Mike and I went sailing for a day with their big brother on Lake Minnetonka before heading home. Joe and John were cute kids. It was a joy for Mike and me to have them with us, and of course they loved every minute away from their parents. We had fun with the Sikorras for years after that, until John went off to the Coast Guard, and Joe went to seek his fortune in Hollywood.

That same year my brother Mark joined the Air Force. My first nephew, Joshua Welsh, was born and I baptized him. My sister Beth graduated from high school in 1978. Around this time, Mike and I bought our first boat, a pre-owned sixteen-foot Larson tri-hull bow rider with an eighty-horsepower outboard motor. Made in Minnesota, it was more suitable for lakes than for the Gulf of Mexico, but the price was right. Like all boats, this one turned out to be a hole in the water you pour money into. Salt water really does a number on the outboard motor and the metal fittings and rails, so you have to flush the engine and rinse the whole boat with fresh water every time you use it. If the battery doesn't lose its charge, the bilge pump refuses to work, or the trailer lights go out. It's all par for the course. Boat owners know what I mean – that's why their happiest days are the day they buy their boat and the day they sell it. Owning a boat in Florida, though, as Mike and I did for years, is still a lot of fun. Everyone in my family has owned a boat. Why not? It's sunny, the water's warm, and chances are you can stand up if you fall out.

It's amazing how many friends you gain when you own a boat. No one ever turns a boat ride down. If we had a dollar for every priest and nun and even a few bishops (they should be worth more than a dollar) Mike and I took out on that boat, we could buy a new one. Once we took some of the altar boys from St. Cecelia for a ride. Later we picked up Monsignor Larkin at the dock. Coming from a meeting, he was still wearing his black suit – not exactly boating attire. We thought we were doing him a favor, letting him sit up front in the bow. But his weight, added to an already full boat, tipped it forward ever so slightly. It was just enough to let water come in the drain it usually goes out – right at his feet. Before anyone knew it, his black leather shoes were under water. With his usual good humor, he took it in stride.

I've flown the boat through the air, both accidentally and on purpose. I've also almost sunk it, completely by accident, to be sure. These perils are all part of the fun. Mike didn't like to ski, but I did. Once I skied right over a very large shark. Needless to say, we both held our breath. We also enjoyed going out on peaceful nights a mile offshore to watch the sun set and the lights come on on the beach. Looking up at the Skyway Bridge from the water is a view most people never get, but we did. One of our favorite places to go was Egmont Key, a large island off the southern tip of Pinellas County. The half-submerged ruins of an old fort, strategically built at the mouth of Tampa Bay to defend it during the Spanish-American War, made for a fun place to climb and explore.

Caladesi Island also has some of the most beautiful white sand beaches in the world. No longer an island, it's now connected to Clearwater Beach. A succession of tropical storms filled in the pass separating these two land masses. Once, while the boat was pulled up on shore and I was leading a troop of altar boys inland, a *St. Petersburg Times* photographer snapped a photo that appeared in color on the front page. Mike and I also used to drive up the

Intracoastal Waterway and come down the mouth of the Anclote River to Tarpon Springs, following the sponge boats till we docked at Pappas Restaurant for a Greek salad. Slowly cruising the cool, crystal clear waters of the Rainbow River to the world's largest springs was perhaps our favorite trip.

The worst thing that happened out in our boat was when heavy fog rolled in from the sea. We had no choice but to creep along till we could find one channel marker, then another. Another bad thing happened when the cotter pin holding the propeller on broke off, leaving us 'dead in the water.' Once we set up a tent and slept on a spoil – an island – in the Intracoastal Waterway overnight. During the night the anchor gave way, and the boat slipped away. In the morning, we spotted the boat being carried out to sea on the tide, but we were able to swim out to it before it got away for good.

On another occasion, we took the boat into the shop for maintenance on the engine. A couple of days later, Mike and I were going somewhere when we saw a truck carrying a boat that looked an awful lot like ours. "Look at that," Mike said, "it looks just like *our* boat!" "Can't be," I said, "ours is in the shop." We called the marina to be sure, and sure enough, it *was* our boat. They admitted that they were taking it to get it fixed after their fork lift driver dropped it. They were hoping we wouldn't notice. But when a fiberglass boat hits the pavement after falling ten feet, it isn't pretty. We got some money from insurance, but an even better deal on a new boat from the marina, now embarrassed about the whole affair. I suppose we could have sued, but this probably worked out more to our advantage in the long run. Our second boat was a 1980 eighteen-foot Chaparral, also a bow rider but with a V-shaped hull better suited for the waters of the Gulf. With a one hundred forty-horsepower outboard, it did about fifty miles per hour. Bryan and Ginny White, good friends, had the name *Tweedledee* painted on one side and *Tweedledum* on the other. Good times on the water kept rolling.

Mike and I gradually learned the ropes, but boats do have a mind of their own. We both enjoyed fishing a great deal in those days, especially around the artificial reefs along the coast a few miles offshore. Fishing by a piling, Mike once pulled up an octopus. We've both reeled in sea gulls that dove at the bait on the hook before it hit the water. Though we never had a miraculous catch of fish, we couldn't stop hauling bowfin out of the Anclote River. They tasted alright, but saltwater fish make much better eating – especially blackened redfish, speckled trout, sea bass, and grouper. Deep sea fishing boats are a lot of fun too. The seminary chartered one once on the Atlantic coast. Only a mile or so out, we hooked into an enormous school of bluefish and caught a ton in just an hour. A lot of guys were seasick due to the swells, and the decks were covered with blood from gaffing these hefty fish. A bit messy, but I'm immune to motion sickness, so I loved it. Back at the seminary, we ate bluefish for a week. Another thrill was catching and releasing my first tarpon – five feet long and eighty or ninety pounds – with my sister and brother-in-law at Boca Grande. Then there was the time that Mike's sister, Lynn, chartered a fishing boat on the east coast. Mike caught a dolphin fish – *mahi mahi* – and I caught a wahoo. They were both delicious. That day we saw dozens of makeshift rafts abandoned by 'boat people' – Cuban refugees picked up by the Coast Guard – floating away to a watery grave. These are my best 'fish' stories. There's nothing fishy about them, however. They're all true.

Something very unusual happened my first winter at St. Cecelia. Coming out of church after the early morning Mass, along with everyone else I was dumbfounded to see that it had snowed. For a few frosty hours, the ground was covered with white. In the forty-five years I've lived in Florida, this has never happened again. It probably never will.

Not long after I was ordained, I was elected to the Priests' Senate – forerunner of today's Presbyteral Council, an advisory board to the bishop. Bishop McLaughlin was not one to waste time on long meetings. That, and his sometimes blustery manner, gained him the nickname 'Hurricane Charlie.' He would get our input on matters affecting the Diocese and the parishes, then make up his mind – often on the spot – and let everyone know his decision. We seemed to get things done a lot quicker in those days. Since I had a good relationship with him, we always enjoyed seeing each other. Once shortly after he was appointed, Bishop McLaughlin came to visit Good Counsel Camp. Since I needed a ride back to St. Petersburg, he gave me one. Unbeknownst to him, he was also transporting some ill-gotten goods in the trunk of his car – a box of those glass insulators I had collected all over Citrus County. A rather intense individual, the bishop had an alarm on the speedometer in his silver Buick set at sixty-five miles per hour. It kept going off all the way home.

I also got involved in ecumenical affairs. This was a cause dear to the heart of Harold Bumpus, a retired priest of the Diocese and a true Renaissance man. Harry could talk the ears off a stalk of corn. His graciousness and his gift of gab suited him perfectly for dealing with assorted Protestants, Orthodox, Jews, and eventually disenfranchised Catholics. A gifted musician and cook, Harry also built pipe organs in his spare time and installed them in several churches. I was his sidekick for a time, and years later, assistant at his parish while I was 'in between' assignments. In the wake of the Second Vatican Council, people were more interested in ecumenism in those days than they are today. Harry was a brilliant philosopher and theologian, but I was no slouch. So Bishop McLaughlin asked both of us to write a simplified paraphrase of several of the Vatican II documents for a book being compiled locally. Apparently I did a respectable job on the *Decree on the Bishop's Pastoral Office in the Church* – the publisher printed it. Harry and I remain friends to this day. In 1983, Mike and I joined him on a trip to Franklin, North Carolina, where he entertained us royally in his rustic mountain home.

My first love as a priest, however, has always been the sacramental and liturgical life of the Church. The knowledge of music and art I gained in my early years has always dovetailed nicely with my experience in the field of worship, church architecture, and environment. My love affair with the liturgy and my involvement in it at the diocesan level has never ceased. One of the first things Bishop McLaughlin asked me to do was to revise the rite of Benediction according to a new document from Rome in 1974 on forms of worship of the Eucharist outside of Mass. This was to replace the old rite still being used in parishes in the Diocese, a rite which had become more elaborate than the celebration of Mass itself. Dad selected suitable music and I selected appropriate readings and prayers to be provided as models. The bishop then authorized the user-friendly package we had assembled for the parishes. The Diocese took another step forward in the ongoing renewal of the liturgy mandated by the Second Vatican Council.

So many years later, it seems strange that a few parishes have slid back to 'the good old days' when Benediction was tacked on to the end of Mass. This seems to be more a matter of convenience than defiance. Some still haul out extra candelabra, copes, and even Latin texts, hoping to add extra solemnity – even though none of this is called for any more. A few throw in Marian devotion for good measure. Doing this only adds to the confusion many Catholics already feel. None of these things increase reverence for the Sacrament because they blur the critical distinction between the celebration of the Eucharist during Mass – its primary purpose – and reservation of the Eucharist, which always remains secondary. Confusion over this issue has given rise to 'wars' over the placement of the tabernacle in churches in this diocese and across the country. I've already related how I learned early on that some people prefer to remain in the dark where they're comfortable, rather than moving into the light where they're not. The Church's stated goal for the liturgy remains the same – full, conscious, active participation on the part of all present. To encourage this is my number one priority as a priest. Short of turning off the lights, I continue doing everything in my power to achieve this goal.

Another thing Bishop McLaughlin asked Jim Russo, a native New Yorker like himself, and me to do was to train Eucharistic ministers. We had to do this from scratch, devising a day-long training session for women and men recommended by their pastors from every parish in the Diocese. For the first time in centuries, lay people were again being empowered to distribute communion at Mass and to the sick, but they needed thorough catechesis on the history and theology of the Eucharist, spirituality, and ministry. They also needed practical guidelines, a hands-on demonstration of the proper techniques, and to be commissioned in the bishop's name. Working in tandem, Jim and I took our show on the road, so to speak, traveling to five central locations along the west coast of Florida. As part of a tidal wave of lay ministry that began to sweep across the Church, the two of us trained at least a thousand Eucharistic ministers for our Diocese. The long lines for communion at Mass were shortened almost overnight. Wherever people were sick, they were able to receive the Eucharist more often.

Back at St. Cecelia, knowing my fondness for the liturgy, Monsignor Larkin tasked me with choreographing the services for Holy Week, the Church's most sacred annual rituals. It was an act of trust on his part to let me do this, and a valuable experience for me. The complex ceremonies of these high holy days went well. So did the re-introduction of the practice of receiving communion in the hand. In the United States, this option was to be restored after an extensive and delicate catechesis on the Feast of Christ the King in 1977. Monsignor Larkin asked me to prepare and give a series of homilies on the Eucharist at all the Masses in the parish four Sundays in a row. Apparently these did the trick, as a majority of parishioners chose this option. This proved to me that traditional Catholics will accept change if it is presented thoughtfully, with good reason, and in a favorable light with sensitivity to their feelings and respect for their beliefs. When these conditions are met, there is little or no resistance. But when they are not, look out.

Receiving communion in the hand today, of course, has become the rule rather than the exception. But at that time, it was viewed with suspicion by some – even as it is today by a handful of holdouts. These are the same individuals who still won't receive communion from anyone but a priest, or who throw themselves down on their knees to receive even though everyone else is content to stand. "O Lord, I am not worthy," they would say. "Of course you're not worthy," I would reply. "The Eucharist is not a reward for being good or perfect. It's the help and strength we all need to be better." At a time when people are highly concerned about the spread of communicable diseases, receiving communion in the hand is clearly the more hygienic choice. Anyone who's ever been bitten or slobbered on placing communion on the tongue knows why.

For a number of years, the Diocese sponsored Dad's and my attendance at various national convocations, to keep up on liturgy and music around the country – in Albuquerque, Chicago, Detroit, Washington, Miami, and Panama City. Looking back, I don't know how I managed to stay so busy and keep my head on straight. Keeping up a feverish pace is not unusual for the newly-ordained. Some come out of the seminary with a 'messiah complex,' believing themselves ordained to save the world and everyone in it. But youthful enthusiasm and idealism eventually wanes. Experience has a way of dispelling myths. Energy levels decline. Reality checks occur, sometimes harshly. The necessity of healthy self-care and a spiritual life emerges. Time off is critical. New priests are fragile. They can break, and they sometimes do. More than ever today, they need gentle guidance – mentoring – so as not to be lost. Affirmation is vital, from the people they serve and from the institutional Church. I'm grateful I got what I needed.

VII   STOP AND GO TRAFFIC

It was 1978 and time for vacation again – this time to the Northeast in my bright red Mazda.   Mike and I took along two senior high school boys, Ed Stein from my parish, and Rick Newsham.   Mike knew Rick and his family from Blessed Trinity Parish and had taught Rick how to swim when he worked as a lifeguard.   Even then Mike was an accomplished guitarist, so his guitar came too, coming in handy around the campfire.   We borrowed the Coleman camper and the inflatable boat again, stopping first on our way up the east coast at our friends, the Reilly's, on Long Island.   The next stop after seeing the sights in Manhattan was Revere Beach near Boston where Rick's aunt lived. Proceeding through the quaint towns on Maine's coast, we took in the maritime scenery of Acadia National Park, before crossing the Canadian border into New Brunswick with its eroded coastal rock formations called 'flowerpots.'   Over lobster rolls, we watched the amazing 'tidal bore' – the leading edge of the world's highest tide – funneling into the Bay of Fundy.   Nova Scotia, with its distinct French and Scottish flavors, favored us with old forts, lighthouses, mines, rocky cliffs, grass-carpeted highlands strewn with wildflowers, and a plethora of fresh seafood – including lobsters fresh off the boat.   A delinquent lobster trap washed up on the beach came across the border with us on the way home, and yards of nylon rope from the sea – so strong Mike and I still use it today to tie our kayaks down on top of his car.   A visit to a few national landmarks including Arlington National Cemetery in the District of Columbia brought that summer's odyssey to an end.

My second assignment was waiting for me.   Returning to my 'home' parish of St. Jude in St. Petersburg – where my family went to church when we moved to Florida and where Dad later became music director – was a change I welcomed.   I had served early Sunday morning Mass there while attending high school just a few blocks up the street, next door to the Chancery. When the Diocese of St. Petersburg was created in 1968, St. Jude became the cathedral church. Built in the 50's, its sheer size and the great round sanctuary beneath its dome clearly destined it to become a cathedral some day. St. Jude was just a mile from home.

Cathedrals are strange places and they attract some strange people. They're a hybrid of sorts – a combination of parish church and diocesan gathering place. People from all over town, often displeased with their own parish, flock to St. Jude – ironically the patron of hopeless cases – seeking orthodoxy, status, or who knows what. As a parish, St. Jude is disproportionately large, and has a grueling schedule to match. Like many parishes in Florida, the population is predominately elderly. Young people, even families with children, are quickly swallowed up in a sea of gray hair. St. Jude still has its own grade school, supported by fiercely loyal parents. My three years at the Cathedral were primarily spent doing grunt work – what assistant pastors usually do. For the first time I got my own office – I didn't have one at St. Cecelia – right inside the door of the hopelessly inadequate little house across the street used as a parish office in those days. The receptionist once chided me for 'bellowing' at her with my door open instead of using the intercom even though she was only ten feet away.

Part of being assigned to the Cathedral was to become what I termed a 'professional' concelebrant, expected to be present – as an ornament if nothing more – at every liturgy the bishop attended. The local bishop is actually pastor of the cathedral, though he usually has no involvement in the day-to-day administration of the parish nor does he usually reside there. My real 'pastor' was the rector of the Cathedral, J. Bernard Caverly, an Irish priest whose brother Patrick, also a priest, was my tenth-grade English teacher at Bishop Barry. Bernie was good to me and to every priest who passed through St. Jude while I was there. There were many – Tom Spillett and Mike Devine among them. Joe Grech came from Rome every summer. The

Cathedral attracted some strange characters among the clergy as well. One of the most cantankerous yet loveable was Monsignor Francis Pack. An elderly cigar-smoking gentleman from Tennessee who lived with his stepmother, Frank always liked me. He was nobody's fool.

Cathedrals sometimes have a haughty air about them, but St. Jude never did. Bernie had his own house, and the rest of us – two or three or four at any given time – lived at Dartmouth, a modest split-level home in a neighborhood half a mile away. Mike and I kept our boat on a trailer in the back yard. Since it was a little too far to walk to the parish three or four times a day, my moped was perfect for running back and forth unless it rained. We definitely had some fun at Dartmouth, watching the reaction of unsuspecting friends to a dribble glass, drinking beer, eating pizza, and playing Uno well into the night. With the Reillys, our friends from New York, we had one rockin' New Year's Eve party – so much fun it's hard to remember. The youngest priest in the house, Bill Lau, could be grumpy. He was not pleased.

During my time at St. Jude, I grew a beard. Actually, I came back from vacation with one, for no particular reason except that I got tired of hearing people say, "You're too young to be a priest." Of course, I'd really love to hear them say that now. There were quite a few *cursillistas* at the Cathedral, and they would not rest until I made a Cursillo weekend. I did, at a sweltering old building at Our Lady of Perpetual Help in Ybor City. I have to admire the faith of these people. Cursillo really changed their lives. Whenever I visit the Cathedral, I see some of them still engaged in one form of ministry or another. More power to them – and to any movement in the Church that inspires people along these lines and to this degree.

The young Diocese of St. Petersburg was rocked by the sudden, unexpected death of Bishop McLaughlin at the end of 1978. My first pastor, Tom Larkin, was appointed Apostolic Administrator of the Diocese, and a few months later, to everyone's surprise – and contrary to the usual custom of Rome in appointing an outsider – he was named

Bishop. The fact that he had been Pope John Paul II's classmate and taught him how to speak English might have had something to do with it. He would have been the people's choice in any case, and no one was more pleased than I. One of the things Bishop Larkin asked me to do for him was to ghost-write his homilies for various occasions. After all, I was familiar with his manner of speaking, his theological comfort zone, and – knowing who his audience would be – it wasn't too hard to pen what a bishop should say. I was smart enough to avoid any overt heresy, and liking the man as I did, I wanted him to sound good. I knew he rarely made any spontaneous comments while speaking publicly. Sure enough, more often than not, he delivered these talks word for word.

It wasn't long before I became a master of ceremonies for episcopal liturgies at the Cathedral. I had observed two priests, Jim Gloekler and Keith Symons, model this role for years. Basically a choreographer, it's the emcee's job to make sure all the players have the right stuff in the right place at the right time. He himself remains as invisible as possible to make everyone else, especially the bishop, look good – as though they know what they're doing. By rehearsing all the players and prompting them individually as needed, he ensures that everything goes smoothly and that God is given the glory he is due. Of course that rarely happens, and God gets a good laugh instead. The worst thing that can happen is when something is supposed to happen but nothing does – or when something is not supposed to happen but does. A pot of smoking incense may set off the fire alarm, for instance, or the sprinklers come on while everyone is processing across the lawn. My experience directing the play in the seminary helped me with being an emcee. There was some fun in telling people, especially those who outranked me, what to do. But for the most part, it was a thankless job. My greatest challenge was directing the largest ordination we've ever had – six priests at the same time. I also recall emceeing the dedication of Our Lady of Lourdes' new church and the groundbreaking ceremony for the new parish of St. Brendan where, as a deacon, I had taken that door-to-door census.

After Bishop McLaughlin died and before Bishop Larkin was installed, two auxiliary bishops arrived – one from Rochester and one from Raleigh – to confer the sacrament of Confirmation around the Diocese. Confirmation tends to become a show in parishes, and the show must go on. These were two very nice gentlemen. I served as their chauffeur and tour guide as well as their emcee for a month. They got a boat ride, too.

The summer of 1979, Mike and I and our friend Dave DeFreitas set out to explore the Pacific Northwest in Mike's brown Malibu. This time, for a couple of hundred dollars, we had bought our own second-hand fold-out camper – a lightweight aluminum Apache. On the way, we saw where pioneers heading west in wagon trains had etched their names on El Morro, a great white slab of rock in the desert of New Mexico. We laid eyes on the groves of giant sequoias in California's Kings Canyon, the unmatched splendor of Yosemite, the lava tubes and paint pots of Lassen. We visited the ghost town of Bodie and the shore of Lake Tahoe, observing the deep blue waters of Crater Lake, haystack rocks off the craggy Oregon coast, and the picturesque waterfalls of the Columbia River Gorge. We took in the rose gardens of Portland, the slopes of Mount Rainier, the Olympia brewery at Tumwater, the rain forests of Washington's Olympic peninsula, and the undeveloped North Cascade Mountains. Finally, we trained our cameras on Grand Coulee Dam, the site of Custer's last stand at the battle of the Little Big Horn, and Devils Tower in the northeast corner of Wyoming – where Spielberg's *Close Encounters of the Third Kind* had been filmed two years before. David didn't stay with us all the way, and Mike and I needed a vacation after that marathon, but a good time was had by all.

To this day I associate the collapse of the Sunshine Skyway Bridge with the Cathedral, because I had just walked into the parish office across the street after Mass on a foggy morning in May, 1980. The story was 'breaking news' as the media calls it today – a term so overused I laugh every time I hear it. I also remember the morning Bernie was not pleased with a comment I had made at Mass about communion taking so long because St. Jude was the only parish in the Diocese that didn't have Eucharistic ministers. Hearing this as he was having his breakfast probably gave him indigestion. It wasn't his fault that our arms were falling off distributing communion by ourselves. Ironically, the Cathedral – the largest church in the Diocese with the most communicants – was the only place Bishop McLaughlin did *not* allow lay ministers. No one was bold enough to ask him why. In theory, a cathedral church is supposed to model state-of-the-art liturgy, music, and environment for the whole diocese. Ours never has. Almost nothing has changed since it was built. There's still a marble altar rail encircling the sanctuary that effectively says "keep out." The giant golden tabernacle in the sanctuary overshadows everything else. The choir is still behind the assembly in the loft. The baptismal font is nowhere in sight. Renovation plans have come and gone over the years. Another is currently being weighed. I'm not holding my breath. My observation is that cathedrals are more often the last places to change rather than the first – an 'unsolved mystery' of the Church.

I've never discovered how the politically incorrect comment I made about Eucharistic ministers in church got to the ears of the rector across the street even before I did. You'd have thought I had spoken heresy. Bernie told me to leave the matter alone since the dead bishop's body wasn't yet cold in the grave. He was right, and I did. However, I'm going to go with 'prophetic' for what I said. It wasn't long before St. Jude got lay ministers of communion like everyone else and my arms finally got a rest.

Desmond Daly, a jolly Irish priest I knew from living at Christ the King in Tampa years before, asked me to do some television Masses. Still being a little wet behind the ears, I wasn't too sure about this but I agreed to. These were videotaped months in advance, three or four Sundays at a time – back-to-back 'episodes' to be put 'in the can.' That meant three or four mini-homilies had to be prepared, aimed at a target audience of homebound folks who due to age or illness could no longer get to church. Local television studios are another world. Timing is everything. I had cue cards in my face counting down the minutes and seconds I had left to finish. It was like having to land a plane on a dime, touching down at just the right second on an airport runway. It was a challenge I got good at. At least I always got invited back – to stare once more with great sincerity into the gaping black hole of the camera's face. Local parishes vied to have their servers, readers, and choir members imported for their 'fifteen minutes of fame' in the next taping session. With stage makeup put on my face, I was afraid of having to get out of my car on the way home, but that never happened. Thus my media career was launched. Though my liturgical sensibilities were offended by the theatrics involved, producing our own TV Mass in those days served a good purpose until it was no longer cost-effective.

The Deegans hosted a party for my thirtieth birthday at their expansive waterfront home, perched on the tip of Island Estates. Over the years, Mike and I made more than a few stops at their dock on our boat, hopping into their hot tub or watersliding into their pool. I don't know why, but my friends had the bright idea to buy me a beer-making kit for my birthday. Nothing tastes as good as beer you've 'brewed' yourself – five gallons at a time. But after a few batches, it proved too labor-intensive. You have to sterilize the bottles each time, then fill and cap each one. The worst part was having to wait five or six weeks for the fermentation process to finish. One notoriously alcoholic priest staying at Dartmouth couldn't wait. After consuming a bottle of peppermint Schnapps, the only booze he could find in the house, he raided the unfermented stash in my room.

Mike and I took a different tack in the summer of 1980, and as crazy as it may seem looking back now, I'm glad we did. As the saying goes, opportunity knocks but once. Eastern Airlines had an 'unlimited mileage' promotion at the time. For a fixed price you could book all the flights you wanted on any of Eastern's routes in the western hemisphere over a period of three weeks. Al Gore hadn't dreamed up the internet yet, so airline timetables were only available in print. Mike and I carefully examined the schedule of flights and destinations. A travel agency on St. Pete Beach helped us reserve a few overnights and line up a few tours from our hotels. It's amazing how much two people can do and see in a limited amount of time – even on a limited budget like ours. It almost became a contest to see how many places we could go. Since Atlanta was Eastern's hub, we flew through it half a dozen times, on twenty-two distinct segments, not once missing a flight (though we had to run through one terminal) or being booted as a result of overbooking. Impressed by our ambitious itinerary, one flight attendant moved us up to first class.

So where did we go? To Denver and Rocky Mountain National Park. To Mexico City, where we took in the folkloric ballet, the shrine of Guadalupe, the ruins of the colonial city of Antigua, the Aztec pyramids of Tenochtitlan, and a riotous ride on the canals of Xochimilco. To New Orleans, where we sipped hurricanes at Pat O'Brien's with Eileen Cornwell, Mike's assistant in the Diocesan Youth Office. To Guatemala City in Central America and a bumpy bus ride to the incredibly colorful indigenous market of Chichicastenango. To San Francisco and its new ultra-modern cathedral, to Alcatraz, and to Monterey Bay. To the beach and a night club in San Juan, and to the Caribbean island of Antigua to visit Tom Armstrong, a member of the Reilly clan and the Christian Brothers. To New York, where we saw *A Chorus Line* on Broadway, with a final stop in Charlotte, North Carolina, on the way home. Long distance phone calls cost money in those days, but in most of these places we were able to stay with friends and save money. This three-week fantasy of flight including tax cost us less than four hundred dollars. I've kept the flight coupons all this time. With a deal like that, it's no wonder Eastern went out of business.

Each of these destinations yielded its own adventures. We had a couple of hours to kill on a connection in St. Croix, for instance. So, walking out of the airport, we found our way to the beach and enjoyed just sitting still for a change, gazing at the clear turquoise waters. The most fortuitous event, if you can call it that, happened on a bus tour out of San Francisco. The suspension broke as we pulled into a winery in the country. I can think of worse places to be stranded. Not too distraught at our fate, we took advantage of the opportunity to sample a bottle of every wine produced there over the next couple of hours. It was a wild ride back to the city. It's strange my memory of this trip isn't foggier than it is. Like most young men, Mike and I drank quite a bit in those days. He quit in 1984. It took me eight more years to wise up.

For most people, that would have been enough. But with a week of vacation left, Mike and I hooked up our new boat and headed for the Florida Keys. Mary, John, and Joe Sikorra pulled our camper with their Suburban, and Bahia Honda State Park – one of Florida's gems near Marathon – became our home. We spent about twelve hours a day out on the water. I tried windsurfing, but it's harder than it looks, so I didn't stay up on the board very long. Of course we had to set foot on the southernmost point of land in the United States, so we drove to Key West and visited Ernest Hemingway's famous hangout, Sloppy Joe's Bar. We tried to lure a few lobsters out of their rocky roost with a mop top, but I don't recall much success. We spent the most time doing what is now called 'snuba' – snorkeling while breathing through an air hose connected to a compressor floating along on the surface, enabling you to stay under shallow water indefinitely as though you were scuba diving. A few miles offshore, the coral reefs around Sombrero Key were the perfect place to do this for hours on end. I remember looking at barracuda right in front of me, nose to nose and tooth to tooth. Three and four feet long, they were motionless, seemingly suspended in the clear warm ocean water.

Taking time to smell the roses in Portland, Oregon.

VIII   FORWARD MOTION

Mike's youngest sister, Patty, died in May of 1980 at the tender age of twenty-two. Everyone takes notice of the death of someone so young. It's tough enough under normal circumstances, but Mike had the courage to celebrate Patty's funeral Mass at St. John, the parish on St. Pete Beach where he was assistant pastor and Dad was music director. The entire parish school came to the Mass. I gave the homily, hoping God would somehow touch the hearts of everyone present through words he would give me. That's all a priest can do. We have to leave the heavy lifting to God, allowing his strength to shine through our weakness.

I stayed at St. Jude one more year. Early in 1981, Mike and I explored the chilly bayou country of southern Louisiana for a week, savoring crawfish and all manner of Cajun delicacies deep down in the delta of the mighty Mississippi. A highlight was touring the McIlhenny Tabasco sauce factory, built over a salt dome in the earth on Avery Island. The acrid aroma of hot peppers in vinegar aging in oak barrels still lingers in my nostrils. Back at the Cathedral, I assisted at the episcopal ordination of Keith Symons in March. Everyone was thrilled at his appointment to assist Bishop Larkin as the first (and so far only) auxiliary bishop of St. Petersburg. I got rid of the beard but kept a mustache as I began my third assignment at St. Patrick in Tampa – where Mike had first been assigned – in June. My first niece, Laura Welsh, was born in October, and I baptized her.

Two more summers brought two more great outdoor adventures. Our new used Cox camper came with a sink and a room air conditioner, but Mike and I 'pimped our ride' with an electric heater, a stereo, a TV, a dual hot-plate for cooking, a faucet operated by a button on the floor, a twelve-volt cooler to keep food, an overhead lamp, and a spice rack and cutting board mounted on the counter. The camper was a piece of work, literally. We were riding in style. Finally we rigged up a collapsible full-size TV antenna and headed west in 1981 with Jim Previtera and Mike Coller – best friends at Bishop Barry and senior servers at St. Jude. After a stop at Capulin Mountain, an extinct cinder cone volcano in New Mexico, we visited the famous mission church of St. Francis in Rancho de Taos. Then we explored the ancestral Puebloan cliff dwellings at Mesa Verde, posed for a photo at Shiprock, drove through Monument Valley on the Navajo reservation, and toured Glen Canyon Dam at the foot of Lake Powell and an old movie ranch at Kanab, Utah. For the first time, we viewed the Grand Canyon from the less-traveled but equally impressive north rim, and the spectacularly colorful high-altitude natural amphitheatre at Cedar Breaks.

Jumping in emerald pools hidden high up on canyon cliffs, we revisited Zion National Park in Utah. After going tubing on the Virgin River, we hiked down to the base of the pink and orange pinnacles rising from Bryce Canyon's floor. We had to put jackets on inside Timpanogos Cave outside Salt Lake, only to warm up again in the thermal waters of Lava Hot Springs in Idaho. After seeing Idaho Falls, Mike and Jim skipped stones across the smooth surface of Lake McDonald inside Glacier National Park. There we took a few days to hike through the forest to some glorious waterfalls beneath Glacier's majestic snow-covered peaks. We visited the historic Jesuit mission of St. Mary in Montana on our way to the wonders of Yellowstone and the familiar fresh air of the Tetons. Heading south through Flaming Gorge, we explored Dinosaur and Colorado National Monuments before a final stop in Denver to see my brother Mark working at Lowry Air Force Base and my godmother Kate, and a tour of the Coors brewery in Golden.

During the summer of 1982, we set a new record for distance – driving all the way to a point on the Pacific coast of Canada just across from Ketchikan, Alaska – this time in my new Dodge Diplomat. Two boys from St. Patrick, my new parish in Tampa, joined Mike and me on this little outing. Pat Dukart and Jay Van Auken knew each other from serving Mass together. Jay's grandparents, Herb and Alice Baybutt, were friends with whom I spent many an evening imbibing and solving the problems of the world. Driving all the way to Calgary in Alberta put us at the base of the Canadian Rockies for the second time in five years. The thunder of massive Wapta and Takkakaw Falls in Yoho National Park, the serene vermillion lakes and mineral hot springs of Banff, the jagged silhouette of Moraine Lake pictured on the Canadian twenty-dollar bill, the turquoise green waters of Peyto Lake, the hanging glaciers and frozen lakes along the Icefields Parkway, the elk herds of Jasper, and the marble canyon of Kootenai – such incredible natural beauty easily overwhelms the senses. Mike and Jay paddled a sturdier inflatable raft down the swiftly-flowing Bow River without incident this time. But Pat and I, taking in the dramatic alpine scenery surrounding Lake Louise in our little boat, were briefly rocked with waves from an avalanche onshore.

Then we headed west across British Columbia. At Kitimat, we toured a copper smelter off the Yellowhead Highway on the way to Prince Rupert on the coast. From locals we learned a delicious new way to grill salmon – wrapped in foil covered with mustard and brown sugar. The four of us hitched a ride in the back of a pickup up a mountain overlooking the town. We gazed out across the narrow fjords we would see again from the ferry we boarded – with car and camper – for the overnight trip down the famed Inside Passage along British Columbia's rugged coast. After landing at Port Hardy the next day, we explored lighthouses and tide pools along the unspoiled shore of Vancouver Island, marveling at halibut as big as we were being lifted off fishing boats. The quaintness of Victoria – with its decidedly British atmosphere – impressed us, as well as the lavishly landscaped grounds of renowned Butchart Gardens. A few hours by ferry through the San Juan Islands put us back in Washington State for the long cross-country trek home. The arid lava wastes of Craters of the Moon National Monument in central Idaho attracted our attention along the way. Near Denver we ascended Mount Evans with my brother Mark, all the way to its windy, frigid summit at fourteen thousand feet. There we observed the oldest living things on earth – rare gnarled bristlecone pines – thousands of years old. Finally, from the roof of Mark's high-rise on the Fourth of July, we had a 'war' with the building next door, shooting bottle rockets back and forth until someone called the cops.

I witnessed my youngest sister Beth's wedding – at St. John where Julie was married – in the fall of 1982. While my first year at St. Patrick had gone well, the second did not. Martin Obert, the pastor, genuinely tried to make me feel welcome. Marty was a big man, his neck so thick he could hardly button his collar. He had been a Franciscan missionary working on a Zuni Indian reservation in New Mexico until coming to the Diocese a few years before. He was also a smoker. We got along fine. There was another priest at St. Patrick when I arrived – a comedic character – but he went back up north as I recall, leaving just the two of us. That changed the whole dynamic.

Much of the work I did in the parish was familiar and routine for me at this point – preparing couples for marriage, for the baptism of a child, writing up annulment petitions, conducting wakes and funerals, visiting parishioners in local hospitals and nursing homes, anointing and taking communion to the homebound, giving instructions in the Catholic faith, teaching children's religion classes, and of course celebrating Mass. One of the dear little ladies I used to visit gave me a can of hollyberry air freshener from the Fuller Brush Company. All I can say is that it smells like Christmas. The can is rusty with age, but I still mist the house with it ever so sparingly at holiday time, savoring its delicious scent. Marty shared my own concern for good liturgy, so he put me to work with the altar boys and the first girls I'd ever seen on the altar, lectors, Eucharistic ministers, and the parish liturgy committee. This has always been my favorite work. What an assistant pastor is spared having to do is administration. That's where the biggest headaches come from. I'd get sixteen years of that later.

St. Patrick was in Tampa. Though only a short drive from Pinellas County – what I've always considered 'home' – Tampa was a foreign land to me. Like a lot of people who live on the west side of the Bay, I didn't care much for Tampa. I go there once a year for retreat, but that's about it. Going to the airport doesn't really count because it's before you really get to Tampa. The parish was sandwiched between MacDill Air Force Base to the south and the larger, more affluent parish of Christ the King to the north. The neighborhood was old, slightly run-down, and mostly blue-collar. Marty depended heavily on a take-charge woman in the parish to run almost everything. The Scoutmaster and the music director rounded out the pastor's coterie. The parish had a striking raven-haired young secretary and two poor old women hanging on as housekeepers. Neither of them could cook, unless you count opening a can as a culinary skill. My clothes came back looking like they had been pounded on a rock, so I started doing my own laundry. Marty and I lived in a duplex behind the ramshackle old house that held the parish offices. My workplace in this maze of cubbyholes was a converted garage.

I've never lived high off the hog. I don't expect any-one to wait on me. I prefer a simple, uncluttered life. The standard of living at St. Patrick was just not what I was accustomed to. Marty was a good priest and a friendly fellow, but he didn't seem to care. We spent less and less time together. I took advantage of every opportunity to eat out.

The parish had a truly dedicated servant in Bill Yarawsky, the maintenance man, later ordained a deacon. In his apostolate to the sea, Bill ministered to diverse crew members on ships passing through the Port of Tampa. Maintenance chiefs are perhaps the least appreciated parish workers. Given little or nothing to work with, they're routinely called upon to work miracles, and rarely receive the acknowledgement they deserve. Bill at St. Patrick, Leon Miani at St. Jude, and Greg Powell at All Saints came to my rescue beyond the call of duty time and time again. To me, these men and their counterparts in every parish stand out as special human beings and real servants of the Church. For that matter, anyone who works for the Catholic Church knows they could probably earn more money elsewhere and has to have a higher purpose for doing so. My Dad did for his whole life. Volunteers deserve high praise, but employees of the Church do, too. Almost every one of the people I've worked with has added joy to my life.

The parishioners of St. Patrick were lovely people. They took pride in their well-worn old church – the front half of a long, low, nondescript building that also housed a hall. One of many built across Florida, this starter building became a permanent substitute for a real church at St. Patrick and other parishes. The sacristan was a no-nonsense sweetheart who led a club of quilters at the parish in a labor of love – making a bedspread I still treasure in my favorite colors, brilliant green and yellow. The parish was also served by a long-suffering director of religious education, and a marvelous St. Vincent de Paul Society that cared for a steady stream of needy parishioners and vagrants. It also had its own school.

Even then, St. Patrick School – still staffed by teaching Sisters at that time – was draining the parish of money, fighting to stay alive. During my second year, Marty found himself increasingly at odds with the school principal. I found myself caught it the middle. The situation deteriorated as the school year progressed. The parish began to feel the effects of this contest of wills. The rumor mill fired up, and people began taking sides. Burdened with having to look after his elderly mother at the same time, Marty became despondent. We spent even less time together. The battle between the pastor and the principal heated up to the point of polarizing the parish. The Sisters threatened to withdraw from the school, and they did. Marty withdrew from public view as much as possible. I tried to help but nothing I said or did mattered. I needed to get out of there before I was sucked further down into the muck. As soon as Easter was over, I asked out.

Whenever a priest asks to be relieved of his assignment, a few eyebrows are raised. I didn't care. I was due to be transferred again in a few months, but the situation had become intolerable and I knew I had to get out now. Marty was also sinking. Eventually he took a leave of absence to get the support he needed. He managed to come back to St. Patrick for a while, but it was a Pyrrhic victory. The parish was the biggest loser of all. I took a short break and flew out to Denver. My brother and I went horseback riding at the Air Force Academy in Colorado. There was still enough snow in the mountains, so we went skiing as well. I'd been out to visit him and my godmother after Christmas when we drove up to Grand Lake and went snowmobiling on national forest roads in Rocky Mountain National Park. I also remember dining on fresh rainbow trout after going ice skating with Mark on a frozen lake. A change of scenery always does a body good.

St. Theresa in Spring Hill welcomed me with open arms in the spring of 1983. Those two months with my friend Harold Bumpus quickly revived my drooping spirit. Populated with retired Midwesterners, St. Theresa had quite a few funerals. Several times a week, parishioners gathered for a potluck after a funeral. They brought their flasks – to salute the deceased, of course.

For all the good they do, Catholic schools today place a tremendous strain on the budgets of even the most affluent parishes. Incapable of sustaining themselves on tuition alone, they require massive subsidies from the 'feeder' parishes of the families that supply their students. This situation is rapidly reaching critical mass for the Church in the United States. While there is impassioned resistance to abandoning a parochial school system that has survived so long, every proposal put forth to ensure its viability seems to be met with opposition.

There's no question that a separate school system served a valuable purpose for generations, at a time when a largely segregated and immigrant Catholic population had not yet found acceptance within the mainstream of American society. Times have changed. My experience interviewing parents seeking to enroll their children in 'Catholic' school is that the majority are really seeking a 'private' school at a bargain-basement price. My observation is that there is little that is actually 'Catholic' about Catholic schools today. Whatever is 'Catholic' about them is not what the parents I've talked to are really seeking. They're looking for more discipline, less violence, and higher academic standards than public schools afford. Little else matters to them. They will go through the motions (jump through the hoops) of registering in a parish and meeting the minimum required level of giving – the bar is usually set ridiculously low – in order to qualify for a tuition subsidy from the parish, often as much as a thousand dollars per child per year. Their annual contributions to the parish rarely come close to this amount. Subsidies are provided even for families that can well afford full tuition and make no real effort to practice stewardship. When I asked the families in my parish if they would voluntarily forego the parish subsidy and pay the full tuition rate themselves, I was told to drop the idea at once. The system of paying for Catholic schools is broken.

The fact is that only relatively affluent families can afford to send their children to a Catholic school today. The noble idea that any child who desires a Catholic school education should be able to receive one, regardless of their ability to pay, is unrealistic. A diocese would need an endowment fund of a billion dollars for this to happen. Parishes can't keep coming up with huge subsidies. The reality is that today, Catholic schools serve far more children of privilege than poor children. A Catholic school that has served the African-American community in Tampa for over a hundred years is fighting for its life. Consultants have advised closing the school because it's costing a quarter million dollars a year to subsidize. Privilege, on the other hand, tends to breed a sense of entitlement. When people with money start thinking their children have a right to attend a Catholic school and that the Church had better provide one, something is wrong. I cannot be the only pastor who's had parents say as much to me.

Pastors routinely report not seeing the families of Catholic school children in church on Sunday, even though regular attendance at Mass is the bedrock of any covenant they sign in order to obtain a subsidy. This was my experience as well. At baptism, parents agree to be the primary religious educators of their children. If parents fail in their fundamental obligation to make Sunday Mass a priority for their family, what is the point of sending their children to a Catholic school?

For all these reasons, Catholics have to ask whether keeping a floundering school system alive is still worth it. Is the value of a Catholic school education, so loudly touted by some, still real or largely a myth? What value do Catholic schools have for the parishes that are their sole surviving lifeline? What value do they have for the Church if they are bleeding parishes to death financially? According to the National Catholic Education Association, during the past decade enrollment in Catholic schools nationwide has declined by twenty percent. Twenty percent of Catholic schools have been consolidated or closed. Tough decisions lie ahead. It seems to me the handwriting is on the wall.

With my days at St. Patrick behind me, Mike and I headed for the west coast with Jay Van Auken again during the summer of 1983. We wandered across a desert of sand dunes, hundreds of feet high, strangely situated at the feet of lofty snow-capped peaks in southeastern Colorado. Then we hiked the south rim of the Black Canyon – the steepest and narrowest in North America – its sheer depth nearly hiding the Gunnison River, still slicing through rock at its bottom. For the first time we laid eyes on the great towers of sandstone in Arches National Park near Moab, rafting down the Colorado River on our first commercial float trip. From nearby Island in the Sky, we gazed down on the White Rim and the vast canyonlands of Utah, with forays into Capitol Reef National Park and even more remote Natural Bridges National Monument. We marveled at the subterranean splendor of Lehman Caves just inside Nevada and the exquisite beauty of Oregon Caves. A quick trip through Yosemite took us to two out-of-the-way national monuments in California – Devils Postpile, with its symmetrical basalt columns, and Pinnacles.

From Monterey, we hugged the coast northward across the Golden Gate Bridge through towering redwoods – the world's tallest trees – to the starfish-studded tide pools along Oregon's rocky shore. After touring a sawmill, we were half deaf and still shaking from the thunder of heavy machinery swallowing trees whole and spitting out lumber. After gazing into the cobalt depths of Crater Lake, we headed south through the arid lava wastes, frozen lakes, and steam vents of Lassen National Park in northeastern California. Stranded nearly a week in the shadow of Mt. Shasta by a failed transmission – one of the few times we've experienced car trouble – after a quick stop in Denver, we finally headed back to Florida. As much as I enjoyed myself on this trip, there were days that were difficult for me. I didn't know what was wrong, but something inside me was hurting. I would find out in time. A few days behind schedule, it was good to be home.

At home with my brother Mark and his wife Pat.

IX   FLYING HIGH AND LOW

It was time to begin my fourth assignment as associate pastor of St. Catherine of Siena Parish in Largo. Glad to be back in Pinellas County, I couldn't have asked for a better pastor than Keith Symons, by that time auxiliary bishop of the Diocese. Only a few months later he was named Bishop of Pensacola/Tallahassee. A lot of us at St. Catherine made the long drive through northwest Florida to his installation that November. Mike Finnegan, already handling much of the administration of the parish, was named pastor. A kindler, gentler soul you could not hope to meet.

Priests generally make a retreat once a year. There used to be so many of us that we had to do this in shifts at the Franciscan Center in Tampa. A bunch of priests can be a tough crowd. The rector of the seminary once said he'd rather preach to convicts than priests because there was more hope for their conversion. It's also been said that whenever the sun comes out on a cloudy day, it means a priest went to confession. Boys will be boys, however. During one of these retreats, Pat Trainor and Jim Herlihy snuck out to go to the dog track in Oldsmar. They took Mike and me with them. I've never been one for gambling, but I do remember having a good old time, winning a trifecta, and coming home with a few bucks in my pocket. The best retreat we ever made was called Emmaus, named after the road the two disciples were traveling Easter Sunday night. They recognized Jesus when he broke bread with them. For several years, Mike and I continued meeting with a small group of priests – six or eight different backgrounds and personalities – with whom we shared our deepest thoughts and feelings. We got to know and to care for one another intimately in this group. We each derived a great deal of support, something priests greatly need but don't always seek.

Mike and I entered a whole new world when we joined our friends the Sikorras in purchasing 1982 500cc

Honda SilverWing motorcycles. These beautiful full-size touring bikes came decked out with matching burgundy saddlebags, trunk, helmet, Lexan windshield, and crash bars – all for twenty-nine hundred dollars. Our parents and friends had some misgivings – Bishop Symons couldn't figure out what a bike was doing in St. Catherine's garage – but I'm glad we got them. We'd so outgrown the mopeds. So much did we enjoy these relatively quiet bikes, we kept them for twenty-one years. Even at that time, in order to ride a motorcycle in Florida legally, every rider had to pass a safety and defensive driving course. Having done so, we were good to go, though I have to admit riding these bikes took a bit of getting used to. My adrenaline kicked in a few times when I found myself stalled out in the middle of an intersection, or trying to stand a five hundred pound machine back up after it tipped over.

Mike and I hooked up with a 'gang' of riders – mostly retired guys – for a while. In those days you could actually enjoy cruising around, going for a ride over the Skyway or driving through the woods in the northern part of the county, for example. There are no back roads any more. Whether on four wheels or two, you take your life in your hands every time you get on the road. I've called Pinellas County home for forty-five years, but even first-time visitors quickly realize there are far too many traffic lights, and they last too long. Consequently, we have the highest number of red-light runners as well. It's almost impossible to make a left turn at your own discretion without having to wait for a green arrow – at some intersections, up to four minutes. Traffic management around here is a real oxymoron.

The most fun I ever had with our little group of riders was cruising across the state in the cool of night to see the space shuttle blast off at dawn. I had offered the parking lot at St. Catherine as a central place to meet up and start out at midnight. The other guys in the house probably didn't appreciate a dozen motorcycles firing up to get rolling. He forgave me later, but I know Arthur Proulx didn't. After all the talk about bringing lady friends along, I've never lived down the fact that I, the priest, was the only one who did. After driving through the night, we crashed – figuratively speaking – on the beach in sleeping bags till blast-off at dawn's early light. Feeling the earth shake with the roar of the rocket was a uniquely exhilarating experience.

In February of 1984, Mike and I saddled up and took in the local color along the back roads of Florida and Georgia on our way to Great Smoky Mountains National Park, straddling the border of North Carolina and Tennessee. We dressed appropriately for the cold ride on our bikes. A winter wonderland awaited us. Freshly fallen snow clinging to every tree branch, bush and twig provided a perfect Kodak moment. After melting and refreezing, the snow had iced some patches of road – bad for cars but even worse for motorcycles. Putting a kickstand down on snow and ice isn't very reliable, either. After parking side by side, we were walking away when we heard, first one crash, then another, as one bike falling over knocked the other one down. That incident was filed away for future reference.

Always hoping to find a way to perform some service for my country, I was commissioned as a chaplain in the Air Force Reserve in October, 1983. The idea came from a priest I had known in high school, Phil Halstead, who was Catholic chaplain at MacDill Air Force Base in Tampa at the time. I was also proud to be following in the footsteps of my dad and my brother. The military had plenty of chaplains but never enough priests. So, with the endorsement of the Diocese, Jim Johnson and I decided to help. We could also use the extra income. I knew St. Catherine could spare me for the twenty-four days a year I would be required to serve. Unlike 'weekend warriors' who train together one weekend a month, I was attached not to a reserve unit but to MacDill itself – a Strategic Air Command base then housing a wing of F-16 fighter jets. I was part of the 56th Combat Support Group that, in the event of war, would not go to the front but stay behind as backfill. That sounded good to me. At that time, in addition to being a SAC base, MacDill was home to two other U.S. Commands. Thousands of personnel from all branches of the armed services worked at MacDill, including a lot of brass.

As a chaplain, I did the same things at MacDill that I would do in any parish – celebrating Mass, counseling, and visiting the small hospital on base. But because I was there so infrequently, knowing what the Air Force expected of me and how to accomplish it wasn't easy. I thought the Catholic Church had a lot a red tape until I discovered the paper trail the Air Force requires for everything. I knew chaplains do not carry guns. I would have been uncomfortable with that in any case. Chaplains are welcome everywhere, so I made it a point to visit a lot of places on base just to meet and greet the troops. This 'ministry of presence' is very important within the military community. I always wanted to go for a ride in an F-16, but there was so much red tape involved in getting certified by the flight surgeon, the only thing I got to fly was a desk. I did get to know a couple of helicopter pilots, so I got to fly in a few Vietnam-era choppers, drilled full of holes by enemy fire. The cargo doors were wide open during these training runs. I loved going along for the ride.

Of course I had to qualify physically to get into the Air Force. So I did the same thing everyone else does – report to the Military Entrance Processing Station in Tampa. That was fine, except that I was the only person over eighteen in sight. Although I had to register for the draft when I was eighteen, I got a deferment as a divinity student. At MacDill, I got to know the base commander's executive officer, Lieutenant Colonel Larry Wood. That opened a few doors. A fine man who became a good friend, I was able to obtain an annulment for him so he could marry Maria Grazia, the charming Italian woman he loved. Though we've lost touch now, Larry and his wife and her family welcomed me and my friends to their home in Naples more than once over the years.

My Air Force career lasted six years. I knew I would have full retirement benefits if I stayed in for twenty, but I was comfortable with my decision to 'retire' after two three-year stints. I still find the most intriguing aspect of my service to have been the fact that, while I knew how to be a priest, I knew nothing about being an officer. I was a First Lieutenant right out of the box. That meant a lot of people would be saluting me when we passed outdoors, and I would have to salute at least a few. I didn't want to get in trouble for not doing what I was supposed to do. The other chaplains jokingly told me not to go outdoors. Most reservists have previous experience on active duty, so they already know the ropes. I didn't. I had to cram just to learn the ranks and how to recognize them in time to salute or not. I got the Army and the Air Force – which are more or less the same – down pat, but I never did figure out the Navy. It was almost two years later – not till the summer of 1985 – that I finally went to Air University at Maxwell Air Force Base in Montgomery, Alabama. The first two weeks were an Officer Orientation Course, an indoctrination into the Air Force way of life and code of conduct. I felt like a fish out of water, but so did everyone else in my class. Our instructors took pity on us. We had to perform calisthenics and go running every morning – not my favorite thing to do at the crack of dawn – but I did it, as well as the prescribed number of push-ups and sit-ups. We even practiced how to march and do a few drill maneuvers, but since most of us were full-time civilian clergy, the bar was set low enough to allow us all to pass. You've got to love the Air Force – they pay you to go to school.

The remaining three weeks were spent in Chaplain School. Perhaps because a third of us were priests, our class was atypically composed of all white male Christian ministers – no females and no minorities. That sped up the bonding, and I learned more about other denominations in those three weeks than I did in eight years in the seminary. Chaplains must be all things to all people regardless of denomination. This was some useful education. Learning to dispel the stereotypes Protestant and Catholic clergy typically have of one another served us all well. The most fun we had was the overnight bus trip for survival training down to Eglin Air Force Base in the Florida panhandle. We had to eat those awful dehydrated Meals-Ready-To-Eat out of foil pouches. The best part was rigging up hammocks made out of parachutes in the pine trees where we had to sleep. That was fine until it rained. Yes, we survived – some lousy food, a poor night's sleep, and a few mosquitoes.

The State of Florida offers reservists a very official-looking vanity license plate. I got one and put it on my new dark blue Dodge Diplomat. My car happened to be the same model and color as the Air Force staff cars that general officers ride around in. I swear this was a coincidence, but riding around Maxwell and MacDill, my car – although bearing no flag – was often saluted just because it *looked* like a general officer's car. I got a kick out of that because I was expected to return the salute, so I did.

Those six years were a unique chapter in my life. In 1987, I was promoted to Captain. It was a proud moment when Dad – going on seventy and still looking good in his Air Force Lieutenant Colonel's uniform – and retired General Earl Peck pinned the insignia of my new rank on me in a ceremony at the base chapel. Two years later I was awarded the Air Force Commendation Medal for Meritorious Service and honorably discharged. Someone will get a flag when I'm laid to rest.

St. Catherine was always a pleasant place, but it had a ridiculous schedule of eight Masses on the weekend. One building housed three or four priests and the parish offices, so you could never really get away from work or people without going off campus. The church was another dreadful multi-purpose building – a long, narrow box that extended across three time zones when the two folding doors were open. People in back couldn't even see the sanctuary, much less the priest. The same building doubled as a bingo hall, with a couple of classrooms tacked on for good measure. After thirty years, a real church has just been built. The music director was a young woman from the Philippines with an angelic voice who had taken organ lessons from Dad. The housekeeper doted on us and actually knew how to cook. It doesn't happen often in a parish that everyone is a pleasure to work with, but everyone at St. Catherine was.

Mike Finnegan was the hardest working pastor I'd ever seen, but he didn't seem to have many friends or much fun in his life, and he almost never took time off. He didn't drink, but he was a diehard smoker. At St. Catherine for twenty years, he died suddenly at only fifty-nine. Mike was always well cared for by Jim and Marie Jeanne McCasland, parishioners who baked him Irish soda bread every week. The McCaslands became friends of mine as well. I spent countless evenings at their home playing piano, having drinks, laughing and telling stories. They really knew how to cook. There was nothing the McCaslands wouldn't do and didn't do for their parish, and for their priests. Life at St. Catherine was a familiar grind. The parish provided priests for Mass at the county prisons every week – I usually went to the women's jail. Being locked in with the inmates, however briefly, was always unnerving, but the ladies seemed to appreciate my being there. I also taught a course in moral theology at St. Catherine when the Diocese first began its Lay Pastoral Ministry Institute.

After eighteen years working for the Church in Florida, Dad retired from his Diocesan work in music and liturgy, but not from parish work, in 1983. Now he had more time for making stained glass. In 1984, the Diocese of St. Petersburg was cut in half, literally, at the Skyway Bridge. I'm glad I was in one of the five northern counties at the time, as everyone and everything in the six southern counties became the Diocese of Venice. The following year, our dear friend Father Gloekler died, twenty years after bringing my family to Florida. Mike had been put in charge of his first parish in Fort Myers. But after only eight months, he was made pastor of Corpus Christi in Temple Terrace, a parish with a school and a reputation for being tough on priests. It took its toll on him as well.

In March of 1984, Mike and I had ridden our motorcycles down to a party in Ft. Myers. We had a good time but we had to get back that night. Neither of us was feeling any pain, but I was worried about Mike. Despite the rain, we barreled all the way up Interstate 75 on our bikes until we went our separate ways. Both of us made it home, but Mike was stopped by a cop for going too fast through downtown Tampa. He was let go, but neither of us should have been on the road to begin with. Mike was simply exhausted, in his own words, "sick and tired of being sick and tired." He asked for help, and a day later, the Diocese had him on his way to St. Louis to heal. Mike knew he had to give up drinking. He has done so successfully to this day. He didn't tell me what he was doing until he was gone, as I'd probably have tried to stop him. However, it was the best thing he could ever have done for himself.

At that point in our relationship, Mike and I leaned too heavily on each other. I missed him a lot, and I was angry about his going away. He would be gone for months. I was starting to let things get to me as well, but I didn't know it yet. I soon found out.

Dad pinning on my Captain's bars at MacDill in 1987.

X   MAKING A PIT STOP

A few months later, I drove up to Citrus County on my day off to see a family I knew. I was almost part of their family, and something of a father figure to their kids. I could be myself with them. Their mom and I had a few beers, and it was getting dark. One of the boys yelled a vulgar name. I thought he was being a punk and dissing me. I grabbed him and threw him up against the wall of his mobile home, knocking his head against it. I didn't hurt him, but I could have. I scared him, I scared his mother, and I scared myself. Worst of all, I left to go home without saying a word. I shouldn't have been on the road. I was angrier than ever.

I don't know what came over me that night. I'd never done anything like that before, nor have I ever again. That doesn't matter, because what I did was wrong. This boy was a kid of thirteen. He looked up to me, and I let him down. I inflicted an emotional wound on his family. I was ashamed, but I was angry. I was angry about Mike being gone. I was angry about other things as well, and I didn't even know it. I used anger as an excuse for a lot of things I said and did. I used anger unknowingly for years to keep people at a distance, wondering all the while why they kept their distance from me. I'd always had trouble with strong feelings and self-control. But I was functional. Alcohol calmed me down. That's what I told myself.

The Chancery heard about this incident and was concerned. The priest charged with taking care of priests with problems came to see me the next day. He made me an offer I couldn't refuse. The Diocese wanted me to take some time off and take a good look at myself. They would pay for it because they valued me. I didn't think much of the idea, but I was hurting. Deep down inside, I knew I needed help.

Since that time, I've come to feel that seeking help for one's problems is a sign of strength, not weakness. Having been there myself enables me to encourage others in the same direction. Accepting this opportunity was the best thing I could have done for myself, even if it wasn't my idea. It may well have saved my life and my ministry. Before I left, Bishop Larkin, who knew me well, assured me that he still wanted me to start a new parish. That made me feel better. The thing I would miss most was taking three boys on a trip out West. We'd been getting ready for it for weeks. But life is what happens when you're making other plans.

Most people knew nothing about what was going on at the time. Now they do. People who knew me well, of course, knew I had a problem handling my emotions. My family did. Mike and my other friends did. They loved me all the same, even the ones I hurt. I was beginning to admit the truth to myself. I concluded I had everything to gain by going and nothing to lose. I put on a happy face and got ready. The parishioners were told I was taking a temporary leave of absence for health reasons. This prompted an incredible volume of mail assuring me of their prayers and support. People understand in their own way. They have great affection for their priests, and great compassion for their problems.

For the next four and a half months – from June to October, 1984 – Whitinsville, Massachusetts, a little town near Worcester, became my home. That fall, I got to see the leaves turn color for the first time in twenty years, and they were no less than brilliant. I was a popular guy right away, having my own car. Weekends were meant to go places, and New England had plenty. There were always several dozen priests, sisters, and a few brothers staying at the House of Affirmation – founded by a priest and a nun – at any given time. We quickly became family, and like any family, old members would leave and new members come. Describing itself as a 'psychotheological therapeutic community,' the House of Affirmation used every means possible to promote mental, spiritual, and emotional growth and wellness among Catholic clergy and religious. In a big old mansion on beautiful wooded grounds, I took part in individual and group therapy sessions conducted by clinical psychologists several times a week. That was the hard work. Like others,

I had to overcome some denial before I began to see the light. We also had a lot of fun together, learning how to line dance, doing relaxation exercises, going to art therapy, and having community meetings night and day where everyone was encouraged to tell their story. We spent a lot of time talking but even more time listening to one another and learning.

One of the greatest common problems priests and religious report is loneliness. Today more than ever, priests are isolated in their own parishes. I used to say I was 'on a short leash' for sixteen years. This provides fertile ground for behaviors that are not conducive to good health, especially for those with addictive personalities. Only a few priests still smoke, but a lot struggle with drinking, overeating, failing to exercise, and not taking enough time off. Some end up in one kind of trouble or another as a result of generally not taking good care of themselves. Too much work, not enough time, and being too tired are always the excuses given. We really have no one to blame but ourselves for this situation. If we don't make taking good care of ourselves a priority, who will? We can blame the Church for some things, but not for this.

Just knowing that others at the House of Affirmation were struggling with the same issues I was helped me a great deal. Not only did I come to understand and accept myself more fully, but I also brought tools home with me to maintain my emotional and spiritual health more effectively than I had been doing. The House of Affirmation did not really address my use of alcohol. I had to do that later. But the months I spent there helped me feel better about myself, and that made all the difference in the world. I've continued to seek professional help in managing my life a number of times over the years since. I'm not ashamed to admit that. Time spent in therapy has improved the quality of my personal and professional life immensely. Anyone who's known me a long time recognizes that.

Mom and Dad came to see me in Massachusetts, and I was able to tell them some things I needed to. That moment was a turning point in my relationship with my father – we've been closer ever since. We enjoyed going to Boston together to see the sights and eat lobster. Over the years I've managed to drop in on a number of the friends I made at the House of Affirmation in my travels around the country. I started a new hobby while I was there as well. With some help from my friends, I made my first Oriental latch-hook rug, five by seven feet – adding tens of thousands of multi-colored pieces of wool yarn, one at a time. After that, I made five more. The beauty of the finished product made it all worthwhile. That's also true of our lives, woven together one day at a time.

There were plenty of places to go besides Boston. On the weekends, I'd take friends to beautiful places like Mount Monadnock in the White Mountains of New Hampshire. On the Fourth of July, we witnessed one of the largest fireworks displays in the country over the bay at Warwick, Rhode Island. We strolled along the famous mansions of Newport on the boardwalk by the sea, and the cranberry bogs and candy factories of Plymouth, Massachusetts. We made it all the way out to Provincetown at the tip of Cape Cod, and all the way up to Colebrook, New Hampshire, just south of the Canadian border, to visit my brother-in-law's parents. With its covered bridges, antique shops, and quaint seaside villages, New England charmed us.

With my time at the House of Affirmation concluded, St. Catherine was happy to get me back and I was happy to come back. After all that, I needed a break first. In November of 1984, I flew to Barranquilla, Colombia, on the northern tip of South America, to visit my sister Julie, her husband Bill, and Josh and Laura, my nephew and niece – still little kids at the time. Besides being a hot and humid coastal city, Barranquilla has a relatively poor standard of living and a thriving black market for most everything. We spent time at the coarse black sand beaches, and took a trip along the coast to Cartagena, where we sampled fresh local seafood and toured the walled old city at night by horse-drawn carriage. Julie and I flew to Bogotá to shop and see the sights, like the great underground salt cathedral in Zipaquira, the view from Monserrate by incline railway, and the largest collection of gold in the world. I brought back a treasure-trove of gifts and souvenirs – hand-sewn leather jackets and boots, adorable enameled fragrant wood sculptures, Colombian coffee, and jewelry – all duty-free as a result of the Caribbean Trade Initiative in effect at the time. The excellent price and quality of the gold and emeralds mined in Colombia made this a once-in-a-lifetime buying opportunity.

I stayed at St. Catherine until September of 1985. On my thirty-fifth birthday that June, while on my two-week tour of active duty, I visited the Coast Guard Air Station in Clearwater. The commander was a member of the parish, so he arranged for me to don a flight suit and fly along on a couple of training runs. First I took off in a giant C-130, the four-engine turboprop military aircraft used for search and rescue and drug interdiction all over the Gulf of Mexico. Then I lifted off in a Coast Guard helicopter equipped with a newly-developed system of navigation known as 'global positioning.' Flying along the Gulf beaches, we eyed schools of cobia and sharks in the shallow waters offshore. The day was a treat for me, and a rare opportunity for the Coast Guard to have a chaplain in their midst.

At St. Catherine I made a lot of friends – Art and Ann Jewett, Gene and Gay Sells – with whom I did a lot of drinking, of course. By then I thought that's what friends were for. I had an awful lot to learn. The summer of 1985, Mike and I took off again, this time with the Kramer boys from my parish – Jeff and Tim – both good kids but unlikely brothers. At Santa Fe, we saw the 'miraculous' spiral staircase in the Loretto Chapel. At the Indian market, we bought turquoise and silver jewelry. We were amazed at how quickly a native woman seated on the ground pulled a credit card machine out from under her skirt without a ruffle. After hiking down into Canyon de Chelly, we took the boys to Cedar Breaks, and to experience the wonders of Bryce and Zion Canyons.

These magnificent places never get old for us. It's amazing how quickly one can gain and lose a couple of thousand feet of altitude going from quaking aspen forests to yucca plants and cactus flowers in minutes. For the first time, we ventured into the remote Escalante region of Utah to pristine Kodachrome Basin and Grosvenor Arch. Ten years later, Bill Clinton would protect the stark beauty of this primordial landscape for posterity by declaring it a national monument. Then it was back to the Grand Canyon, and the primitive nearby ruins of Wupatki, Sunset Crater, and Walnut Canyon. Together with Montezuma Castle – an out-of-the-way cliff dwelling dramatically carved into a sheer cliff face – these national monuments preserve North America's ancestral heritage.

After a not-to-be-missed glimpse of giant steam shovels clawing tiers of exposed earth a mile wide, grasping at veins of copper, we wandered across the sparkling gypsum flats of White Sands National Monument in New Mexico, hoping to see a missile test-fired. We didn't, so we went underground instead, touring Carlsbad Caverns by day and watching thousands of bats fly out of its gaping mouth at dusk. Finally, we roamed the ranges of Big Bend National Park in Texas, surprised at the pink and purple paddles of the Santa Rita cactus. After a soak in the natural hot springs on the edge of the muddy Rio Grande, we paid a Mexican with a rowboat a few pesos to be ferried across this not-so-mighty ribbon of river. We didn't know how shallow it was, until he *walked* us across. The four of us hopped on burros and rode a couple of blocks to a broken-down cantina in the tiny town of Boquillas, where we ordered tacos, beers, and cokes. Though the temptation to wade across the Rio Grande again is strong, today it's a violation of federal law. Hiking out of the desert up into the free-standing Chisos Mountains brought brief relief from the heat. Looking up while creeping along the base of Santa Elena Canyon's striking rock walls made us feel very small. Big Bend is one of a kind. Photos from this trip, like those before, make us laugh today. They show us grilling shish kabobs, wearing the short shorts and long socks boys wore in those days.

Around this time, I quit smoking for several years. Mike, of course, had quit drinking. At times we nearly drove each other crazy. I did the drinking, and he did the smoking – for both of us. True friends can weather any storm, however, and we did. Another storm we weathered together was Hurricane Elena, on the way back from North Carolina in September of 1985. After hopping on our Hondas for a few days off, we ended up taking only one bike when the other had a flat tire on the way out of town. This turned out to be a blessing in disguise. Our combined weight on one bike gave us the traction we needed to keep both wheels on the ground as we battled the fierce winds of Elena's outer bands all the way from the Georgia border. Someone was looking out for us. It was neither the first time nor the last.

In January of 1986, Mike and I set out on a journey to the center of the earth – to the equator, that is – this time with my sister Julie, who was still living in Colombia. Julie flew to Quito, Ecuador, where we were to meet her, but Mike and I only made it as far as Miami. We were put up in a sleazy hotel near the airport while *Ecuatoriana*, the national airline of Ecuador, sent another plane from South America to replace the one we were supposed to take because the door had fallen off in flight. The concierge at the delightful indigenous hostel in Quito where we were to stay – named *Los Alpes* for the typical alpine scenery in this land of lofty snow-covered volcanoes – found out what had happened and let Julie know. Despite her gringo-esque blond hair and blue eyes, my sister was able to navigate by herself just fine, surprising locals with her perfectly-accented Colombian Spanish. My Spanish was good enough to get us to the hotel, only to be stunned by the breaking news and unbelievable video of the disastrous explosion of the space shuttle *Challenger*. After this rocky start, the real adventure began.

Quito proved to be a marvelously cosmopolitan city nestled in a long valley nearly two miles above sea level in the Andes, and an unbeatable travel bargain. The Cathedral literally glistens with Spanish gold. A monumental statue of the Virgin Mary that figured prominently in the movie *Romeo and Juliet* overlooks the city on a hill. We ate for a song one night at a French restaurant – nothing but crepes, first stuffed with seafood fresh from the Pacific, then with tropical fruits for dessert. We were going to take an antique train trip famous for leaving people breathless as it creeps along sheer cliffs, but apparently God had other plans – the tracks had washed out just before our arrival. So we trekked east instead to Baños at the headwaters of the Amazon River on the edge of the jungle. We were amazed to see poinsettias blooming amid the exotic tropical flora and fauna near hot springs at the base of a waterfall hundreds of feet high. While we didn't have the nerve to sample the national delicacy, *cuy* – guinea pig – we saw these rodents roasting everywhere on spits. We settled for roasting the internal organs of chickens, pigs, and other small animals on skewers over a hibachi. Morning coffee was powdered with boiled milk. A riotous bus ride back to civilization followed.

We would have liked to visit the Galapagos Islands off Ecuador's coast, but the cost was prohibitive and tourism severely restricted even then. Instead, we hired a guide with a car for the day to take us to the famous Indian market at Otavalo, similar to the one we'd visited in Guatemala, where we bought hand-sewn alpaca rugs, wool sweater vests, and tapestries. The guide also took us to small towns in the region noted for their leather goods, wood carvings, and brightly painted bread dough ornaments. We brought back crowned heads of Christ carved from tree limbs still covered with bark, and miniature pairs of wooden work boots – a national symbol. Mike was taken with an exquisite if modest diamond, handsomely set in an eighteen-karat gold ring.

Most memorable, however, was the day we rented a four-wheel drive vehicle and starting climbing thousands of feet up Cotopaxi, an extinct volcano, leaving the heat of the city behind. We kept driving along a rutted track right up into the clouds until we found ourselves above them, looking down. Three miles above sea level, we were in the permanent snow zone in a national park in the sky at the equator. Llamas and alpacas, the only residents in the vicinity, came to greet us. We didn't know but soon learned they spit. Their fur is irresistible to pet, but all that saliva got messy. And then, it snowed. Just like that, a little blizzard blew up – enough to ice the sparse vegetation, and us. We had little to protect us from the elements when the first signs of anoxia appeared. The air was so thin and the oxygen so depleted, we started feeling funny. That's the highest any of us had ever been on earth. We were parked on such a sharp incline that Mike and Julie were afraid to get back in the jeep. They thought it would just roll off the side of the mountain. I actually had to start driving away without them before they got back in. In minutes, we were all fine. A rainbow appeared. The view coming down from the clouds, and the whole day's experience, was out of this world. The three of us knew what Peter, James, and John must have felt like on Mount Tabor.

Mike and I in the rain near Seward, Alaska, in 2009.

XI TWISTS AND TURNS

To celebrate my tenth anniversary of ordination in May of 1986, Mom and Dad hosted a lovely party at home in St. Petersburg. I had been at St. Catherine for three years, so the entire parish staff came, as well as a dozen parishioners who had also become part of my life. It was warm, but everyone gathered in the back yard after dark for a slide show highlighting the beauty of the national parks and other places I had been privileged to visit over the years. Mike entertained with his guitar and song. Nothing in life is better than having family and friends close by on occasions like this – people you've come to know and love, and people who've come to know and love you. It was almost summer. Mike had his own plans. The camper was ready to go, and I had no trouble finding three boys from St. Catherine – thirteen to seventeen – eager for a Western adventure.

Climbing an hour in the car up to the blustery, frozen summit of Mt. Evans, one of the highest peaks in the Rockies, had become a tradition in itself by this point. So that's what Jeremy, Bryan, Bill, and I did with my brother Mark as soon as we got to Denver. We treaded carefully around patches of tiny, fragile flowers by the alpine lakes, still covered with ice. Then the gang of us headed south to Salida where Mark had arranged a serious whitewater rafting trip through a steep canyon a thousand feet deep known as the Royal Gorge of the Arkansas River. It proved to be a long, wild, cold, wet ride, one of the most daring and thrilling runs in the country and a first for all of us. Mark headed home as the four of us headed off to the Great Sand Dunes of southeastern Colorado. A truck I had passed deliberately clipped the back corner of the camper, but the damage was slight. Next we made our way along the rim of the narrow Black Canyon, surveying the silver thread of the Gunnison River half a mile below. Park rangers guided us through the well-preserved cliff dwellings of Mesa Verde. I took the boys into Monument Valley to experience the timeless stillness of its mammoth monoliths. We climbed Fisher Towers along the muddy Colorado and explored Mother Nature's marvelous architecture in Arches National Park in Utah. One of the boys had a history of behavioral problems I had hoped would not recur on this trip. But when the Moab police picked him up prowling the streets after the rest of us were asleep, I knew it was time for him to go home. Much as I hated to put him on a bus for that long and lonely ride, he'd have time to think and, I hoped, grow up a bit. Sooner or later, we all have to.

To see the high desert plains of the Southwest bloom in summer is always a treat, and we did on this trip. Spectacular bursts of color appear across the horizon – yellow biscuitroot and wild blue flax, fiery red-orange paintbrush, lacy white cow parsnip, pink fireweed, and purple iris. We wandered along dusty washes beneath the three great sandstone spans in Natural Bridges National Monument. We followed an old jeep trail out of Moab through an unearthly landscape of rock, past salt flats and potash mines onto the perilous White Rim – encircling Canyonland's Island in the Sky a thousand feet above and overlooking the Colorado and the Green Rivers meandering a thousand feet below. Great caution was required crossing foot-deep fissures in the stony desert surface, ascending slippery gravel inclines, and negotiating uneven sandy patches without damaging the car, but we were rewarded with unparalleled views of the naked earth. The high anxiety of this adventure continued as we climbed in first gear up the one-lane Shafer trail, straight up the solid rock face of a high plateau by way of a dozen hairpin turns on a series of switchbacks, each affording a more striking view than the last. This off-road adventure – together with the whitewater of the Royal Gorge – made this trip one of my all-time favorites and one of a kind.

Shortly after I had begun my fourth year at St. Catherine of Siena, Bishop Larkin put me in charge of St. Patrick Parish in Tampa in September of 1986. Since he had previously indicated his desire for me to open a new parish, returning me to a place I had already been – even as 'priest-in-charge' – was not exactly what I was expecting. This was hardly 'the big break' I was looking for. From the day he's ordained, every priest longs for the day he's made a pastor, the day he 'becomes his own boss' – or so he thinks. This is pretty much the undeclared goal of ordination. Others aspire to attain an honorific title or office of some sort – monsignor, dean, vicar – or perhaps the episcopacy itself, long perceived as the pinnacle of ecclesiastical success. At least this used to be the case, though with all the headaches bishops have these days and so many dioceses finding themselves in trouble, it doesn't seem to be as much any more.

One reason priests instinctively want to become pastors is that they are trained to be leaders, not followers – though some, like drivers, don't seem to be very good at leading or following, just at getting in the way. Another reason is that pastors gain a certain status in church law that priests do not otherwise possess. Their parish used to be termed a 'benefice' – such that you could describe a pastor as a priest 'with benefits.' Not unlike those who touted the *Titanic* as 'unsinkable,' some pastors believed they were 'irremovable.' Until a generation ago, most priests were well on their way to becoming old men before being appointed pastors, and by that time more qualified for retirement than energetic leadership. Regardless of age or experience, it isn't usually long – only a few months – before priests appointed pastor for the first time rue the day they were, once they find out all the headaches that come with the job, including the unrelenting burden of administering property, personnel, and finances. New pastors rapidly discover that instead of being their own boss, now everyone has suddenly become their boss, and everything bad that happens in a parish is their fault. The buck stops at their desk, and when it does, for any reason, they're in trouble – with everyone. It's a longstanding joke that the couple of hundred extra dollars a month pastors receive just isn't worth it. No amount of money is.

Nevertheless, after a well-deserved 'roast' and some tearful good-byes, I moved on to my new assignment somewhat regretfully. It soon became apparent that no one had told me what was really going on. St. Patrick was in shambles. The former pastor had been whisked away to an undisclosed location, the renovation of the abandoned convent into a rectory and parish offices was underway, debt was piling up, and the Scoutmaster was now managing the parish. I was told to expect detectives making inquiries and not to do or say anything without contacting a Tampa attorney or the Vicar General. This was my rather abrupt introduction to the world of administering a parish.

Soon after crossing the Bay I learned who was really in charge of everyone and everything. Laurence Higgins was the Man. His was a path not to be crossed. Long dubbed the 'bishop' of Tampa, his tenure as pastor of St. Lawrence Parish was unequalled. A tough-talking Northern Irishman, the Monsignor was politically well-connected. From the inception of the Diocese, he had opposed Rome's designation of St. Petersburg rather than Tampa as the see city. Larry was widely regarded as 'the power behind the throne' during Bishop Larkin's administration of the Diocese. Controversy still surrounds the fact that he single-handedly wielded so much power. It did not exactly endear him to the rest of us.

Be that as it may, I did the best I could to improve conditions at St. Patrick over the four months I was there. I had a friend and partner in Venard Moffitt, a Franciscan priest who was at the parish when I arrived. Quite a few people remembered me from the two years I'd spent at St. Patrick, from 1981 to 1983 – also a difficult time for the parish. I provided parishioners with full disclosure of the financial challenges the parish and school were facing. Even with limited potential, the parish responded to my steward-ship appeal with enthusiasm. I furnished the new work and living quarters as economically as possible. Overseeing the final phase of the long-awaited renovation was my first experience with construction, one that would prove helpful later. I believe I made a lasting contribution in getting the parish back on its feet. Not everyone welcomed my efforts. People naturally want to protect their own interests – their 'turf.' They're not about to let a temporary administrator get in their way. Shortly after my departure at the end of 1986, St. Patrick was given over to a religious community that has administered it ever since.

South Tampa was not particularly kind to my car, either. With only an exposed carport in a rundown neighborhood, vandalism was commonplace. During my first tour of duty at St. Patrick, my car was flooded by an early evening thunderstorm. The second time around, another storm blew the gravel off the tarpaper on the roof, raining it down on my car, chipping the paint. It's a good thing the Diocese pays our car insurance. It would have been more cost-effective to provide a safe place to park to begin with.

With the Diocese still not ready to open the four new parishes being planned, it would be a year before I'd get on with the work that would occupy the next sixteen years. I approached David MacNamara, one of two deacons working full-time for the Diocese and an old friend of Bishop Larkin from his days as pastor of Christ the King in Jacksonville. When I proposed working with Dave in the Office of Communications, Bishop Larkin appointed me to do just that. I resided at St. Raphael Parish in St. Petersburg. I was glad to be back on this side of Tampa Bay.

St. Raphael is located right on the Bay on Snell Isle, an affluent section of the city that nevertheless submerges every time it rains heavily at high tide. During the summer, that can be almost every day. This is probably not what developers had in mind when they named surrounding areas Shore Acres and Venetian Isles. Being a peninsula nearly surrounded by water, Pinellas County has an excellent stormwater runoff system, but much of it lies only a few feet above sea level. At high tide, storm drains can't empty, so the rainwater backs up, making St. Pete look like New Orleans after Katrina until the tide retreats. By coincidence, Mike's youngest brother, Steve Lydon, was youth minister at

St. Raphael. The pastor, Anton Dechering, gave me a warm welcome and a light schedule. Mike and I were grateful to Anton for coming to our rescue when my old Corvair broke down once in Arcadia in the center of the state on our way home from the seminary. Always a gracious man, Anton was the first computer geek I ever knew. He and I shared the rectory with Angel, his gentle if highly nervous prized whippet. Bea Williams was the housekeeper and cook. I had become the godfather of her twin grandsons years before when Father Gloekler was pastor of St. Mary.

So began 1987. One of the things I've always enjoyed as a priest is teaching adults. Kids are fine, but adults need faith formation, too. From what I hear, I'm good at this. Promoting the teachings of the Second Vatican Council has always been my top priority. I carry a torch for them, and I always will. They are what my whole priesthood has been about. Since these documents detail who we are as a Church and who it is we are called to become, nothing saddens me more than seeing how enthusiasm for them has waned. It seems that over the past thirty years – roughly corresponding to the pontificate of John Paul II and his successor – the documents of Vatican II have been misplaced altogether somewhere in the dusty basement of the Church. Whatever happened to Pope John XXIII's mission statement for the Church? "We are not on earth to guard a museum. We are here to cultivate a flourishing garden of life." It seems to me that the 'garden' is withering.

Small as St. Raphael is, parishioners came out in droves for the evening series I presented on Vatican II and the Church today. Two dear Friends, Howard and Mary, snowbirds from Philadelphia I'd come to know from St. John on St. Pete Beach, also trekked down to Snell Isle each week. With his inquiring mind and gift for gab, Howard provided as much entertainment each week with his ingenious questions as I did with my talks. Friends of my parents, Mary was a devout Catholic, and Howard – schooled in every known Christian religion – a man without guile. Mary's pastor up north wasn't quite ready to receive

Howard into full communion with the Catholic Church, but I was – and Howard was ready and willing. So a few months later at St. John Church, with their two sons present – one a Presbyterian minister and the other Methodist – Howard Friend officially became Catholic. After he laughed, God cried with joy.

During my stint as spiritual moderator of the Diocesan Communications Office, I reprised my role as TV Mass priest. I worked primarily in radio, however, since as everyone knows, you don't have to be good-looking to do that. The Diocese had just launched it's own 'Catholic' radio station, housed in a shack adjacent to Christ the King in Tampa, with the call letters WBVM – dubbed 'the Voice of Mary.' The original idea was that a Catholic radio station could become a valuable tool for evangelization, as well as a way to make the local Church present in the life of those who could no longer get to church. WBVM came to be seen largely as 'preaching to the choir,' and as costs rose, the format changed to Christian rock music. For my part, I wrote and recorded a dozen mini-homilies on the parables and miracles of Jesus that were broadcast morning, noon, and night, along with the audio track of the TV Mass, endless promos, and other pre-recorded staples. I had the most fun, however – as well as achieving that all-important on-air status as a 'personality' – providing commentary for live events, usually with station manager Tom Derzypolski, who occasionally let me play with the sound board. Of course, the now nearly-defunct *Florida Catholic* newspaper photographer always came around to take a picture of us on site, thereby providing yet another layer of largely in-house publicity. My favorite photo is of a friend of mine, Robin Jewett Emery, a young woman ready to give birth in the delivery room on Sunday morning – watching me celebrate Mass on TV. No wonder that baby, Jonathan, is now in the seminary.

Tom and I took our show on the road, so to speak – to Calvary Catholic Cemetery for the annual Memorial Day Mass, and of course to the Cathedral. The ordination of the first class of thirty deacons in May was a huge event for the Diocese. Every parish was tuned in to the live broadcast of this history-making event for the local Church. From my perch in the glass-walled balcony, I tried to paint a picture with words, providing a visual narrative of the action taking place in the sanctuary. Doing this for a couple of hours with Tom was not unlike a couple of sportscasters narrating a baseball game, though I'd like to think we sounded a bit more intelligent and – at least in our finer moments – a little more clever. It was especially important to fill 'dead air' time – when nothing was going on – with scintillating conversation that would no less than enthrall the aural churchgoer. I also worked with the co-founder of WBVM, Debbie Scarberry. For ten days, she and I teamed up to provide live radio coverage of Pope John Paul II's second visit to the United States, before live television coverage became the norm. After all these years, I ran into Tom not long ago at a Life Teen Mass at the parish where his daughter is youth minister, and Debbie at the baptism of my friend Tom Baker's new baby boy.

My youngest sister Beth remarried in June of 1987. A dental hygienist, she married a dentist, Charles L. Ford III. The wedding was a family affair in her parents-in-law's back yard, and the reception Florida-style at a club right on the beach. Watching their two kids grow up, my nephew Charlie and niece Carol Anne, now both in college, has brought joy to my life. That fall, I traveled to upstate New York to visit my sister Julie, her husband Bill, and my older nephew and niece, Josh and Laura – still kids at that time. Todd Jewett, a young man from St. Catherine, tagged along. The autumn scenery was at its peak, with a few patches of early snow. We all piled into the car and headed to Niagara Falls. As we donned raincoats to climb around the base of the falls and to feel its blast from the deck of *The Maid of the Mist*, Julie and I recalled having done the same things there as children. Todd and I headed farther up to the St. Lawrence River where we took a scenic boat tour of the Thousand Islands straddling the Canadian border. We checked out a few picturesque covered bridges, a granite quarry and a maple sugar factory before heading home.

Mike and I took our own trip earlier that summer, re-visiting some of our favorite destinations in the Northwest, enjoying once more some of the most spectacular scenery in North America. The thunder of waterfalls, the serenity of icy lakes, the abundance of wildflowers, the diversity of wildlife, and the majesty of the alpine scenery in this part of the world are unsurpassed in their beauty. We wandered in solitude along the tranquil shores of Avalanche Lake in Glacier National Park and the slippery slope of Athabasca Glacier. We surveyed the ice fields of the Canadian Rockies and the rainforests of the Olympic Peninsula, all the while spotting elk, bighorn sheep, moose, bear, mountain goats, and marmots. We savored a couple of huge Dungeness crabs – each over three pounds – before exploring North America's deepest river gorge, the inaccessible Hell's Canyon along the border of Oregon and Idaho. A jetboat trip through the wilderness bordering the Snake River, nearly eight thousand feet below the surrounding peaks, proved to be one wild ride.

During 1987, as a result of my six-year stint in the Air Force Reserve, I got roped into becoming chaplain of the Clearwater chapter of the Military Order of the World Wars. As the name implies, this organization of retired military officers consisted primarily of World War II veterans, with a few from Korea and Vietnam thrown in for good measure. I have to admit admiring these tough old soldiers and sailors, mostly of my dad's generation, not only for their service to their country, but also for their efforts to revive patriotism in our society, especially through the schools. Although I'm a lifetime member, I hadn't been active for years until Pearl Harbor Day, 2009, when Dad was chosen to be honored as a survivor. After regaling the crowd with his recollection of that infamous day, he picked up a baton to conduct the band – what he went around Europe doing during World War II almost seventy years ago. It was a proud moment for father and son.

My friends won't let me forget that around this time my hair started getting lighter and lighter, until I became a dirty blond. I don't really know what got into me. I guess I wanted to find out if blonds really do have more fun. Perhaps it was the onset of early middle age. Who knows? Anyhow, I found out that when you have dark brown hair, lightening it gradually is problematic. It looked pretty good when the transition was completed. But after a year or so, I went back to my natural hair color – dark brown – this time with professional help. I was shocked when I looked in the mirror. People who knew me did a double take, but they were kind enough not to say anything to my face. You might say it was the end of an era. So was 1987 for that matter. Things were about to change.

Overlooking the Grand Canyon at Toroweap.

XII   OPENING THE THROTTLE

It was the best of times and the worst of times – the next sixteen years of my life, that is. I met some of the nicest people I've ever known, and some of the nastiest. At this point in my life, I believed starting a new parish was what I was ordained to do. I had been looking forward to this for several years. The time had finally come. I was thirty-seven years old.

During the annual priests' retreat in October, Bishop Larkin gave me a map of northeastern Pinellas County with proposed boundaries outlined – parts of Clearwater, Palm Harbor, Safety Harbor, and Oldsmar – at least a dozen zip codes, including the east side of Lake Tarpon. The population of the area had grown tremendously during the previous decade. The building of new homes and condominiums was still booming. As priest-in-charge of the new parish, I proposed three names for it. Bishop Larkin chose All Saints. Actually, my mother suggested the name, since my brother was born on the Feast of All Saints, and the Diocese didn't have a parish by this name. So All Saints, referred to as a mission at this point, was officially established on November 1, 1987. Three other new parishes were created at the same time, and Mike was appointed to start one of them – St. Justin Martyr in Largo. The Diocese had a grandiose plan to open dozens of new parishes over the next few years, but only a handful ever came to be. The shortage of priests and a lack of money took care of that.

The task I was given, not unlike God's own work in Genesis, was to create something out of nothing. All Saints was given nothing to start with – and when I say nothing, that's what I mean. It was not a satellite or an offshoot of any other parish. The only thing the Diocese 'gave' me was an interest rate of eight percent on every dollar I borrowed from day one. No seed money – not a single dollar. The Diocese later changed their way of doing business with new parishes, but All Saints was created independently and had to

105

sustain itself from the start. Neighboring parishes contributed a few usable liturgical items and office supplies, but no funds. Then, for the most part, they ignored us as long as they could. We didn't pose much of a threat to them initially, but they weren't particularly happy that All Saints had been carved out of their territory. Some people went around saying the bishop had made a mistake. Understandably, pastors are rather territorial, and turf wars – especially where revenues are at stake – are not uncommon. I had landed in a relatively affluent neck of the woods. New kid on the block, I couldn't help but be viewed as a potential 'sheep-stealer.'

There is something distinctly apostolic about starting a new community of faith. After all, that's what Paul and the other Apostles did. In order to do it, they had to be 'sent' – which is what the word 'apostle' means. They also experienced opposition and occasionally outright rejection. They had to beg, borrow, and probably even steal in order to get the job done. They had to beat the bushes to see who was out there and who would sign up. I had to do all these things and then some. I often described what I was doing those sixteen years as "making it up as you go along" because that's exactly what I had to do. That's the mission of the Church. The mission is not supposed to be mere maintenance. Too many pastors and parishes acquiesce in maintenance, forgetting about mission altogether. All Saints was in developmental mode the entire time I spent there. When the work I was given to do was finally finished at the end of sixteen years, I had the good sense to move on.

Another metaphor that works for me is having a baby. Starting a new parish was a lot like giving birth. For nine months, all kinds of strange things happen. Then you have to stay up half the night figuring out what your child needs. There are growing pains along the way. Eventually the child learns to walk and you have to back off, but still be there in case he starts to fall. You have to show him what he needs to know. Finally, the child comes of age and no longer needs you, except to know that he is loved. That's what this 'Father' tried to do. Priests need to remember they are called to be real fathers. There are already too many deadbeat dads.

I quickly discovered no one had a 'how-to' book for starting a parish. But that's the beauty of it – you're not bound by the way things have always been done or the way someone else wants them done. In other words, you're completely free to make your own mistakes, and I did, of course. Bishop Larkin told me only to look for a place to celebrate Mass, and for a place to live – whichever came first. I found and bought a modest home I really liked in a neighborhood just a couple of blocks from the parish site – ten acres of high and dry virgin pine forest on a gentle slope overlooking Curlew Road, one mile east of U.S. 19. After eleven years of living in a house with other priests – an unnatural and usually less than satisfying arrangement – I couldn't wait to live by myself. I bought a Soloflex exercise machine to help stay in shape and look good. I still use it. But I also started smoking again. I bought a hot tub to soothe my muscles and relax in. The parish didn't pay for these things, I did.

I was able to lease a storefront in the Shoppes at Clover Place – an upscale shopping center on Tampa Road, two miles north of the parish site. The leasing agent, Joan Forrester, gave us a deal on the thirty-two hundred square-foot space we rented. The first year came free, but the second we paid the going rate. We painted the walls pink, and for two years shared those walls with a pizza parlor and a video repair shop, affectionately coming to be known as *Saints 'R Us*. All two-hundred seventy chairs were filled when we 'opened for business' at noon on New Years Day, 1988, celebrating Mass for the very first time. In the front window hung the beautiful stained glass panel Dad made, depicting the familiar logo I had chosen for All Saints – the Cross and Crown – inspired by Revelation 2:10. "Be faithful unto death, and I will give you the crown of life." Dad played piano and organ, accompanied by my friend Zsuzsanna Varosy, veteran cellist with the Florida Orchestra.

Local Knights of Columbus provided the obligatory honor guard for the procession. A flurry of publicity in the local media heralded the day 'the Saints came marching in.'

Several key people helped me get All Saints off the ground. Debbie Scarberry, whom I had worked with at WBVM, stayed at my side for seven years as pastoral assistant. There was nothing that woman couldn't and didn't do. I didn't want to start the parish all alone, and I didn't have to, thanks to her. She was as much the mother of our baby as I was the father. Then there was a retired gentleman who turned out to be the deacon from hell. He had to be let go. Two other young retired folks signed on to run the tiny storefront office and do the books – Ginny Pellaumail and George Netterfield. Three of the five of us came from Toledo. These people were part of my life in a big way. Along with a kindly man by the name of Ray Fulton, they founded the parish with me. For sixteen years, All Saints *was* my life.

One of the major factors that contributed to the success of All Saints was the emphasis I placed on stewardship right from the beginning. I didn't hesitate to invite people to set aside a significant percentage of their income for the work of the Church – to 'tithe' according to the teaching of the Scriptures. I don't see how a parish that fails to do this can really experience much success. I'm not talking about a hard sell here, or incessantly begging for money – just presenting the facts and providing a spiritual motivation for sacrificial giving. As a rule, Catholic congregations are notoriously reluctant to do this. Pastors hate to get up and talk about money. If stewardship is presented properly, however, they should never have to. I never did. The first step in raising funds for a capital campaign, for example, is to tell people what you need. Step two is to tell them what it will cost. Step three is to tell them how they can help. If you tell people the truth, they will supply your need. I found that emphasizing authentic stewardship turned a few people off but a lot more people on. If you're going to raise a couple of million dollars to build a church, this is what you have to do. All Saints did – quite successfully, I might add.

In sixteen years, there was never more than one collection at All Saints. New parishioners were encouraged to register and support the parish regularly through the use of envelopes. We studiously avoided almost all requests for fundraising, no matter how worthy the cause, in order to focus on the primacy of stewardship. Sacrificial giving succeeds when the giver is motivated by his own need to give a generous portion from his substance rather than from his surplus, as a way to demonstrate his faithfulness and gratitude. Ultimately, stewardship must become a way of life.

I'm convinced that one of the main things that turn people off when going to church, and one reason they stop going altogether, is having to run through an endless gauntlet of tables where stuff is being sold, from raffle tickets to rosaries. Everybody and their brother has a hand out, and everyone wants a piece of the rich and creamy fundraising pie. These are the latter-day 'money-changers in the temple.' Jesus drove them all out, but a lot of pastors are just afraid to say no. When pastors fail to restrain all this peripheral activity, how can they be surprised when all people put in the collection are a few loose dollar bills? That's all they have left in their wallets by the time they get in church. I'm proud of the fact that parishioners at All Saints were spared most of the fundraising nonsense that passes for stewardship in favor of the real thing.

Life in our temporary home was a uniquely enjoyable experience. In addition to coffee and donuts on Sunday morning, wine and cheese were served under our awning on the sidewalk after Mass on Saturday night. Hospitality was not neglected. Making people feel welcome constantly attracted new members and gained the parish a friendly reputation. A Catholic church in a shopping center was a novelty that attracted more than a few curious passers-by. A lot of time was spent trying to explain to people what we were doing there. Seeing chairs instead of pews and observing the absence of kneelers, people would ask, "Is this a Catholic church?" This was amusing at first. As time went on, it was just annoying.

Everything we did in that all-purpose one-room store-front was secondary to the celebration of Mass. Parish life was clearly centered on the Eucharist. How else could a new Catholic community successfully take root and grow? We were fortunate to be given a travertine marble altar, ambo, and tabernacle by the House of Affirmation – though sadly as a result of having to close the doors of their new center in Clearwater shortly after having opened them. With my background, good liturgy and music consistently were given top priority. Communion was always offered under both species. Baptisms took place during Mass. Children made their first communion with the parish on Sunday. A parish – new or old – not properly centered on the Eucharist will flounder. I also formed a pastoral council and appointed a finance committee almost immediately so that parishioners could 'own' their parish from the beginning. They needed to understand that developing stewardship, promoting hospitality, and encouraging ministry were as much their responsibility as mine.

People also need to understand that a pastor cannot always explain his reasons for doing something they may not like. Confidential or legal matters may be involved. A pastor may have a very serious reason for making a decision people have no business knowing. Doing something you know is going to be unpopular is not easy. One of the toughest things I had to do was to let a popular music person go just before Christmas. Inappropriate conduct with a minor was the reason. Because I was unable to provide an explanation for the sudden departure, people thought I was being autocratic or mean. Some held it against me for years. Pastors almost always deserve the benefit of the doubt.

People who come forward to start a new church are a breed apart. I hold them in high esteem. Those who laid the foundation for All Saints during those first two years in the storefront were fiercely loyal. They were true pioneers.

During the summer of 1988, Mike and I headed northeast for a change – all the way to the island of Newfoundland. After taking the ferry across from Nova Scotia, we explored this rugged, sparsely-populated land of picturesque tidal bays full of screeching seabirds, placid deep-water harbors, and foggy inlets where killer whales play. Quaint seaside villages are nestled in every crag along the coast. We watched an endless procession of fishing boats chug past wharves stacked high with lobster traps, preparing to unload their precious fresh-caught cargo. Everywhere salted cod were laid about on wooden racks to dry in the sun. The rocky coastland was dotted with lighthouses, waterfalls, and cliffs. A friendly fisherman gave us a bucketful of mussels which we promptly steamed open and devoured. We made our way to Cape Spear, the easternmost point of North America, outside the capital of St. John's. In the tiny town of Avondale so far from home, we were welcomed by my brother-in-law's parents and grandparents, happily trading stories for a day.

Once I got the storefront launched, I began working with Diocesan personnel and an architect on the final design of a new multi-purpose building to be erected on all four new parish sites. Mike and I collaborated on this with the other two new pastors. The Diocese handled all the red tape involved in the permitting process, securing the annexation of the parish site into the city limits of Clearwater. A contractor was selected, and groundbreaking for All Saints' new home took place on the parish's first anniversary, November 1, 1988. Still a chaplain in the Air Force Reserve at that time, I invited my boss from MacDill, an Assemblies of God minister, to give the invocation. The mayor of Clearwater officially welcomed us to the City. All Saints continued to grow.

My grandmother, Marie Andrews, who had lived with my family in St. Petersburg for some time, died in January of 1989 at ninety-eight years of age. Though Bishop Larkin announced his retirement in November of 1988 after ten years on the job, in February he came to All Saints, one of the parishes he had created, to confer the sacrament of Confirmation for the first time in a storefront church. That winter, Mike and I got away to Denver where we went skiing at Keystone with my brother. Even though Mike is nearly three years older, he has more stamina than I do when it comes to things like rollerblading. We still laugh, however, about the trouble he had getting on and off the ski lift. I think he spent more time lying down on the snow than standing up on it, but we had great fun. The change of climate and scenery did us good. Coming to us from his native Louisiana, John C. Favalora was installed as third Bishop of St. Petersburg in May. Again we were blessed with a good and gracious man. My second nephew, Charlie Ford IV, was born in October.

For the first time, neither Mike nor I got to take our usual summer vacation in 1989. Both of us had to monitor the progress of construction on our parish sites – consulting project managers, approving requests for payment, and making decisions in the field that would permanently affect the outcome. I enjoyed working with an interior decorator on the finishes for All Saints and St. Justin, selecting materials and colors for the floors and walls. This proved to be a necessary but constant distraction from working directly with parishioners. It was fun but increasingly burdensome. A baptismal font and presider's chair had to designed and built to match the marble altar and ambo. Dad was commissioned to create fourteen original stained glass 'windows' depicting the Stations of the Cross. Seven hundred interlocking solid oak chairs upholstered in seafoam green, burgundy, and mauve had been ordered. The nitty-gritty details of opening a new church required constant attention. With time running out on our lease, we had to move out of the storefront by the end of the year, and the new building had to be ready to occupy. The usual insane rush to the finish line was on.

Prayers were answered, however, as the new Parish Center opened just before Christmas. Bitter cold gripped Florida that winter. My nerves were frazzled. Only hours before Mass was to be celebrated for the first time, I was frantically trying to set the programmable thermostats in the building for heat. Somehow I succeeded. On my mother's sixty-fifth birthday, December 23, 1989, the new worship space was christened. I gave Mom a dozen red roses during Mass, as well as my pastoral assistant, Debbie, and our former leasing agent, Joan. Bishop Favalora and Bishop Larkin both came to bless the newly-opened Parish Center in February, followed by a champagne reception and a week of festivities. A short time later, three of us who had established the new parishes wrote to our boss asking him to make our appointments permanent. He did. On May 1, 1990, I was officially appointed Pastor of All Saints. After fourteen years, I'd finally grabbed the golden ring.

In June it was time to go camping again, so Mike and I saddled up. This time we brought two sixteen-year olds along for the ride – Jay from my parish, and Tim from Mike's. The boys were so excited when we got to Denver that they didn't notice how cold it was getting as we made our way up Mt. Evans. They were getting silly breathing the thin air and playing in the snow amid the gnarled bristlecone pines and the ice-covered lakes. It was hot in Salida where we went for another cold, wild ride on the whitewater of the Arkansas River through the Royal Gorge with Mark. After flirting with freefall along the rim of the Black Canyon and staring into its misty depths carved over millennia by the Gunnison River, we climbed up under Landscape Arch near Moab – the longest stone arch in the world. Taking the obligatory photos beneath even more famous Delicate Arch after the steep climb up to it, we threaded our way through the sandstone skyscrapers known as Fisher Towers along the Colorado. Poor Jay fell into some nasty cactus. We had to pull the spines out of his backside with pliers. I had hoped this trip would cheer him up after his parents separated, but ironically, all he wanted to do was to go home. So we packed him up and put him on a bus.

Tim Wagner was the nicest kid Mike and I ever brought along on a trip. After Jay went home, the three of us had even more fun on the warm waters of Lake Powell, stretching two hundred miles through Glen Canyon National Recreation Area in southern Utah. Joining John and Beth Gallant, friends from Florida, and their friends Jack and Cele, the seven of us had a blast – on a houseboat. There are few places that invite discovery like Lake Powell. Its raw beauty inspires awe. For a week we plied the still waters of ever-narrowing sandstone-walled canyons, one after another, making camp each night in an alcove along sandy shores, and sleeping under the stars. We visited titanic Rainbow Bridge – the largest natural bridge in the world – a national monument few people ever see, accessible only by water. At Hole-in-the-Rock, we climbed twelve hundred feet up from the water along a steep, narrow crevice in the western rim of Glen Canyon to the top of the Kaiparowits Plateau, retracing the treacherous route Mormon pioneers took a hundred fifty years ago. With a speedboat in tow, we went skiing and riding on an assortment of water toys to our hearts' content. This was one of the best weeks of my life.

Mike, Tim, and I then ventured across a swinging footbridge over the muddy San Juan River to search for some dusty old ruins. From a lofty vantage point, we surveyed a series of tightly-coiled serpentine bends in the river known as 'goosenecks.' Then we went off-road through the 'Valley of the Gods' – a remote landscape of solitary sandstone monoliths and 'monuments' – where the thrilling opening scenes of the third installment of *Back to the Future* were filmed. Mike and I wanted Tim to experience the thrill of seeing Zion National Park's majestic canyon. Its massive orange cliffs conceal several emerald pools filled with rainwater that has actually percolated hundreds of feet through the porous rock. Curiosity led to the discovery of our own private pool, idyllically hidden among the lush vegetation at the base of overhanging Weeping Rock. On the way home through Arizona, we revisited the open pit copper mine at Morenci, that gaping hole carved out of the earth by mechanical monsters. Not far away, a mile higher in elevation, nature's own incredible

display of wildflowers at Hannagan Meadow brought back
pleasant memories of vacations past.

Giving Mom roses at the first Mass in All Saints Parish Center.

XIII   SETTING THE PACE

Whenever a list of parishes needing new pastors comes out, there are three things priests prefer to avoid – a school, a hospital, and the Knights of Columbus. I had to contend with all three. Mease Countyside Hospital was small when I started All Saints, but quadrupled in size over the years. The way the system works, primary responsibility for taking care of a hospital is determined by parish boundaries. It doesn't matter if most of the Catholic patients belong to other parishes – all of which had more than one priest – as they did in my case. I was alone at All Saints for years before Espiritu Santo finally came to my rescue. In the meantime, I was run ragged trying to start a parish, build a church, and run to the hospital night and day – often on what turned out to be a wild goose chase or a non-emergency, due to poor communication. The system is flawed.

It would help a great deal if people would ask to be anointed at their own parish before they go to the hospital, especially when they know they're going to have surgery that's potentially life-threatening. It would also help a great deal if families would accept the fact that their loved one is dying, rather than remaining in denial and refusing to call a priest until the last minute. Priests cannot raise the dead, so there is no point in calling a priest to come after a person has breathed their last. The days of priests waiting in line like taxis to be dispatched on a moment's notice – or like genies to be summoned on demand from a magic lamp – are over. A person who is conscious and still in possession of their faculties will benefit from the Sacrament of the Sick far more than one who is in a coma or on their deathbed. To a large degree, Catholics have yet to update their understanding of the sacraments sufficiently. In light of the sharp and continuing decline in the number of priests, Catholics must revise their expectations accordingly. In my opinion, the Church has so far largely failed to help people do this to any meaningful degree.

I've previously aired some widely held views about Catholic schools today. Even under optimum conditions, which rarely exist, a pastor who has primary responsibility for a school takes on another whole set of headaches. The buck stops not at the principal's desk but at the pastor's, so he cannot remain uninvolved. Even more daunting a challenge than having to administer a school is having to build one. To ask a heavily-indebted young parish still struggling to get on its feet to help build a school doesn't make much sense to me. But that's exactly what Bishop Favalora asked All Saints to do. When I first heard this, I couldn't even believe it. Could this be one of the 'joys' of being a pastor? I certainly never saw it coming. Even with three other parishes carrying much of the load, the growth and development of All Saints would be severely tested.

We all have to do things we don't particularly want to do, even things we may not be sure we believe in. I've never been one to avoid a difficult task or to do things half-heartedly. Instead of taking a back seat, with the capable leadership of Ken and Mary Ellen Emery, All Saints took the lead. Grabbing the bull by the horns, so to speak, the parish led the way in the capital campaign to build Guardian Angels School in 1995. We were the only parish to exceed the ambitious goal we were given. The 'goal' of course was really an assessment. We either had to raise the money now or add it to our existing loan and pay interest on it. Against the odds, we were successful. False humility aside, the enthusiasm I demonstrated and the wholehearted support I gave to this project is what made it succeed. I was determined that, if it had to be, the school and the parish could establish a mutually supportive relationship and co-exist peacefully. That's exactly what we did. By the time I left All Saints in 2003, the parish had contributed a half million dollars to build and operate Guardian Angels School, and to enable its expansion in 1998.

I can only describe my experience with the Knights of Columbus as nightmarish. I don't believe it was typical, but it was real. After a start-up I encouraged that was initially successful, the leadership of the newly-formed council was hijacked by a few individuals who had axes to grind against the Church. Their bizarre antics and subversive behavior resulted in the whole council going rogue, to the embarrassment of the national organization. All Saints endured this ordeal early on. To be worthy of the name Christian, apparently every new community of faith has to do the same. That's what kept St. Paul so busy writing all those letters in the New Testament.

The longer organizations of any kind exist without renewal and reform, the sooner they become obsolete. The same holds true of organizations that are associated with the Catholic Church. All organizations and movements within the Church have a natural lifespan. Unlike the Church, their charter is neither divine nor eternal. There is no guarantee that organizations that served a valuable purpose in the life of the Church in the past do so today. Times change. The world changes with the times. Because the Church is a living, breathing organism – the Body of Christ in the world made up of frail and sinful human beings – the Church is continually changing and constantly in need of purification and renewal.

The Knights of Columbus – and all organizations that seek to serve the needs of the Church today – must ask themselves some hard questions. In a Church that desperately needs to become more inclusive, is there still a place for organizations that are gender exclusive? In a Church that desperately needs to cast off the veil of secrecy that shrouds so much of its internal affairs, is there still a place for organizations that conduct their affairs secretively? Is Christopher Columbus – under scrutiny for inhumane treatment of indigenous peoples in the New World – an appropriate icon today? What possible value can a group of men, parading in capes and swords and plumed hats, have for the Church today? What Church do these organizations serve – a triumphalistic, clericalistic Church that is dying? Or a humbled, contrite Church that is still being born? Organizations that find themselves getting underfoot in parishes and crossing swords with their pastors need to look for answers to these questions.

The new Parish Center was quite a step up from a crowded one-room storefront in a strip mall. All Saints now possessed an expansive, easily expandable worship space, a dignified Blessed Sacrament Chapel, a nursery, ample offices and storage space, a sacristy and a half, multiple bathrooms, and more than one place to meet simultaneously – all under one roof. The natural beauty of the parish site – in a forest of oak and pine – was priceless, though much of it later succumbed to infestation. Two much-loved retired priests, Leo Dobo and Clem Carroll, helped me out. Parishioners enjoyed coming together for pizza parties, picnics, and a couple of deep-sea fishing trips that yielded some hefty grouper. Speaking of fishing, around this time I joined my sister Beth and her husband at Boca Grande, tarpon fishing capital of the world. Plying the crowded deep waters of the Pass before dawn, all three of us managed to hook, reel in, and release enormous fish – in the eighty to hundred pound range. Like a lot of other things in life, tarpon fishing is about being in the right place at the right time. Sometimes you are, and sometimes you aren't. But when you are, look out.

Then there were our trademark roller-skating parties. Each year before the vinyl tile floor of the Parish Center was waxed, all the chairs were removed and a five thousand square-foot roller rink appeared. It was a multi-purpose building, after all. With a cotton candy and a popcorn machine, the kids – big and little – loved it. Even the Friday morning ritual of dust mopping the floor of the worship space fostered fellowship, as did 'the ministry of mulch' that contributed so much to the beautification of the grounds as time went on. A rustic Way of the Cross wound its way through the woods, and benefactors contributed countless memorial gifts, including an exquisite statue of Our Lady Queen of All Saints, hand-carved in Italy and burnished with gold, symbolic wood carvings of the seven sacraments, eight Slabbinck tapestries from Belgium, and Stadelmaier vestments from Holland. Memorial gifts remain an inspiring testimony to the faith of the people, including my family, who made them, and to their extraordinary dedication to stewardship.

After getting over the hurdle of construction and the euphoria of dedication, I needed a break. Bishop Favalora, in fact, had suggested that I take one. On short notice, I called up friends in England and Ireland and went to visit. From Heathrow, via bus, subway, and train, I found my way to Margaret Meston's home in Warwick – a cozy cottage with an honest-to-God thatched roof. Margaret, a widow, was a nurse. Among the places she took me were Warwick Castle, Stratford, and Coventry, which was badly bombed during World War II. I savored a bit of Beefeater's, Yorkshire pudding, shepherd's pie, and British fish-and-chips – greasy in brown paper with malt vinegar and salt. I remember ducking into a courtroom to see if the barristers still wore powdered wigs. They did. It was still February, and I was so cold I think Margaret heated a brick in the fireplace and put it in my bed. I took another train to Hartlepool, a town near the northeast coast of England. There I met Tony Cornforth, a priest who used to come to St. Catherine every summer, who showed me around his parish. We saw the sights of Newcastle, splendid Durham Cathedral, and the ruins of ancient settlements along the gale-whipped North Sea, where I nearly froze again. Then I flew across to the Emerald Isle to meet my host Brendon Kennedy at his parish in county Galway. Needless to say, there's no shortage of things to drink in Ireland. The pubs were warm, and so was the Guinness stout. Among other things, Brendon and I stood on the Cliffs of Moher, admired the glass at Waterford, toured Bunratty Castle near Limerick, and you just know I had to kiss the Blarney Stone.

The birthday party I had at the rectory when I turned forty in June, 1990, was a lot of fun. Besides family and friends, parish staff members joined me for the celebration, showering me with gag gifts – including a whip – as a perverse token of their affection. Along with bacon-wrapped filets on the grill, Mike concocted a fabulous Cedar Key salad – fresh hearts of palm, pineapple, dates, peanut butter, and pistachio ice cream on a bed of lettuce. This may not sound like a congenial combination, but it's one of the most delectable treats you can put in your mouth.

All Saints was honored to have Bishop Favalora visit us on the parish's fourth anniversary and feast day in 1991. Engulfed in a sea of children wearing saints costumes, he wore his own – pointy hat, shepherd's staff, and a big smile on his face. With families in mind, we created our own two-year multimedia series based on Franco Zeffirelli's moving 1977 motion-picture portrait of *Jesus of Nazareth*. Shortly after the Persian Gulf War began in 1991, the parish hosted a patriotic gathering known as 'the Massing of the Colors' to honor military personnel past and present. The following year we sponsored a special tribute to law enforcement and public safety personnel in the community. Parishioners diversified the color scheme inside the Parish Center, adding an oak chair rail to the worship space and common rooms as a labor of love. Doors were opened to the public as a polling place for the first time in 1992. For the first time that year at Thanksgiving, we joined three Protestant congregations and the local Jewish synagogue for an interfaith prayer service – a cherished annual tradition ever since. All Saints proudly celebrated its fifth anniversary with a hugely colorful outdoor Mass, *Saints 'R Us* tee-shirts, an afternoon of fun and games with the pastor in a dunking booth, and an authentic Tongan pig roast at night.

My second niece, Carol Anne Ford, was born while Mike and I were roaming around the Pacific Northwest in the summer of 1991. These days we were camping in style in Mike's Hi-Lo travel trailer, more commonly called a recreational vehicle today. When I used to see these on the road, I referred to them as 'midget motels' because of their low profile. But that's what makes them so easy to tow. I never knew they had a hydraulic lift system that raises the roof once you're in your campsite. These campers have become Mike's pride and joy and our home on wheels ever since. Over the summer I let my hair grow long enough in back to sport a mini-ponytail for a while. I don't know why, but I did. Making our way along the rocky northern coast of California through the tall trees, we took in lighthouses, tide pools, noisy seals, and an unusual canyon lined with fifty-foot high walls of five-fingered ferns. Oregon treated us to raging rivers and fields of foxglove. Mossy rainforests and bogs filled with insect-eating cobra lilies and skunk cabbage greeted us in Washington. We were awed again by the pristine beauty of Crater Lake's azure depths and the snowy peaks of the North Cascades. The sight of Mount St. Helen's flattened ash-gray slopes – eleven years after its famed eruption – was a gruesome reminder of nature's potential for destructive fury.

The Alstons welcomed Mike and me to Salt Lake City by cooking up elk steak for dinner. They also took us on an enlightening tour of the famed Mormon Tabernacle and Temple Square. We got to hear the mighty organ play, if not the mighty choir sing. We stopped to go jet skiing with their son Jack, our friend from Lake Powell, on a chilly lake north of Denver. A rugged outdoorsman and a pigeon breeder, Jack also took Mike and me on a whitewater run, ironically on the Blue River, through the White River National Forest a couple of hours west of Denver. Together in an inflatable kayak, I was so scared I grabbed on to an overhanging tree limb to escape, leaving Mike plunging headlong downstream alone. He and Jack made it, however. They found me an hour later on the side of the road after clawing my way through brambles up the steep bank of the river. I'm usually up for a wild ride, but this was a little too much adventure even for me.

In February of 1992, I took my first trip to Naples, Italy, and to Sicily. With me came Dom and Deenie Renzi, friends at that time from All Saints, to visit my friend from MacDill, Larry Wood and his charming wife, Maria Grazia. With their three-year old son, Fabian, they lived with Maria Grazia's parents, who opened their home in Portici to us as well. Southern Italy has got to be one of the liveliest and most colorful places in the world. The crowded old neighborhood where we stayed was a noisy place, full of young men on motorscooters and barking dogs, where people routinely shouted greetings and hung their laundry out their windows to dry. The musty stuccoed walls and narrow alleys reeked of garlic and pungent herbs, the aroma of tomatoes drowning in olive oil and peppers roasting wafting through the air. Cooking is an art form here and dining a pageant, flush with wine and lasting well into the night. Then our hosts produced home-made, anise-flavored liqueur, to tame the tummy and warm the heart for bed.

Since Larry had to work during the day at the NATO base, the rest of us piled into his sporty Saab, and I got to drive the mean streets of Naples, where driving is a free-for-all. In this game without rules, you have to huff and puff and bluff your way through traffic that would make a blind man blush. My temperament suited me perfectly for this. Everyone in the car got into the act – gasping one moment, shouting and gesturing the next. Such sweet madness. After attaining the windy summit of Mt. Vesuvius, we savored the breathtaking vertical scenery of the Amalfi highway, winding down tiny cobbled lanes to pastel seaside towns. We also traveled to the magnificent palace and gardens of the Neopolitan kings at Caserta – on a scale as grand as Versailles – and to the silent, lifeless ruins of Pompeii.

Before coming home, I went to Catania in Sicily where the Rizza family welcomed me as though they'd known me all their lives – in-laws of my friend Tom Baker from All Saints. We drove around the island to the spectacular amphitheatre of Taormina, perched high in the hills overlooking a turquoise sea gently lapping the shores of this coastal resort. Not far from these Greek, Roman, and medieval ruins, we could see even in daylight fiery lines of lava flowing down Mount Etna. While I've never been to Greece, I can't imagine ancient temples any more impressive than those at Agrigento, where flowering almond trees scented the air with their pink blossoms. The sea surround-ing Sicily yielded its fruits, and with crusty bread freshly-baked in a brick oven and smeared with olive oil, I savored every one.

Mike and I had a trip to the Canadian Rockies planned for the summer of 1992. Tim Wagner, and another young man named Tim who had just graduated from high school, were going to fly up to Montana and meet us before we crossed the border. All our gear was packed. As usual, we could hardly wait. After Mass on Sunday morning, we hit the road. Mike started out driving and I sipped a drink. It was July 19. We didn't get very far. Something happened that changed both our lives, especially mine.

Springtime in the North Cascades in Washington State.

XIV   HITTING THE BRAKES

Hot and humid as it always was in Georgia this time of year, the sun was getting lower in the sky when we stopped for gas early that evening. I finished my beer and crunched up the can – I'd never drive with a drink in the car. We'd been on the road four or five hours. After you've been on an interstate for a while, you get used to the speed. Mike's brand new Hi-Lo camper was actually bigger than his car, a Chevy Blazer. But it towed so easily it was easy to forget it was even there. We weren't in a hurry. We just wanted to get as far as we could before dark. It was my turn to drive. I was fired up and ready to go.

There were a lot of trucks on the road as usual – always in a hurry, always getting in everyone's way. One came barreling up behind me while I was passing someone. He just couldn't wait. He almost gave me a push. I got back in the right lane when I could, but I took my sweet time to make him wait. He just about ran me off the road flying past. I decided to show him who was boss. I sped up and pulled back in the left lane. It would take a minute to get up enough speed, but I'd crawl up on his butt and see how he liked it till I could fly past him.

That decision was the worst one I ever made. We almost made it. But fast-moving trucks displace a lot of air and leave a vacuum in their wake. At the speed I was going, the Blazer never had a chance. The Hi-Lo began to sway back and forth, gently at first, then more violently. The Blazer started to fishtail. The Hi-Lo danced until it flipped. The Blazer, still attached, went with it. Spinning around, it rolled over, again and again – off the road and into the grass. Rubber and glass and metal bounced and scraped and cracked. The world turned upside down. Finally, it stood still.

The scene was surreal. At some point the camper came off the car. There wasn't much left of it – just a field of debris. The car was wrecked. Mike and I were still breathing. We were speaking. Dazed and confused, unsure of what had happened, we were unharmed when we should have been dead. When a cop stopped to see what had happened, it never occurred to us to say that Mike had been driving. Mike had quit drinking eight years before. It never occurred to us that my blood alcohol content might be over the legal limit but the cop was suspicious. It never occurred to me that Mike and I might *both* be arrested and put in handcuffs in the back of a patrol car. Not what I was expecting, but this is what happened. Life is what happens when you're making other plans.

Sooner or later bad habits catch up with you. I was charged with driving under the influence – just barely – but enough to make my life miserable for a couple of years. I can't say it was the first time I'd ever been guilty of this, but I can say it was the last. Worse than the disgrace of being handcuffed was the shock of being put behind bars in a holding cell for half an hour. The only saving grace in this bizarre succession of events was having enough cash in our possession – nearly a thousand dollars – to bail ourselves out.

There has never been a time in my life when I felt worse about myself than this. I could have killed my best friend as well as myself. I destroyed his car and his camper. I ruined our vacation. He was paying the price for my poor judgment. The possibility that I could be sent to prison for a year – highly unlikely as that was – terrified me. My driver's license had been confiscated. Mike stood by me through it all. I don't know what I would have done without him. I called Brendan Muldoon. He kindly offered to help.

The next morning Mike and I picked up the pieces of what would have been our vacation at the salvage yard where his car and camper had been towed. We also returned to the scene of the accident to look for his video camera. Adding insult to injury, it was nowhere to be found. We rented a vehicle for the long ride home. We were grateful to be alive. I was already beginning to see the light. I knew things had to change. This was my wake-up call. I'd had my last drink. It was high time.

A very high percentage of cases involving driving under the influence result in conviction. Mine was no exception. The charge against Mike – bogus to begin with – was dropped as part of the deal. For a year the legal ordeal dragged on. It cost me a small fortune. Then Florida suspended my license for a year, though I was allowed to drive for 'business purposes.' I interpreted that to mean everything but joyriding, but I always wore a clergy shirt in the car in case I was stopped. I was able to get insurance but it didn't come cheap. My second biggest fear was being recognized by someone at DUI school, but I wasn't. I told people I was in an accident. No one knew more than that.

In retrospect, excessive speed, the laws of physics, and drinking all played a part in the crash. But my bad attitude played the biggest part of all. Alcohol had been fueling that for a long time. I just hadn't seen it. My grandiosity and aggressiveness behind the wheel – and elsewhere in life – were the result. My relationships had been suffering for a long time. I sensed something was wrong but I didn't know what. I was never a falling down drunk, so I didn't have a problem. I was in denial – not intentionally – I just didn't get it. I underestimated the powerful and baffling effect alcohol was gaining in my life. I didn't recognize the increasing impairment of my thinking, feeling, speaking, and acting. A few other people – like Mike – did, but until *I* was ready, that didn't do me any good. Finally I was. The appointed time had come. Like Paul, God finally got my attention. The scales were beginning to fall from my eyes.

I found a wonderful counselor, and I turned to Alcoholics Anonymous for help. I asked Mike to take me to my first meeting. After putting up with me for all those years, that was probably one of the happiest days of his life. This proved to be one of the best decisions I ever made. The beauty of A.A. is that the only requirement for membership is a desire to stop drinking. That's the one thing everyone has in common. Now I had it too. To stop drinking wasn't terribly difficult for me. For me, it was harder to quit smoking once and for all and stick to it. I did that a few months later. I haven't had a cigarette since.

The other great thing A.A. did for me was help me realize I was not alone. Not unlike the 'fraternity' of the priesthood, there is a 'fellowship' to be found there. People who have come to depend too heavily on alcohol as an all-purpose lubricant for their lives develop similar behaviors and ways of thinking. Recognizing these for what they are goes a long way in getting your life back, but it also takes a long time. For me getting sober wasn't the hard part. Even staying sober wasn't. Finding serenity was. Being at peace with myself and with other human beings was. Recovery is an ongoing process. I discovered that only I could do it, but that I could not do it alone.

Another realization A.A. led me to is that I am not really in control of anything. I could barely control myself. Letting go of the myth that I was in charge of my life and my parish – and the anger that went with it whenever I was reminded I was not – was a big step. Pastors typically joke that the sign on their door should read 'Damage Control' since they spend so much of their time putting out fires and trying to manage crises that arise. I sure did. But I may have unwittingly fueled some of those fires and aggravated some of those crises by my own inflamed feelings and lack of clear thinking, by my perfectionism and need for approval. My intense personality did not lend itself easily to an admission of powerlessness. That would require humility. But I had just been humbled in a big way.

It isn't every day a priest actually grants God absolute power and cedes control of everything in his life to Him. But that's what I did. I started growing a better spiritual life – an interior life, not just a religious one. For the first time, I admitted to myself: 1) I can't. 2) He can. 3) I think I'll let Him. The truth is always so simple, yet I was forty-two years old before I really saw it. Now I remind myself every day.

This was the conversion process I went through that has changed my life. I don't mean to suggest for a minute that I'm finished. I won't be till I'm laid to rest, and then it will really be God who's finished with me. But sobriety – and the serenity I've found through it – continues to improve the quality of my life. That's apparent to anyone who's known me a long time. I'm no longer concerned about anyone who can't or won't see the change in me. I've given up trying to change other people's minds. At least I'm less intent on it. For a change, I'm trying to accept things as they are rather than as I'd like them to be. The Serenity Prayer has become my best friend. There are days I find myself saying it a hundred times, to remind myself of the 'creed' by which I now choose to live my life – one day at a time.

A.A. for me is a means to an end – a happier life in this world and in the next. It proposes a simpler, more honest, more spiritual way of living than most people are accustomed to. Its spirituality is perfectly compatible with Christianity and has found its way into my preaching. I don't advertise my affiliation with A.A. but I don't need to. People in recovery can tell as soon as I open my mouth. Alcoholics Anonymous has brought me closer to the people I love. It has helped me become a better person and a better priest, and for that I am grateful. My gratitude is primarily toward God, for he is my ultimate end as he was my beginning. As I get older, I find God assuming more importance in my life, not less. I find myself more grateful all the time. I'm not as active as A.A. would have me be. I don't go to many meetings, but I am staying sober. And I am being faithful – to myself, to my vocation, and to my family and friends. Life doesn't get much better than that.

I don't think of myself as an alcoholic any more than I think of myself as a priest, or as having one sexual preference rather than another, or as being a degreed person, or in any of the other ways people sometimes define themselves. Now if I could just see everyone else from the same magnanimous perspective, the world would be a better place. My definition of an alcoholic is simply a person who has a problem when he drinks and is better off when he doesn't. That includes me and an awful lot of other people. Academic and clinical definitions don't do much for me.

As far as being a priest goes, I was a person for twenty-five years before becoming one, and I'd like to think I still am that person. It used to bother me that my father always introduces me to people as his 'priest/son.' I knew he wanted to be a priest as a young man, but he also loved music. He was told he could not do both, and that he had to choose between the two. He chose music. I know how proud he is of my being a priest. Still, I wish he would introduce me as his son – who also happens to be a priest. Men especially tend to define themselves by what they do rather than by who they are. Priests are no exception. A lot of priests see themselves all but exclusively in their role. Some develop a subtle arrogance about it. They get so caught up in the *persona* of priest they hardly exist outside it. When I see young priests today running around even on the street in cassocks, I wonder what's going on. You don't see older priests doing that.

One thing priests and alcoholics have in common is that once you become one, you are one forever. But that's not all you are. For me, learning to accept who I really am and staying true to myself has been the work of a lifetime. Most titles and labels just get in the way. In an imperfect world, I suppose we're stuck with them. The slower we are to wear them, however – much less pin them on others – the better.

Mike and I were able to salvage some semblance of a vacation during the summer of 1992 after the crash. I had to get started on my new sober life if I were ever to catch up with him. On rather short notice, we jumped in my red Dodge Shelby and headed northeast to visit friends and family. After welcoming us to their two-hundred year old barn house near Philadelphia, Howard and Mary Friend escorted us on a walking tour through Independence Hall to the Liberty Bell. Then it was on to Narragansett, Rhode Island, where Mike's brother, Dave Lydon, welcomed us and took us deep-sea fishing on the way to Block Island. After straining to haul fish in on barbed hooks, a couple at a time, we docked and dined on mussels *al fresco* before scootering around the island. In Newport, I took Mike to see the oceanfront mansions and historic Trinity Church where George Washington used to worship. After passing a couple of lighthouses on the way out to Provincetown on the tip of Cape Cod, we visited some snowbirds I knew from All Saints, Jim and Louise McDonough. Strictly by accident and not as payback, Mike had a slight mishap with my car, tearing off the front ground effects panel after bumping a berm. Needless to say, I didn't make much of it after what I had done. After taking the car for a ride on a marine ferry, we enjoyed visiting not one but two oceanside aquariums – in Massachusetts and North Carolina – on the way home.

Then we headed in the opposite direction – southwest, all the way to Costa Rica. Mike and I had stopped at the Costa Rican port of Limon a few years earlier on our first Caribbean cruise. Unable to go through the Panama Canal as planned, we went whitewater rafting instead on the formidable Reventazon River. On another visit to Costa Rica, we went zipping across valleys and through the tree tops of the rain forest on a series of cables strung through the canopy. This time we flew with Dominic Renzi to his brother Gene's home in the capital of San Jose. Mike and I concelebrated Mass in Spanish at a parish church in Alajuela on the feast of the Assumption – Mother's Day in Costa Rica. The next day we got a personal tour of the enormous Coca Cola and Firestone tire plants that Gene managed, supplying all of Central America. After experiencing a minor earth tremor the night before, we hiked through a steamy 'cloud forest' punctuated with brilliant tropical flowers in the highlands. From the heights we walked along the rim and stared down into the boiling lake in the active volcanic crater of Irazu. Crossing lush tropical rain forests on some barely passable, muddy, potholed roads to the Pacific coast, we sampled local seafood delicacies like ceviche and previously unseen tropical fruits while watching the surfers. Before coming home, we visited an orphanage for abandoned and disabled children with Gene's boss, a wealthy American expatriate, industrialist, and philanthropist. Seeing the impoverished conditions these poor kids lived in moved us to empty our pockets as well.

At Christmas time, I joined my sister Julie and her family on the dock of their waterfront home to watch Treasure Island's noisy and colorful lighted boat parade. In January, Tim Wagner joined Mike and me on a quick winter trip to the Smoky Mountains. Wrapped in blue haze, the Smokies never fail to live up to their name. For a few chilly days we just relaxed, wandering past frozen waterfalls through leafless forests, as far as Cades Cove. A change of scenery always does a body good. In March, Mike and I headed for Rome. This was the trip that almost wasn't. Besides being overbooked, flights up and down the eastern seaboard were backlogged for days from the unnamed 'storm of the century' that had raked the Atlantic coast. TWA was begging for volunteers in Tampa to be bumped in exchange for a free flight voucher. Though our time was short to begin with, Mike and I took the deal. It was too good to pass up. We left the next day instead.

No matter how many times you've been there, the Eternal City is always a fun place to visit. It has arguably the best food in the world, if you like to eat. But you've got to walk to see the sights. After managing to get where we wanted to go by bus or subway, Mike and I spent hours just roaming the streets. One of Rome's best kept secrets is the inexpensive tour of major sights around the city offered by the municipal bus line, with an English-speaking guide, departing from the central train station. While Rome is a great place to visit, I wouldn't want to live there. I was offered the opportunity to pursue further studies there twice. I would have had to stay several years, then come back to teach in the seminary for at least a few more years. I'd already 'done my time' there – eight long years – and had no desire to return. Rome was just too far away from Florida for me, and all the people that make this home. That's why I joined a diocese, not a religious order. I always wanted to be a parish priest, not a seminary professor.

Vatican City is like no place else on earth – in more ways than one. Seeing rays of sunlight strike the baldacchino over the main altar of St. Peter's, strolling across the roof of the Basilica, climbing up into the dome, looking out from the cupola, kissing the marble foot of Peter's statue worn smooth over the centuries, visiting the tomb of Pope John XXIII and the Vatican museums, and admiring the ceiling of the Sistine Chapel and the Pieta – any one of these thrills alone is worth the trip. People who are hung up on churches having pews and kneelers and giant tabernacles should visit St. Peter's. They'll be terribly disappointed.

In Rome, Mike and I visited an old friend, a woman we knew from Mike's days at St. Patrick in Tampa, Maria Whitley. She kindly put us up at her flat for a few days and made us the most wonderful bruschetta – slabs of fresh tomato, mozzarella, and basil drizzled with olive oil on crusty bread – a meal in itself. Then we hopped on the *rapido,* a super-fast train to Naples two hours south, to see our friends Larry and Maria Grazia Wood again. This time we soaked up the sights, the sounds, and the smells of the noisy waterfront, bustling with activity on Sunday morning with the fish market in full swing. We gawked at stall after stall of fishmongers hawking their wares, showing off their still-wriggling catch, passionately bargaining for the best price. Then we boarded a hydrofoil bound for the Isle of Capri. After taking a taxi to the top for a stellar sea view and a snack, we hired a rowboat to take us inside the celestial Blue Grotto. Ducking our heads, we were able to sneak inside through a crack in the rock between the waves. Seeing this huge cave illuminated by the sun's reflection off the white sand beneath it is an unforgettable sight.

Here we were again, driving the twisting road along the Amalfi coast, clinging to sheer cliffs shrouded in the cool mists of March. We proceeded slowly down a narrow lane lined with shops to the cobbled beach below where dogs and children played. This time I guided Mike through the fabled ruins of Pompeii where the idle rich indulged themselves before being buried alive in ash by Vesuvius in 79 A.D. Forgotten by time, Pompeii's crumbling temples, faded frescoes, rutted stone pavement, chipped plastered columns, abandoned arches, and mute mosaics all conspire to create an ominous, strangely silent landscape.

The summer of 1993 found Mike and me on our way through the prairies and grasslands of the Great Plains. Groves of quaking aspen, soggy fields of bear grass, semi-frozen lakes, cold rushing streams, and gushing waterfalls all awaited us at Glacier National Park in Montana. After we crossed the Canadian border, the stately Prince of Wales Hotel came into view, framed perfectly by the towering snowy peaks along windswept Waterton Lake. Amidst an endless array of summer wildflowers along the Icefields Parkway connecting Banff and Jasper, we sighted deer, moose, elk, mountain goats, bighorn sheep, marmots, buffalo, black bear, and stellar jays. The untamed beauty of Alberta's Moraine Lake, snow falling softly on Cameron Lake, the liquid turquoise waters of Peyto Lake, the breathtaking setting of jewel-like Maligne Lake, and the serene stillness of the Vermillion Lakes make the Canadian Rockies a favorite destination in North America. After hiking up to Angel Glacier, we set foot once more on massive Athabasca Glacier, before soaking in Banff's thermal hot springs, and strolling around glistening Lake Louise. Deafening up close, the thunderous roar of Wapta and Takkakaw Falls on the British Columbia side of the Continental Divide is a sound not quickly forgotten.

Dropping back down into Montana, Mike and I couldn't resist the charm of Montana's cloistered caverns named after explorers Lewis and Clark. In Yellowstone, we took in steamy geyser basins, impressive waterfalls, and roving bison herds. Then we went to sleep with the sheep – literally thousands of them grazing on the open range – at a primitive campground high in Wyoming's frosty Bighorn National Forest. In the Black Hills of South Dakota, we had to crawl on our hands and knees at times to get through some tight places inside Wind Cave, where a ranger led us on an arduous underground adventure. After visiting Mt. Rushmore, we managed not to slide off a muddy back road we took through the Badlands to revisit Devils Tower in Wyoming. At last, we were ready to head home.

Mike, Tim, and I on a wild ride through the Royal Gorge in 1990.

XV   MOVING RIGHT ALONG

My pal Tom Baker and his fourteen-year-old son Tommy teamed up with Mike and me on a trip to the desert Southwest the following summer. On our way out of town, we stopped at the mall in Crystal River to get our ears pierced – at least Tom and I did. Less is more for me in the body piercing department – one hole in one ear was enough. Tom had already taken me with him to get my first and only tattoo at a parlor on Clearwater Beach. Then there was the time he introduced me to a 'yard' of beer – poured in a very tall glass shaped like a funnel. A guy needs to have at least one 'bad boy' as a friend. I've got Tom, or depending on your point of view, Tom's got me.

So in 1994 we explored some less traveled roads, driving across Texas to Chiricahua just inside Arizona, where we disappeared into a vast jumble of rock spires. Amidst prickly pear cactus, morning glories, and flowering yucca, we rested at the old Spanish mission of Tumacacori. Raising their lofty arms in greeting, saguaro cacti, luring all manner of winged creatures with their succulent fruit, welcomed us to Tucson. While prickly 'teddy bear' cholla cacti invited petting, and the swaying tentacles of ocotillos tempted us to touch them, the spindly spines of barrel cacti warned us away. Sighting the occasional long-eared jackrabbit and lightning-fast lizard, we watched the 'White Dove of the Desert' – Mission San Xavier – rise up like a mirage. After a quick walk across the border into Mexico at Nogales, we found respite from the haze and heat ascending the heights of Mt. Lemmon and taking in its dizzying views.

Though off the beaten path and with access now restricted due to illegal immigration, Organ Pipe Cactus National Monument on the Mexican border offered magnificent Sonoran desert scenery. With Tom and Tommy turning back, Mike and I headed for cooler climes, but not before visiting the National Observatory at the top of Kitt Peak where we observed astronomers studying the planets, the stars, and the sun with telescopes of every description. Driving through great sand dunes at the southernmost tip of California, we passed the Salton Sea and took in Joshua Tree National Monument. We marveled again at the ancient groves of giant trees in Sequoia National Park and the raging rivers in the ravines of Kings Canyon National Park. From Glacier Point in Yosemite, we thrilled for hours at the most beautiful scene carved from stone on earth, second only to the Grand Canyon. Leaving the Sierra Nevadas behind, we hurried east to Capitol Reef in Utah, hiking up to a dizzying walk across Butch Cassidy Arch. Crossing Lake Powell brought us to more out-of-the-way places – Natural Bridges, nearby Valley of the Gods, and scattered ancestral Native American dwellings at Hovenweep and Canyon de Chelly.

Meanwhile, back at the 'ranch,' things were coming along nicely at All Saints. In keeping with the rustic nature of the site and its original use as ranchland, a split-rail fence and gates were built across the front in 1993. A gazebo added the following year honored the saints and provided a focal point for celebrating Mass in 'the cathedral of the great outdoors.' Still growing, the parish reached out to help missions in Mongolia, Ecuador, and Africa, as well as struggling St. Peter Claver Parish in Tampa. To build community, parishioners posed for a third parish directory, proudly hosted pizza parties to welcome newcomers, and even originated a Christmas card capturing the beauty of the sanctuary. At the end of 1995, Robert Lynch was named fourth Bishop of St. Petersburg. Hundreds of curiosity seekers were serenaded by carolers as they drove through the parish's first living Nativity scene. I drove through in my new bright blue Pontiac Firebird Formula, a 'muscle car' I kept for nine years. I just loved the T-tops.

I spent a memorable week with my brother in the spring of 1995. After crossing the Rockies from his home in Denver, Mark and I passed through Colorado National Monument on the way to Moab. It was warm enough to wear tee-shirts hiking through Arches and Canyonlands and along the base of Fisher Towers. Not too late for winter sports, we had time for some Kodak moments skiing at Copper Mountain and snowmobiling in Arapaho National Forest near Grand Lake. In June, I was honored to speak at my niece Laura's graduation from St. John School on St. Pete Beach. After that, Mike and I returned to some favorite haunts in Rocky Mountain, Black Canyon of the Gunnison, and Mesa Verde National Parks. Coming from the heat and humidity of flat Florida, we always look forward to the simple joys of walking through snow, sitting beside rushing waterfalls, admiring the delicacy of larkspur and lupines, and recognizing the chirp of marmots.

For the first time in Zion, we made the gravity-defying climb twelve hundred feet up to Angels Landing – hanging on for dear life to the chains near the top. This has become my favorite hike in the national park system. Deer flies pestered us hiking through the soft sand along La Verkin Creek, on a long trek out to a gargantuan arch hidden away in the remote Kolob Canyons of Zion. We wandered once more through the maze of pink sandstone columns on the floor of Bryce Canyon – named after a man who lost his cow. Successfully negotiating the steep switchbacks of the Burr Trail, we hiked for the first time deep into one of the canyons of the Escalante until we finally cooled off at Lower Calf Creek Falls. Then we stopped for a drink at a true oasis – Pipe Spring – an obscure national monument where Paiute Indians and Mormon pioneers found a life-saving source of water in the desert. Mike's Suburban survived the nearly impassable rutted road through eighteen miles of virgin forest to a spectacular view of the Grand Canyon at Point Sublime on the north rim. In another first, we made the all-day five-mile descent of thirty-two hundred feet down the North Kaibab Trail to Roaring Springs and back. Sidestepping the foul discharges of mules along the way was the hardest part.

On this trip, we learned that the most striking view of the mother of all canyons was not to be had here. After leaving pavement and civilization behind for two hours, and braving mile after bone-jarring mile of dusty washboard gravel, desert sand, and eventually sheer rock, we discovered Toroweap. To be sure, crossing this barren no man's land is neither for the faint of heart nor for the feeble of vehicle. Water and an extra spare tire must be carried. But the dramatic views from this overlook – up and down the Canyon, here less than a mile wide, and of the Colorado River raging three thousand feet below – will take the breath of all but the dead away. Few views on planet Earth compare.

Mike and I pooled our savings to become property owners for the first time in 1995. Apart from the rectories where they live, quite a few priests own their own homes or condos. We wanted a place on the water to get away to on our days off, maybe even to retire to. We knew that location would make this a good investment. We scoured the Gulf beaches in 1994. Prices hadn't started going through the roof yet, but nothing seemed quite right. A year later, we found the perfect condominium overlooking the Gulf a few floors up on Sand Key. With a sparkling pool, a great view up and down the beach, and rarely seen neighbors, it was a great place to visit every week even if we didn't live there. Beachcombing and bike riding kept us busy. Relaxing on our balcony watching thunderstorms approach was a thrill. Sunsets were never better. Life may not always be a beach, but life at the beach was great.

Just about everyone in Florida enjoys fishing and boating at some point. A parishioner with a charter boat offered to take Mike and me fishing on the grass flats around Caladesi Island. Mike is the more avid fisherman, but both of us brought home some beautiful fish. With an inshore 'grand slam' – snook, redfish, and speckled trout – I even got my photo in a fishing magazine. The snook weighed eleven pounds, and it was delicious. My friend Margaret from England and her new husband Niall invited Mike and me to join them at their beautiful penthouse condo in Naples and go boating with them. We later returned the favor, though they had to settle for going out on our much more humble boat and staying at our much less lavish condo.

All Saints inaugurated two new traditions in 1996. The first of seven annual Gold Crown Galas was held. The parish's one and only fundraising event, this elegant evening was a dress-up affair featuring fine wines, hors d'oeuvres, and live music, plus a ten thousand dollar giveaway. Involved in the parish from the beginning, Mom and Dad looked forward to coming to the Gala every year. Dad even provided some of the keyboard entertainment. At a hundred dollars apiece, tickets were limited to five hundred, but they sold like hot cakes. In the spiritual realm, I created the Garden of Life Memorial Mosaic to honor living and deceased parishioners and friends by inscribing their names on the wall of the narthex. Formed by three thousand tiles in twenty-seven colors, the Mosaic, patterned on a geometric Roman design, became a popular 'work in progress.' By the time I left All Saints in 2003, two thousand donations had been made and two thousand names inscribed, putting the Mosaic well on the way to completion.

You might think Mike and I had worn out our welcome in the West by now. Nevertheless, we went skiing again at Keystone with Mark in February. Mark Raffinan, a young man from Clearwater working in Denver, joined the three of us for a few spills and thrills snowmobiling on the western slope of Rocky Mountain National Park for a day. On a clear day you can see forever, and once the snow stopped blowing, it left a winter wonderland in its wake. The days were cold, but the warmth of the sun felt great on our faces. Of course Mike and I trekked across the mountains to the high desert country of Utah, finding it nicely dusted with snow. Having the national parklands almost entirely to ourselves at this time of year, we hiked peacefully under a cloudless winter sky through the arches and canyons we love.

Dividing our vacation time during the summer of 1996, we explored some new frontiers in addition to revisiting familiar territory. It's amazing how much snowfall varies from year to year and from place to place. The sharp peaks and round valleys of the Tetons – rising so abruptly from the surrounding flats of Jackson Hole – were still blanketed with snow except where bright yellow balsamroot flowers poked through. Snow banks on the higher peaks of Glacier further north were mostly melted. Ice still covered Fourth of July Lake in the jagged Sawtooth wilderness. A rainbow-colored mist hung in the air over Yellowstone's steamy thermal pools. Steep grades deterred us from descending into the foreboding depths of Hell's Canyon, but crossing Idaho's panhandle led us to discover the resplendent breadth of Kootenai Falls in Montana's northwest corner. Mike and I bagged plenty of moose, a few pronghorn antelope, and even a family of foxes – on film, of course.

With our friend Rick Newsham and his family eagerly awaiting our arrival, we made it to the great land of Alaska for the first time at summer's end. Fall comes and goes quickly here. Daylight dwindles, temperatures drop, and color explodes from sky to ground. The Chugach Mountains pin Anchorage up against twin embracing arms of the sea. The brilliance of the flora on our first hike through them made us giddy with excitement. The air was so clear that Mike and I could see the outline of Denali – Mount McKinley – two hundred and fifty miles away. A train took us through a tunnel to a dock in Whittier where we boarded a steel-hulled vessel that could ply the berg-laden waters of College Fjord. The magnitude of the towering tidewater glaciers along this inlet of Prince William Sound was staggering. Harbor seals lounged haphazardly on pads of ice, even as great slabs came crashing down, 'calving' right beside them. We watched screeching kittiwakes swoop down to their nests along finely-forested cliffs, and rafts of otters float past on their backs, occasionally diving for a hard-shelled treat.

Most of Portage Glacier, spilling down a valley to the water's edge, was concealed by low-hanging clouds. A pod of beluga whales played in Turnagain Arm. We headed south to foggy Kenai Fjords, a national park of massive glaciers accessible only by sea. Under a cold sun we cruised south out of Resurrection Bay – discovered by Captain Cook on Easter Sunday – past the shipyards of Seward toward the fjords. Nature treated us to a feast of fauna – nesting bald eagles fishing for herring to feed their young, Dall's porpoises racing alongside our craft, oystercatchers and puffins, stellar sea lions and leopard seals huddled in heaps on the rocks, and killer whales – to name a few. Dwarfed as we pulled up to a glacier's face, we were shocked by the sudden crack of an iceberg breaking off, rocking our boat. Near Seward, we got a marvelous look at the luminescent blue ice along the heavily crevassed toe of Exit Glacier.

Then we headed east through the Matanuska Valley, passing sparse spruce trees leaning to and fro, struggling to stand upright, like drunken soldiers. Worthington Glacier actually let us feel its slick, cold, ice-blue edge. From the top of Thompson Pass on the way to Valdez, we were awed at the vast expanse of land stretched out below. The sight of supertankers bloated with oil at the terminus of the eight-hundred mile Alaskan pipeline conjured up the sullied specter of the *Exxon Valdez*. Onboard another steel-hulled vessel, we crushed and crunched our way through the eerie polar landscape of Columbia Bay. Clearly visible beneath the surface of every iceberg was its billowing blue base. The temperature plunged as we approached the face of Columbia Glacier, as tall as a fifty-story building, mightily grinding down mountains from time immemorial on its march to the sea.

The lofty summits of the Wrangell Mountains beckoned in the distance, but they would have to wait. The peaks of the Alaska Range loomed ever larger on the horizon as we moved north, then west across the Denali highway – the most beautiful hundred unpaved miles in America. Under a crystal sky, we ventured in an old school bus into the pristine interior of Denali National Park, where the tallest peak in North America glistened in the sun, reigning supreme over tundra carpeted with living color. Around every bumpy bend, incredibly broad valleys and majestic rows of mountains came into view. Grizzly bears, Dall sheep, antlered caribou, and moose all appeared as if on cue. On our last day, we made a mad dash three hundred miles further north, dodging rocks thrown up by speeding trucks, until we reached the Arctic Circle. Along the way, amber ribbons of aspen and silver braided rivers threaded their way through a sea of evergreen. Nowhere else in the United States can beauty be measured on such a grand scale as in Alaska.

Years after he began his studies, Jack Lyons was finally ordained a deacon in June of 1997 for service to All Saints. The restoration of the diaconate was one of the finest accomplishments of the Second Vatican Council. Jack quickly took over preparing people for baptism and marriage as well as actually administering these sacraments, taking a load off my shoulders. Most of the deacons I work with in parishes today are truly dedicated, prayerful men. Their service to the Church rivals that of any priest. Joachim Msaki, a priest from Tanzania, arrived that summer as well. His 'visit' – at first during the summer and then year-round – lasted for six years, until he returned permanently to his diocese in Africa. Joachim was an invaluable help to me, and we became good friends.

Bishop Larkin came out of retirement to celebrate All Saints' tenth anniversary at a testimonial Founders' Day Mass and brunch on the first of November. The parish celebrated its first ten years under the tall pines with a picnic and another festive outdoor Mass, captured for posterity in a photo on the cover of the weekly bulletin. Seven hundred registered families were now supporting the parish. New hardwood flooring enabled the expansion of the sanctuary, drawing everyone closer to the altar. The year ended sadly with the passing of All Saints' devoted sacristan, Winnie Cole.

A parish that dedicates itself to genuine stewardship will experience one blessing after another. At the end of ten years, All Saints' original loan of one and a half million dollars had been reduced by two-thirds. The parish wisely accepted and profited from Bishop Lynch's offer to match diocesan funds with parish dollars to accelerate the reduction of the debt. This saved not only money but time. For the first time, All Saints began saving for the future, daring to envision anew the original dream of a permanent church.

Mike and I took one more trip to Italy in July of 1997, taking advantage of my brother's employment with United Airlines. This time, instead of trouble getting there, we had trouble getting back. Driving up the coast to Washington, we left my car there with friends and flew to Milan. There we hopped on the express train to Naples, where we met up with a couple from Mike's parish with a cute but hyperactive kid. With our friends Larry and Maria Grazia's two kids, that made three. This time we joined them at Pozzuoli on the sparkling blue Bay of Naples. Though the water was surprisingly cold, Mike and I made an incredible discovery snorkeling offshore. All of a sudden we were right over ancient Roman ruins – crumbled columns and floor slabs tiled with mosaics – like a scene from the lost city of Atlantis. Instead of revisiting Pompeii on this trip, we spent a day strolling under a burning sun among the smaller but better preserved ruins at Herculaneum.

We also enjoyed visiting some monumental churches and catacombs, savoring the fresh seafood, driving along the coast, and tasting limoncello – a sweet local liqueur made from lemons. But it was getting harder and harder to enjoy a vacation with three needy kids. How my parents ever managed with four of us I'll never know. I have to admit I let the kids get to me, but I was outnumbered three to one. Instead of heading to the beach with our friends, at my urging Mike and I bid farewell and boarded the train back to Milan. We got away from the kids, but flying standby, we couldn't get back to the States – for days as it turned out – without *buying* a ticket. It cost a small fortune. To make matters worse, we had to fly to New York, and then book another flight to Washington where my car was. Not expecting us to be back for another week, the friends I had given my car and keys to were out of town. So we had to hire a taxi to take us to my car, parked on a street somewhere in the neighborhood. At least I had a hide-a-key to open the car door. Mike and I spent a stuffy, largely sleepless night reclining in my bucket seats. In the morning, I had to get to a Pontiac dealer to make an ignition key before we could finally drive nine hundred miles home. God may have been laughing at this colossal comedy of errors, but I wasn't. I was beginning to learn how making such elaborate plans in order to save a few bucks only sets things up to go wrong.

With precious vacation time left, Mike and I headed once again for familiar territory in my Firebird. We left the T-tops off most of the time, hightailing it out to Colorado and Utah as though going to visit old friends. After climbing to the chilly roof of the world at Mt. Evans, we went rollerblading alongside the Colorado River, churning through narrow Glenwood Canyon, on the way to Arches National Park. There we obtained a backcountry permit to explore the Fiery Furnace region, which really lived up to its name with temperatures over a hundred degrees. After nearly getting lost wandering through its sandstone 'fins,' we spent a lazy day at Newspaper Rock on the way to Canyonlands National Park's barren Needles District, which was all but devoid of human visitors in the heat of summer.

Morning glories greeted us on our way out to find mighty Corona Arch, and another new landmark near Moab, Negro Bill Canyon. It's rare to find a stream in the desert, but we cooled off more than once in one that runs through a sandy gorge leading to massive Morning Glory Arch. After looking down on the magical monoliths of Castle Valley from the forested heights of the LaSal Mountains, we took in more bird's eye views from Island in the Sky. Finally cooling off in Rocky Mountain National Park, we took our time climbing from ten to twelve thousand feet, where tiny pink and blue alpine flowers dot the treeless tundra. From that altitude we descended to Denver, catching Michael Flatley's engaging performance in *Lord of the Dance* before making a beeline home.

XVI   GETTING UP TO SPEED

With my brother working for United Airlines, Mike and I decided to see how far we could go at a discounted rate with a free upgrade to business class on a space-available basis. We considered circumnavigating the globe just to say we had done it, but we didn't know anyone and wouldn't have had time to see much in the several cities we would have passed through. After I looked up a classmate from high school who said he'd be glad to see us, we settled on Australia. We were able to board all four connecting flights for the ten thousand-mile journey across the U.S. and the Pacific Ocean to get there. With a lengthy layover in Los Angeles on our way to the land 'down under,' where the seasons are reversed, we filled the time riding a city bus to Santa Monica, where we wandered around Venice Beach and the famous Pier seen in so many films. Having crossed the equator and the International Date Line for the first time on the flight from Los Angeles to Melbourne, with a stop in New Zealand, we found ourselves in a time zone sixteen hours *ahead* of the one we had left. Christmas, the heat of summer, and the end of 1997 were all approaching.

Trying to keep my balance, just as in life.

Ed Kirby brought us home to his quaint cottage in Pakenham, a little town an hour east of Melbourne where he taught school. His red-haired Aussie wife and two freckled little girls welcomed us with their charming accents. Mike and I had two weeks to explore Victoria, Australia's southernmost state. Ed couldn't accompany us, but he sent us off in his ancient Volkswagen bus – on the left side of the road, of course. Mike did a better job of driving than I did navigating, especially through all the roundabouts. First we headed south to the granite headlands, mountains, forests, and fern gullies of Wilson's Promontory, a national park encompassing eighty miles of coastal wilderness at the southernmost point of the Australian mainland. After relaxing on the pure white quartz sand of Squeaky Beach, we climbed to the top of Mt. Oberon for a panoramic view across the wild and windswept Southern Ocean. A walk through a eucalyptus forest filled with passionflowers yielded our first sighting of a koala in the wild. Giant tree ferns in the misty rainforest dwarfed us. Kangaroos, emus and wombats grazed freely wherever grasses grew.

Making our way along the coast, we explored star-fish-studded tidal pools, blowholes, sea caves, and lighthouses. We observed rows of pastel surf shacks lining the beach, lawn bowlers on the green, and hundreds of shearwaters, also known as muttonbirds, soaring overhead. The nests of these migratory seabirds are patrolled by cobras scavenging their unattended eggs during the day while the birds are out to sea fishing. Lyrebirds sang to us as we walked through Sherbrooke Forest in the Dandenong Ranges. Brilliantly colored parrots streaked through towering eucalyptus trees, also known as mountain ash. Fast food – especially Kentucky Fried Chicken – is available everywhere in Australia. Chips come with everything, and everything is take-away. Moderately priced restaurants are few and far between. We found one in an old caboose.

Then it was on to Phillip Island to witness a natural phenomenon that people the world over come to see at dusk each night – the extraordinary parade of fairy penguins. To the delight of hundreds of hushed onlookers huddled on bleachers, first a few, then a line, and finally a wave of birds ride in gently on the rolling surf. Homeward bound, they wobble by the hundreds across the sand and up the dunes. After foraging at sea all day, they march tiredly but triumphantly, sloppily waddling to their burrows with single-minded purpose. Amusement quickly turns to amazement at their unabashedly public displays of affection. Apparently this penumbral spectacle takes place nowhere else in the world.

The mountains, trees, and waves grew to storybook proportions as we moved west along the Great Ocean Road, Victoria's dramatic coastal highway. Driving past flocks of thick-wooled sheep grazing on the grassy heights, we overlooked the aqua waters of Anglesea's crescent beach. In a blustery wind we made a steep descent to the soggy beach at Moonlight Head, famous for shipwrecks. We found the ruddy sand there strewn with cuttlebones and abalone shells, iron cannonballs too heavy to carry, and rusty ship's anchors protruding from the pounding surf. As the sun came out around a bend, the ageless faces of the Twelve Apostles came into view. An awesome sight, these massive craggy limestone stacks rise up out of a foaming ocean held back by sheer cliffs. After strolling along the soft sand at their grottoed base, we stopped to marvel at London Bridge, Loch Ard Gorge, and other monoliths dotting the coast – arched islands of stone carved by a relentless sea.

Heading north into Victoria's interior we came to the Grampians, a striking series of small mountain ranges abruptly rising out of the surrounding plains. Enshrined in a national park, these low-angled sandstone ridges feature jutting peaks, rocky outcroppings, a hidden canyon, lovely waterfalls, flowing streams, hazy blue vistas reminiscent of the Smokies, and forests filled with screeching white cockatoos and laughing kookaburras.

Perhaps Mike's and my most memorable outing in Australia occurred in the middle of nowhere, in the dead of night, and in total darkness, feeling our way blindly along a shaky handrail with only a few other hearty souls on a boardwalk though a damp gully. Intrigued by a description of glow worms we had come across, we asked the proprietors of the quaint bed and breakfast we were staying at where they might be found. They directed us to this dank place where, after we stumbled along some distance, our eyes finally adjusted to the absence of light. Almost imperceptibly at first, thousands of tiny points of light began to appear around us, embedded in the dirt walls of the gully we were walking though and becoming brighter with each footfall. Glow worms are actually the larvae of a gnat found only a few places in the world. Unlike lightning bugs that flash intermittently, they glow continuously to attract prey into strands of silk they spin and hang as snares. Almost mystically, their bioluminescence creates the impression of walking under a starry sky at night. Witnessing this obscure phenomenon made our trip down under even more memorable. Flying standby once more, we managed to get on all four flights home, though in Melbourne Mike and I were the last two people called to board the jumbo jet.

My brother Mark gave us a scare in April of 1998 when at the age of forty-two he suffered a heart attack. His voice on the phone was so weak I decided to leave for Denver immediately. I jumped in the car, and thirty hours later, I was at his bedside in the hospital. He didn't ask me to come, it was just something I felt I had to do. Besides keeping him company, I took care of his cat, Otis, despite being allergic to cats, watered his plants, and shoveled spring snow off his driveway and sidewalk. I brought him home a few days later. As a result of making a few changes to his lifestyle, as we all have to do from time to time, he's been fine ever since.

Being alone in our parishes, as Mike and I were for years, always required careful planning in order to get away. In addition to my brother's connection with United, we also mastered the award travel system of Northwest Airlines and its partners. This enabled us to go a lot of places we could not have afforded to go otherwise on the income of a priest.

We were able to stockpile frequent flyer miles by using a business credit card to charge as many parish expenses as possible, in addition to our own personal credit cards. Our parishes simply paid the bill each month. Never carrying a balance resulted in no cost to the parish at all. The system of booking award travel online was clearly not designed to be user-friendly. I found it challenging, but once I became computer literate, I got quite good at it.

When my friend George Fasching, an Army colonel retired from MacDill, and his wife Mary Anne moved to St. Thomas in the U.S. Virgin Islands, Mike and I decided to use the free flight vouchers TWA had given us when our trip to Rome was delayed a day. St. Thomas was listed as a destination on the back of the voucher. However, when trying to make reservations, we were informed that TWA no longer flew there. I was determined not to take no for an answer. I can be adamant when I have to, and I was about this until I prevailed. TWA routed us from Tampa to San Juan, but by way of New York. They had to ticket us on another carrier – at their expense, of course – for the hop from Puerto Rico to St. Thomas. We had to change terminals at JFK, which meant going outside to catch a shuttle from one to the other. It was winter, and Mike and I hadn't thought about this. There we were, standing outside JFK in the snow in shorts and flip-flops, waiting for the bus. We finally got to our friends on the island. We had a great time, renting a boat for a day to visit the beach and the Soggy Dollar Bar on Jost Van Dyke, a British Virgin Island. On the way to St. John, the island east of St. Thomas, we suddenly found ourselves in the midst of a pod of whales. Killing the engine, we sat spellbound and watched them play, listening to their plaintive song.

Over the years at All Saints, I became part of a group of parishioners who were close friends. I was able to be myself with them and just have fun. When Halloween rolled around, I was bound and determined not to be recognized in costume. I've dressed up in some wild outfits before – a clown, King Arthur, a dowager, Santa, even a playboy on stage – but nothing like this. I put on a huge wig, a vintage pumpkin-orange polyester leisure suit with flared pants, high-heeled boots, and enough gold rings, bracelets, and necklaces to sink a ship, not to mention tortoise-shell sunglasses, a giant gold earring, and a gold front tooth. Then a friend, costumed as Dolly Parton, helped me apply stage makeup on my face, neck, and hands. My arrival met with shock and awe. They had no clue who I was. The photos will probably turn up on the web one of these days.

The best deal I ever found on travel to faraway desti-nations was Northwest World Vacations. Mike and I took four of these trips in all, we enjoyed them so much. The first, in May of 1998 – and the last, in November of 2008 – were to Bangkok, Thailand. While we only spent five days there – not counting a day coming and going ten thousand miles each way – the long trip was worth every minute of it. The price was surprisingly low, with airfare, six nights at a hotel, transfers, and then some all for less than eight hundred dollars. As if that were not enough, we covered enough miles to earn a free domestic round-trip.

Singing in the rain in a rhododendron garden.

151

The Royal River was a first-class hotel, filled with orchids and fresh flowers, right on the banks of the Chao Phraya River, the bustling main artery of transportation through the city and the country. Bangkok is reputed to be the hottest city on earth. Even though it was not the hottest time of year, I'd agree with that – I've never perspired so much in my life. You can't drink the tap water, but anything bottled is fine, readily available, and inexpensive. The hotels take great care with food preparation. Like Florida, Thailand caters to tourists. While the streets are kept almost fanatically clean, the air is dreadfully polluted by trapped auto exhaust from unbelievably congested traffic – the only unpleasant aspect of Bangkok. Tens of thousands of overloaded scooters and *tuk-tuks*, canopied open-air three-wheeled carts crammed with passengers and cargo, ply the streets and alleys. Bangkok is notorious for its sex and drug trades, but these were outside our scope of interest. People are friendly but no one speaks English except the tour guides, who were humorous, knowledgeable, and grateful for even a modest tip. The hotel had its own longboat, so Mike and I rode up and down the river on it, to go shopping and just to take in the exotic sights, sounds, and smells of the waterfront. We did the same wandering the streets, once we realized they were safe.

The hotel put out an enormous Thai as well as American breakfast buffet that became our mainstay every day. Whether it was bacon and eggs, an omelet made to order, pancakes, cereal, fish, noodles, rice, sweet rolls, or fresh papaya and pineapple, you could have it all – and we did. This was part of the vacation package, together with a splendid tour of the city. Bangkok is all about the temples – four hundred of them in all – almost all Buddhist, and all architectural works of art on a grand scale. They literally glisten, inside and out, with cut glass, polished metal, and glittering gold. Their décor rivals that of the finest European cathedrals. Pagodas shaped like giant bells, ceilings, doors, walls, statues of Buddha, garudas, and other mythological creatures are all covered with gold leaf, giving a fantastic appearance to their surroundings. Buddha is never depicted as a squat, pot-bellied figure, but variously standing, reclining, or seated in the 'lotus' position. Lotus blossoms, sticks of incense, and votive candles are typically offered by devout worshippers, kneeling about the temples with bowed heads as Christians do, but always with shoes removed. No one in Bangkok wears shoes anyhow, only flip-flops. We never wore anything but sandals, tee-shirts, and shorts, which were suitable everywhere.

Each morning saffron-robed monks roam the streets, seeking donations of food in bowls they carry to feed the poor. What is left over is their food for the day. Bangkok is filled with canals. People who live on them easily find their humble dwellings inundated, especially when monsoon rains upcountry swell the river. Thai food is simply among the world's best and spiciest. It is inexpensive by our standards, even in the hotels, and incredibly fresh, much of it seasoned with coconut, ginger, lemongrass, fish oil, and chili peppers. A meal is never farther than a few steps away, as food vendors line the streets with their woks and grills, cutting up tropical fruits and vegetables, and frying up the catch of the day. You can buy almost anything on the street, especially inexpensive knock-offs of designer-label clothes and watches. Textiles are manufactured locally. Silk shirts are a steal.

The day trips Mike and I took couldn't have been easier to arrange or more convenient. We were picked up and dropped off by minivan at the door of our hotel each day. The 'Floating Market' – recently featured in *Bangkok Dangerous* starring Nicholas Cage – is only a couple of hours away. Here dozens of vendors sell everything from lampshade-shaped hats to giant hand-painted fans from loaded wooden boats jammed side by side like sardines on a network of canals. In addition to lush landscaping, the 'Rose Garden' showcases traditional native dancers in costume, Asian elephants, as well as a demonstration of kickboxing and other martial arts. We stared in amazement at a troop of young people daring enough to step in and out of bamboo rods being clapped together to elaborate rhythms, hoping to avoid any painful misstep. Along the way we marveled at the artistry of woodcarvers, exquisitely sculpting everything from teakwood furniture to finely finished fish, and making paper embedded with flowers and leaves by hand from mulberry paste.

Nothing quite prepares the casual sightseer in Bangkok for the opulence of the Grand Palace, a walled complex of spectacularly decorated temples and ornamental gold-towered buildings, including the official residence of the kings of Siam. A summer palace in the peaceful setting of the country outside Bangkok's urban sprawl also delighted us. Next to an ornate red and gold reception hall guarded by Chinese dragons, a temple rises out of a flower-ringed lake on glittering pillars of gold. Mike and I succumbed to the urge to ride on an elephant's back – careening uncomfortably to and fro with each slow stride – on our visit to Ayutthaya. This former capital of Thailand, stripped of gold and now overgrown, was sacked by the Burmese two hundred years ago and left in oddly picturesque ruins. Our first trip to the Far East would not have been complete without experiencing a genuine Thai massage. A petite masseuse worked skillfully not only with her trained hands but also with her feet, walking in all the right places on our backs – just what the doctor ordered before leaving the mystique of the Orient behind and re-entering the Western world.

From reading these travelogues, one might get the impression that I didn't spend much time working at the parish. Nothing could be further from the truth. As the only resident priest for the better part of sixteen years, I was on a very short leash – on call twenty-four hours a day, seven days a week, even when I was 'off duty.' Priests typically take a month off in the summer, though I prefer alternating between spring and fall. They also take a day off each week, usually overnight, and a few other days here and there – such as after Christmas and Easter. Most people view priests as overworked and underpaid. Like all stereotypes, this one is exaggerated. I have never known a priest who was not amply provided for by the Church. If a priest is overworked, he has no one to blame but himself.

Learning to manage time well is a critical survival skill for priests, just as it is for other professionals. Despite clerical ranks being depleted by retirement and lack of replacements, taking time off and getting away is more important for priests than ever before. Finding coverage for one's parish is not all that difficult with a little advance planning. Much parish work is predictably routine and no one would read a book just about that. For me, lining up places to go and things to do and looking forward to getting away for a time is at least in part what's kept me going for thirty-five years. Striking a healthy balance between work, prayer time, and play time is what happiness – and life – is all about.

A stringer of fish caught from our kayaks.

XVII GOING WITH THE FLOW

All Saints and I were about to embark on our last and greatest adventure together, one that would take a full five years. Our ambitious goal was to recapture the original vision of building a permanent church – by way of a major structural expansion and renovation. It took several years of evaluation and consultation with an architect before a consensus emerged to proceed in this direction as the most cost-effective alternative. Preliminary plans for a new ten thousand square-foot worship space seating a thousand people, as well as additional meeting rooms, courtyards, and gathering spaces, were drawn by Alexander & Associates in 1998.

Of course, the approval of the Diocese had to be obtained before such a project could ever hit the drawing board. As a member of the Diocesan Commission for Liturgical Art, Architecture, and Environment, I already knew how to go about this. Bishop Lynch originated DCLAAE to assist parishes and pastors by guiding them through the process of designing and building or renovating spaces used for worship. Working with the staff of the Worship Office headed by my long-time friend John Tapp, DCLAAE was there to help, not hinder, architects, contractors, and parish building committees in every way possible, from start to finish. Pastors often don't realize when they begin how much help they're going to need with their project, but they soon learn. I had in fact helped compile and present the very guidelines governing projects like mine for the Diocese. Being the wiser in this regard at the beginning of my own project made for smoother sailing than many parishes experience.

A few times in the course of the ten years I served in this capacity, the important work we were trying to do seemed like pulling teeth. Some individuals resented having to deal with anyone from the Diocese at all. Some came to DCLAAE with their plans cast in stone and their minds made up, without ever having read what Church documents had to say on the matter at hand. While members of DCLAAE do not like being branded the 'liturgical police,' there were times we resorted to playing games like 'good priest, bad priest' to prevent costly mistakes from being made. Most pastors who came to us were more open to suggestion, and willing to adhere to the various Church documents in force. All this aside, this work became dear to my heart and still is. I served on DCLAAE for ten years. The practical experience I gained working with professionals and parishioners still comes in handy from time to time.

A highlight of my stint on DCLAAE was attending a national conference known as Form/Reform in Chicago during the summer of 2001. For one thing I got to know what a gifted architect and fine human being Will Alexander was. Mike and I attended seminars from dawn to dusk on every conceivable aspect of building and renovating churches. We thoroughly enjoyed a walking tour of downtown Chicago's marvelously diverse architecture, and an exhausting all-day trek by bus to architectural landmarks in the vicinity, including the incredible Bahai Temple. After the conference, Mike and I drove up to Harbor Springs, Michigan, to spend the Fourth of July weekend with the Emery family. For the first time since I was a kid, we drove across the iconic Mackinac Bridge. Once in the Upper Peninsula, our friends took us out to Whitefish Point on Lake Superior and to lovely Tahquamenon Falls. I relived another childhood memory navigating the famous locks on the Canadian border at Sault Sainte Marie.

Before I took the next step toward getting a new and improved All Saints off the ground, Mike and I headed once more for the tranquility of St. Mary Lake on the eastern slope of Glacier National Park. Little snow rested on the peaks by August, but wildflowers at Logan Pass were in full bloom. The dancing flames of our campfire warmed the chill night air. Several hours of climbing revealed Iceberg Lake living up to its name. After being ferried across Lake Josephine, we joined a ranger for a five-mile hike to Grinnell

Glacier, finding our footing cautiously along the edge of a vast blue crevasse. From Montana we drove north into the Canadian Rockies for a week, enjoying familiar vistas at Waterton Lakes, Banff, and Jasper. To the mournful strains of an alpenhorn echoing across the water, we ascended to the rock-strewn snow-covered heights of the glacier that forms the spectacular backdrop of Lake Louise, literally disappearing into the majestic alpine scenery.

In September of 1998, when Asia was in the midst of a recession and travel to the Far East was cheap, Mike and I went on another week-long junket, this time to Beijing. Staying in another first-class hotel on one of the city's main drags, we enjoyed taking in all the sights, sounds, and smells walking affords, all the way to Tiananmen Square. There we joined a fast-moving line of hundreds of people on the way in to Chairman Mao's monumental tomb. With no talking allowed, the almost reverential silence was broken only by the shuffling of feet, briefly passing by Mao's glass-encased body lying in state under the watchful eye of heavily-armed soldiers. Seeing so many bicycles and pedestrians on the move rather than cars took some getting used to. Most people just stared straight ahead rather than smile or nod. Though we nearly got lost in the great crowds, we visited the Forbidden City and the Temple of Heaven. I found these magnificent structures, so overrun with tourists, somewhat dulled by age. Then it was on to see the famed bamboo-munching giant pandas at the zoo. A trip to the Summer Palace in the country and a boat ride on a peaceful lake provided some relief from the trapped heat and air pollution from which Beijing suffers, just like Bangkok.

Perhaps the greatest thrill China offered was walking along the Great Wall, winding and disappearing across the hills like a serpent, only to reappear stretching into the distance. A rickshaw ride through the *hutong* – a neighborhood maze of alleyways and courtyards – gave us a close-up view of everyday life in Beijing. At night we savored Peking duck before taking in the tedious clang of highly stylized Chinese opera, and an utterly amazing performance by a troupe of Chinese acrobats, world-renowned for their unbelievably daring balancing acts. We watched highly skilled artisans applying delicate metal inlays and ceramic enamel to cloisonné figurines, as well as stringing necklaces of opalescent fresh-water pearls by hand. Like Thailand, China yielded a treasure trove of souvenirs, none more lovely than a serene watercolor painting of two sandhill cranes. We bought it as we were about to leave with the last faded banknotes folded in our pockets.

As the end of the millennium approached, enthusiasm began to build at All Saints. Bollenback Builders was chosen for the expansion. Children's and handbell choirs were added by music director Harryette Williams. Parishioners loved being able to do business at the parish office on weekends, and parents loved the respite they and everyone else at Mass gained by leaving their little darlings in the nursery on Sunday morning. Recognizing the need to celebrate daily Mass in a more intimate space, we had a new altar and ambo fashioned out of oak and began using them right away. Alcoholics Anonymous began on-site meetings, and Father Tom Allender drew record crowds at his first parish mission in Florida. Mike and I had been so impressed by his down-to-earth style of preaching at a church we visited in Colorado that we invited him on the spot to come to our parishes. The long-overdue widening of Curlew Road in front of All Saints, though messy and inconvenient, only served to attract attention to the parish and accelerate our growth. For the first time in 1999, Bishop Lynch honored a single parishioner, Greg Powell, with the St. Jude medallion at a ceremony in the Cathedral. At the same time, on behalf of the Pope, he bestowed the first Pontifical award ever given in the Diocese to my father, Carroll, in recognition of his lifetime of service to the Catholic Church.

One of the lasting contributions I made to All Saints was establishing a strong tradition of sacrificial giving. Time and time again when put to the test, parishioners responded overwhelmingly. Despite my reservations, they did so when the Annual Pastoral Appeal was restored in

1998, replacing the 'parish tithe' system previously used to fund diocesan spending. They did so again two years later, marking the elimination of the original parish debt, years ahead of schedule, with a ceremonial 'burning of the mortgage.' This milestone paved the way for the *Garden of Life* capital campaign in the fall of 2000. Even though a third of the proceeds were reserved for diocesan capital improvements, All Saints raised an astounding one million two hundred thousand dollars in pledges. This 'piggy-backed' campaign was so successful Bishop Lynch asked me to give a pep talk to the entire presbyterate. I did, encouraging the rest of the parishes to follow our lead. With just enough savings in hand, the parish finally got the green light to proceed with construction.

In July of 1999, I went back to Costa Rica with my friends the Renzis and their daughter. Dom's brother Gene put us up at a lavish hotel high in the lush mountain forest overlooking San Jose. Brilliant flowering tropical plants – helliconia, birds of paradise, and bromeliads, not to mention orchids – abound everywhere in the tropics. From high in the rainforest above the clouds, we peered down into the steaming mint green lake in the caldera of the dormant volcano, Irazu. Heading off into the interior, we stayed both in Arenal – where a perfectly shaped active volcano made its presence heard and felt – and at a resort in the jungle literally crawling with giant green and brown iguanas. Monkeys chattered and swung through the canopy of trees overhead. The girls stayed behind while Dom and I climbed to the base of a magnificent waterfall at LaFortuna. Between the humidity and the spray, we were soaked by the time we got there. I plunged into the pool at the base of the falls. The moisture unfortunately did my video camera in. Dom and I went on to a seaside resort, exploring the Pacific coast of Costa Rica for a couple of days. For the first time, I took a kayak out into the surf and loved it.

When I got back, Mike and I hooked up the camper and headed out to Flagstaff. Using Tom Allender's house as a base, we visited familiar national monuments at Walnut

Canyon, Sunset Crater, and Wupatki. We also braved the crowds and the confounding shuttle bus system at the south rim of the Grand Canyon – more like Grand Central Station during the summer months. Tom had arranged for us to stay a night at Phantom Ranch in the bottom of the Grand Canyon, but heavy rains just a few days before had washed out the trail and forced its closure. Disappointed at missing out on this once-in-a-lifetime opportunity, we took less traveled roads, stopping to admire the mottled bark of sycamore trees at Montezuma Castle National Monument, and the mammoth limestone natural bridge in Tonto National Forest. Hundreds of century plants in bloom dotted the landscape with their huge stalks of yellow flowers. Near Sedona we found a slippery rock chute to slide down into some cold river water. People rave about this area of Arizona, but it doesn't do much for me.

More to my liking is the truly majestic Zion National Park. There Mike and I scaled the heights of the awesome Canyon, and clawed our way once more to the top of Angels Landing. From a lookout east of the canyon, we heard voices rising from a jumble of huge boulders beneath us. Closer inspection revealed a thin silver stream flowing down to the Virgin River. Deciding to explore this unmarked region, Mike and I headed into the brush toward a row of massive old cottonwood trees which always grow by water. There we came upon a series of secluded freshwater pools, created by natural rock dams, refreshingly cool and deep enough for diving into. Thus we escaped the heat of the afternoon, making this secret place our own oasis and leaving no trace of our presence. On this trip we also discovered Tuacahn, a fabulous outdoor amphitheatre set in the red rocks of St. George, Utah. We savored an old-fashioned Dutch oven supper there before enjoying a stellar musical performance of *Seven Brides for Seven Brothers* under the stars.

Despite the millions of flies ringing its shoreline, we went for a float on Utah's Great Salt Lake on the way home. Though finding little of note on Antelope Island, we took in its spectacular setting from high up in the Wasatch Mountains on a rocky road out of Bountiful. Eighteen years after our first visit, we returned to admire the rare and delicate helictite formations of Timpanogos Cave in the hills above American Fork. Finally, with most of the snow on the Grand Tetons melted by August, we hiked miles up Cascade Canyon to Lake Solitude where we did find snowy patches along its rock-strewn shore. These valleys and streams never fail to yield sightings of grazing black bear, marmots, and moose, as well as pale yellow glacier lilies, white columbines, and wildflowers galore.

In November of 1999, I reached a milestone of sorts, touching down in the only state I hadn't yet set foot in – Hawaii. A young couple Mike and I knew in Honolulu came to greet us in typical island fashion with leis made of carnations and frangipani flowers. We stayed at the hotel on Waikiki where Christine worked. Mike Romeo took us around to see the sights. It was a joy to baptize their first child at their parish church during our stay. Right away we climbed to the top of Diamond Head, Honolulu's most famous landmark, to get our bearings. The fantastic combination of warm sun, soft sand, gentle breeze, and rolling surf that is Hawaii is hard to beat. But another world – that of the tropical rainforest that carpets the island's ancient volcanic slopes – lies only minutes from the city. That's where we headed next.

Lush green ferns, mosses, and vines covered every rock and overhanging branch. Hiking through coconut groves and stands of bamboo, we followed a muddy trail to lovely Manoa Falls, tumbling over a lava cliff. After braving the cold water of the pool at its base, we marveled at the sweet song of unseen birds and the delicate scent of wild orchids and hibiscus. Out of a sea of anthuriums and ginger plants, bananas and papayas, a wild boar emerged with a snort. The reality of Hawaii's wartime past was brought home as we visited the National Memorial Cemetery of the Pacific and passed Wheeler Field, surrounded by pineapple and coffee plantations. Dad had run for his life across it seventy years ago when the Japanese were strafing Schofield Barracks. Going out to the USS Arizona Memorial at Pearl Harbor moved us deeply. Oil can still be seen leaking from the sunken hull of the battleship. The size of the guns on the battleship USS Missouri surprised us, as did the close quarters onboard the submarine USS Bowfin nearby.

Wherever you are on Oahu, you can almost always hear the roar of crashing surf in the distance, but you have to watch your step walking out to blowholes on the sharp lava rock. Surfers, struggling to stay up on their boards, can be seen everywhere. Beaches on the Pacific are rather intimidating compared to those along the Gulf – the water is cold, the undertow powerful, and the waves huge. We couldn't help but notice the flamboyant red-orange royal poinciana trees lining Honolulu's waterfront. Donning rubber boots and aprons, Mike and I were admitted to a commercial fish market where forklifts carried around pallets of fresh-caught tuna and mahi for auction to wholesalers. Our only culinary adventure was trying *poi* – a traditional Hawaiian staple made from taro root – a bland, faint purple dish the consistency of cream of wheat. I won't be ordering it anytime soon.

We took a day trip to Kauai, primarily to see the famed 'Grand Canyon of the Pacific.' The play of light, shadow, and color on the lush volcanic chasms deep within Waimea Canyon – much larger and deeper than one would expect to find in the middle of an island in the Pacific – was indeed impressive. While we had to settle for seeing the foreboding cliffs of the Na Pali coast from the air, Kauai – nicknamed 'the garden isle' – was worth the visit. A slow boat took us down the Wailua River to a natural fern grotto and another lovely waterfall. Back on Oahu, the day we spent with our friend Mike at the Polynesian Cultural Center on the scenic north shore was especially entertaining. We wandered through the villages of seven distinct Pacific cultures where hundreds of natives, primarily Mormon university students, demonstrated traditional crafts and skills – making clothes from bark, carving outriggers, scaling coconut palms, building bamboo huts, and rubbing sticks to make fire. Performers in native dress danced and drummed their way into the night with lavish shows, including authentic Hawaiian hula and ukulele. People in this part of the world really know how to play with fire – they eat it, throw it, and walk on it.

Besides taking trips together, Mike and I usually spend our days off together as well, riding bikes or rollerblading along the recreation trail that runs the length of Pinellas County or through the wilds of Starkey Park in Pasco. Three years older than me, Mike once had an angina attack that seemed to come out of nowhere, but we were only minutes away from a hospital. The same thing happened another time when, exhausted from hiking in the heat, we jumped in some water that was a little too cold. We learned not to do that again. Having a stent put in remedied the situation. Mike just has to watch his heart rate a little more closely now.

Mom and Dad sharing a drink as they did everything in life.

The other recreational activity we've enjoyed for years is kayaking. Our bright yellow molded polyethylene 'sit-on-top' kayaks bail themselves out with any forward motion. With no moving parts to wear out except our upper bodies, they're perfect for exploring the shallow waters of the Gulf Coast and Tampa Bay. Besides the Tsala Apopka chain of lakes in Citrus County and Pasco County rivers like the Anclote and the Pithlachascotee, we've gone 'way down upon the Suwannee' and through mangrove forests along the Black Water River in the Everglades. We've glided along on the crystal clear waters of the Weeki Wachee, the Rainbow, and the nearly pristine Silver River. Following these to their source – the largest natural springs in the world – is always a relaxing way to spend a day in the 'real Florida' few people see. Observing alligators, manatees, and snakes in their native habitat sometimes only feet away can be a bit disconcerting at first. Near Silver Springs where Lloyd Bridges filmed 'Sea Hunt' in the '50s, you can even be entertained by a colony of cavorting rhesus monkees. Not native to Florida, they were introduced in the '30s by a tour boat operator to enhance his 'jungle cruise' ride.

Kayaks are a great eco-friendly way to stay in shape and in touch with the natural world. Fourteen feet long, our narrow one-person boats are fast on the water, so we can go for miles. At forty-eight pounds, they're light enough to pick up and carry and easy to tie down on top of Mike's GMC Yukon XL. In a kayak, you get to observe not only what's around you but what's moving under and over you at the same time. The summer of 2000, Mike and I took ours to three National Recreation Areas – Lake Powell in Arizona, Flaming Gorge in Utah, and Curecanti in Colorado.

After sitting in the car for a couple of days, I couldn't wait to get out on the water. Though Mike was not as enthusiastic, doing battle with the wind and the waves and the powerboats crossing Lake Powell felt good. Wearing nothing but a pair of shorts, we kept our hiking boots, cameras, and canteens dry beneath the waterproof hatch. The desert region surrounding Lake Powell is harsh and nearly inaccessible by land, but extremely colorful and inviting to the waterborne explorer. Once the boats were pulled up on a sandy shore at the mouth of one of the dozens of canyons within range of our campground, we'd begin hiking in to see what we could find. In one, a hawk and an owl were having an airborne duel. In another, we discovered petroglyphs and some long-abandoned cliff dwellings. In addition to eagles' nests, we spotted one rattlesnake sunning itself on a rock and another hiding on a sandstone ledge in the shade. The silence makes it easier to remain alert and aware of your surroundings.

Another day we ventured twelve miles downstream through Glen Canyon, starting at the base of the seven hundred foot-high dam that confines two hundred mile-long Lake Powell. Leaving the car at Lee's Ferry, we hitched a ride with our kayaks – looking like a couple of aging surfers with their boards – on a pontoon boat headed back upstream after ferrying sightseers down the Canyon. The water coming out at the base of the dam where we put in was ice cold but warmed up quickly as we made our way downstream. We passed between cliff walls rising more than a thousand feet, along a peaceful meander of the Colorado River known as Horseshoe Bend. A vantage point from the highway south of Page, Arizona, provides a dramatic bird's-eye view of this scenic wonder.

Back in the car again, we crossed over the Colorado at Marble Canyon, passing along the Vermillion Cliffs and through the forests of the Kaibab Plateau to the north rim of the Grand Canyon. In remote northeastern Utah, we stood on the rim of the red rock canyon through which the Green River flows near Flaming Gorge. This long, low, exceptionally colorful sandstone cliff face really lives up to its name, glowing radiantly in the morning light, especially up close from the water. Here too we explored miles of tall, twisting, silent rock-walled canyons in our kayaks. A surprise of sorts awaited us on a popular stretch of the Green River we kayaked down – some whitewater we had not really been expecting. As the volume of water flowing over the rocks was sufficient, this exciting but nerve-racking ride did not result in any mishap, though our kayaks are not designed for this type of activity. Another lesson to be learned: make sure you know exactly where you're going before putting in.

The Green River converges with the Yampa River inside Dinosaur National Monument in the northwest corner of Colorado. A gigantic monolith called Steamboat Rock sits near the confluence. The horseflies there were the worst I've ever experienced, and with a thunderstorm approaching, we had to hurry back up a treacherous dirt road before it turned to mud. Besides a lot of dinosaur bones, this out-of-the-way place offers stunning views of an unexplored labyrinth of canyonlands as far as the eye can see. At the top of a hill in a national forest nearby, Mike and I climbed up to a working fire tower. It was a clear day, and we could almost see forever, looking out in all directions, marveling at the sheer beauty of the land before us.

Finally we headed once more for the deepest canyon in North America, which affords extraordinary vistas of its treacherous depths. At the bottom of the Black Canyon lies the Gunnison River, still slowly slicing through the rock of ages. With whitewater far too wild for our kayaks, Mike and I settled for a jetboat ride along its calmer course instead. We did explore several arms of Blue Mesa, the largest lake in Colorado, where we took in another panoramic view from the top of an island. Picking up some thin, flat slabs of sandstone, we carried them back down to the kayaks, across the water to the car, down the dirt road we'd come up, and eventually back home.

People still argue about exactly when the new millennium began. But after all the hype, Y2K arrived quite uneventfully – depending on your point of view – either six months before or six months after my fiftieth birthday in June, 2000. While some might prefer to ignore an event like this, I decided to do something different – throw a party for myself, my family, and my friends at a Mexican restaurant. Mom came pushing Dad, recovering from successful colon cancer surgery, in a wheelchair, but they were able to enjoy the taco-fest along with everyone else. My two sisters Beth and Julie came with their husbands and kids, and my brother Mark came from Denver. Time marches on for all of us, so we may as well do things we enjoy with people we care for while we can.

Trying a few new things along the way on the road of life is good, too. Thirty-five years after spending my last Saturday at the Toledo Museum of Art, I decided to try my hand at painting. My sister Julie paints finely detailed watercolors. I love impressionism. Drawing inspiration largely from photos I've taken in America's national parks over the years, I've worked exclusively with acrylics so far, painting nearly a hundred scenes of various sizes on heavy paper and canvas, even a few on those flat stones Mike and I brought back from Colorado. I've given some away and sold some at an art show at Mike's parish, but quite a few still hang on my walls. Trying to capture reflections of nature's glorious beauty on canvas has brought great joy to my life.

The four Andrews siblings – Greg, Julie, Mark, and Beth.

XVIII LAND CRUISING

Getting to go places you've only dreamed of has a way of expanding your horizons and, every now and then, changing your view of the world. My trip to east Africa in September of 2000 definitely did that. Using a big chunk of the air miles we'd earned with our parish credit cards, Mike and I joined our friend Joachim Msaki, the priest who worked with me at All Saints, in Tanzania for seventeen days when he went home on vacation. Formerly known as Tanganyika – once a colony exploited by Germany, then by Britain, and finally by a failed experiment in socialism – Tanzania is now a republic that remains economically challenged. September is the driest month and the best time of year to see wildlife. Only a few highways are paved. Most roads are dirt tracks or bare rock scattered with crushed rock that eats tires and cracks windshields. Gaping potholes make for painfully slow going and a bone-jarring ride. September is also when the stubble of corn plants remaining in the fields is burned. As there is little else to eat, people eat the corn. Livestock, kept inside in pens, are fed only the stalks. The air is thick with a smoky haze, made oily by the heavy diesel burned by vehicles. It sticks to your clothes and skin and gets into your lungs. Monster trucks, dimly lit, prowl the night. Doorless minivans, overcrowded with workers jumping on and off, careen around street corners. Toyota Land Cruisers are the vehicle of choice, though heavy import taxes make vehicle ownership a luxury.

Our arrival was heralded with great fanfare by the villagers of Kirua, on the slopes of Mt. Kilimanjaro. Some had never seen Caucasians before, much less video cameras. We were crowned with leafy floral wreaths and garlands, applauded, sung to and danced for by the women – Joachim's family and friends – at the new house he had just had built. Most people live in huts made from sticks and mud with rusty corrugated metal roofs, without running water or electricity. There is no refrigeration and cooking is done over an open fire or on a wood-burning stove. This only aggravates the problem of deforestation. We were also ceremoniously presented with a partially fermented beverage made from mashed bananas to drink out of a gourd.

Joachim was held in high regard as an elder and head of his clan, as well as a priest and successful native son. His homecoming called for a celebration, and he was expected to provide the goat that would feed everyone. Mike and I were invited to slay the goat, but we chose instead to record this and the other events of the day on our video cameras. Having asked to keep the skin of the goat for a souvenir, we watched the men, only too happy to oblige, undertake the elaborate process of stretching and preparing the hide with salt. It was ready for us two weeks later when we said goodbye, still soft enough to be folded up in a suitcase. Then it was time to eat, mostly vegetables. The goat, however, provided meat not only for us but, steamed with rice and bananas in a huge iron pot, for dozens of others. Joachim comes from the Chagga tribe who eat the small and sweet bananas growing everywhere with everything. So did we. In a country where a third of the population are Muslim, and another third animistic, the Chagga are primarily Christian. Quite a few are Catholic.

Shortly before leaving for Africa, Mike and I went to the Pinellas County Health Department to get shots for yellow fever and hepatitis. We also happened to see a National Geographic special on Tanzania that featured a quarry near Moshi – the small city by Joachim's home – where workers cut building blocks of soft volcanic rock out of the earth, entirely by hand. We found the place. Tourists were not allowed, so Joachim told the manager we were American producers scouting a film location. That plus a couple of bucks gained our entry. Video cameras in hand, we watched in amazement as large blocks were pried loose, carried by women on their heads up and out of the quarry, then hewn with chisels to size. There is little mechanization in Tanzania. Almost everything is accomplished by manual labor. I could hardly believe what I was seeing when I watched workers sitting in the bed of a road being built around the nation's capital. With hammers, they were breaking rocks to make gravel.

All Saints had provided me with a check for eleven thousand dollars to bring to Joachim's bishop for use in his diocese. Knowing this was coming, after having us for dinner at his residence, Bishop Msarikie gave us a Land Cruiser to use during our stay, and a man to drive us wherever we cared to go. Joachim escorted us everywhere. One place he took us to was a farm he had started for the Diocese of Moshi at Kilacha that became a model of agricultural science and animal husbandry for the whole country. We were lucky to get a slice of ham and roast pork there – a rare treat. We stared in amazement as a diesel-powered machine, looking like a giant meat grinder, crushed rocks we threw into it and spit out coarse and fine gravel. Joachim's diocese also owns a machine that slowly compacts natural materials into building blocks – two at a time. This is where he got the blocks for his house. In Moshi we stayed at a lovely residence for priests in the shadow of Mt. Kiliman-jaro, whose famous snowcap is rapidly melting away. Here we learned how to sleep under a mosquito net. Electricity was off as much as it was on. Needless to say, we couldn't drink the water. Breakfast consisted of a purple porridge made from millet – the main ingredient in bird seed – with raw sugar, warm milk fresh from the cow, and fresh eggs from the chickens in the back yard. Tanzanians have a thing about washing your hands before you eat, a cultural ritual everyone is expected to observe. Outdoors, there's a basin and pitcher. Indoors, as odd as it looks, there's a sink sticking out of the wall in almost every room.

National park fees are steep and payable only in U.S. dollars. Mike and I had to pay twenty-five dollars each time we entered a park, but to see what we got to see was worth far more. Entry today is more restricted and costs much more – one reason safaris are very expensive. We had to remain inside our vehicle at all times, for good reason – we could have been stomped, bitten, mauled, or eaten if we hadn't. Game wardens patrol to ensure compliance. We also had to hire a native guide who rode with us and told us what we were likely to see, when, and where. The first park we headed for was Lake Manyara, a shallow body of water famous for the thousands of pinkish-orange flamingoes that flock to its shore. Almost instantly, we found ourselves captivated by monkeys munching their way through the acacia trees, roving bands of bright-eyed baboons with their young, wallowing water buffaloes, gangly giraffes, skittish impalas, tusked warthogs, graceful gazelles, spoonbills, crowned cranes, and vultures soaring overhead. It wasn't long before zebras appeared, then a gray wall of elephants – constantly flapping their massive tattered ears – lumbering through the woodland in family groups. Giant baobab trees, with their telltale upside-down appearance, dotted the landscape.

I never thought Africa would be cold, but it was at night at Joachim's house and at the lodge we stayed at on the rim of Ngorongoro Crater. Nine miles wide, this steep bowl holds grasslands, forests, swamps, and lakes. Here is to be found the greatest concentration of wildlife in the world. After a bumpy descent into the volcanic basin, we watched herds of wildebeests appear on the horizon, leaving long trails of dust in their wake. A pair of ostriches engaged in a graceful mating dance. A parade of guinea hens passed by, carefully observed by a cheetah stretched out in the shade, motionless in the grass. We sighted a few endangered black rhinos at a distance, a solitary hippo half-submerged, then a whole flotilla. Joachim hailed a game warden who piled us all into his jeep and drove us up to see a species on the verge of extinction – a cluster of white rhinoceroses. A white pelican drifted by on a pond, trailed by a crocodile. A few spotted hyenas loped along on the prowl. Under a cleft rock, we peered into their den and watched a mother nurse her playful pups. Finally the king of beasts came into view with his queen, alternately roaming about and lying down again. We came across a whole pride of lions who were content to dismiss us, not with a roar, but a yawn.

Elephants lurked at every turn as we came out of the forest onto a grassy plain where giraffes, grazing with their long necks craned awkwardly, broke into a gangly slow-motion gallop. A pair of waist-high secretary birds – so called because feathers on their head look like a pencil tucked over the ear – came strutting along, looking for snakes to kill by picking them up and dropping them from the air. Ngorongoro literally teems with predators and prey engaged in a delicately balanced struggle for survival. Leaving that amazing place, we arrived wide-eyed at our next destination – an open-air lodge on the Serengeti. As dusk approached, a whole pack of friendly mongooses came scurrying by, seemingly to greet us.

The savannahs of the Serengeti, dotted with acacia trees and rocky hills called *kopjes*, yielded every sort of big game. Almost immediately we came upon a pride of lions that had just brought down a zebra. For nearly an hour we stood up through the sunroof of the Land Cruiser, video cameras in hand, watching the lions feed a stone's throw away, only occasionally bothering to glance at us. One of the females took off, returning shortly with a half dozen cubs in tow who, after the adults had torn the zebra apart, worked their way into the still-fresh meat. Red-faced and finally sated, the lions rested, reclining in the shade, licking themselves and their cubs clean, as all cats do. A herd of zebras sipped skittishly from a crocodile-lined watering hole. Baboons walking on all fours carried babies on their backs and bellies. Herds of gazelles, ostriches, and elands grazed, as lions laid in wait. A hyena slept beneath a sausage tree. Hiding in the shaded grass, a cheetah eyed a pack of elephants crossing the plain. We watched a pair of hippos cavort shamelessly in a river so choked with them you could walk across it on their backs. The Serengeti did not disappoint.

Camels appeared in the desert as we entered Kenya. Dust devils spun out of a distant sandstorm and danced at the base of Mount Meru. Here and there we passed Maasai tribesmen, wearing the traditional red shukas in which they're so often photographed, tending their herds. Clinging to a traditional lifestyle, they roam all over the Rift Valley attracting tourists, though they're generally regarded as unfriendly. Crossing the border with the Land Cruiser was a bit of a hassle. We would have to return through the same port of entry, not by way of Mombassa as Joachim had planned. Some nuns he knew in Nairobi put us up for the night. Over an open fire indoors, they slaved away cooking dinner for us, even heating water for Mike and me to bathe, which we did by pouring it over ourselves after soaping up over a drain in the concrete floor. This took place in the dark no less, as the power was off for the night – par for the course. Brief as our visit was, Kenya struck me as a heavily industrialized version of Tanzania. The air in Nairobi was so choked with factory smoke and diesel exhaust from stalled traffic it was barely breathable. We made a visit to the cathedral and to a wildlife orphanage, passing the American embassy bombed by terrorists two years before.

Back at Kilacha, the diocesan farm near Moshi, we joined the bishop, dozens of priests, and hundreds of people at a colorful outdoor Mass. The only Caucasians present, Mike and I stuck out like two sore thumbs, but we were welcomed as honored guests. We did our best to concelebrate in Swahili, enjoying the lively native singing and dancing to drums that were part of the liturgy, as well as the picnic that followed featuring the farm's own produce. Then we headed east to Tanzania's capital on the Indian Ocean, Dar es Salaam, meaning 'Haven of Peace.' The huge seafood market right on the beach was bustling with activity. Hundreds of people were milling about, mending their nets, cleaning their catch, and selling whatever they had to sell, right out of their boats pulled up on shore. The influence of the Arab world on the predominantly Muslim population here was immediately evident. Traditional Arab sailing vessels called *dhows*, with graceful triangular sails curved into the wind, were plying the waters offshore. Smaller boats, roughly hollowed out of wood by hand, were pushed along by poles. Whether it was our white skin or our video cameras, Mike and I seemed to attract some curious stares. The sea shells were the most beautiful we'd even seen, and for next to nothing, we bought an assortment. In Dar es Salaam, we stayed at a guest house sponsored by the Tanzanian Bishops' Conference.

People pushed cartfuls of coconuts, lemons, and papayas through the downtown streets lined with vendors selling nuts, rice, and vegetables. Others went about stripping and squeezing sugar cane for its sweet juice. Everyone walking seemed to be carrying something on their head. After a visit to the Cathedral of St. Joseph, we watched artisans skillfully carving statues, animals, and bowls out of ebony. After driving a hard bargain, we had our souvenirs. Though Tanzanians don't go to the beach, coming from Florida Mike and I couldn't resist. Hibiscus, coconut palms swaying in the breeze, and the warm salty ocean water made us feel right at home. Then we boarded a hydrofoil to an even more exotic locale, the island of Zanzibar, where a nun picked us up for a wild ride through the narrowest streets I've even seen. Here we stayed at the rather decrepit cathedral, standing alone in a sea of mosques. More closely related to the Arabian peninsula than to Africa, Zanzibar, once ruled by sultans, was the center of the infamous slave trade on the east coast of Africa. Huge fig trees tightly wound with 'creeper' vines bearing vanilla beans cover the island known for its spices, especially its cloves. After walking through Scheherazade's tomb, we chewed on cinnamon bark, cardamom seeds, nutmeg, cumin, and ginger root, washing it all down with milk straight from freshly hacked coconuts.

Before leaving Tanzania, we spent a day gently climbing five miles up Mount Kilimanjaro, to an elevation of nearly nine thousand feet at Mandara Hut – halfway to the top. Fog kept us cool most of the way up its forested slopes, brimming with orchids, ferns, and lush tropical plants, all watered by trickling streams of snowmelt. To the southwest we ventured to Tarangire National Park, which is watered by a shallow river that draws huge numbers of game in dry season. So many elephants, waterbuck, baboons, gazelles, zebras, and monkeys came out of the bush we could hardly keep up with them. We were fascinated watching giraffes spread their front legs apart to bend down and sip water from a stream, and by tiny antelope called dik-diks. Mike and I couldn't leave Tanzania without buying the precious deep blue gemstone known as tanzanite mined only there. Wearing the gold rings we bought in Arusha always brings back treasured memories of this trip.

Back in Moshi, we bounced around in the back of a jeep going to visit the cathedral and the chancery, before returning to Kirua for a dinner of free-range chicken and rice, lentils, cucumbers, peas, and carrots. Near the village we stopped at a terribly impoverished medical clinic. I have more supplies in my house than this government-run facility had. Upon our return, volunteers from All Saints took up this cause, managing to send a whole shipping container of medical supplies to provide relief. Joachim's relatives showered us with parting gifts, including a set of paintings depicting a boy's passage to manhood by spearing a lion. Mike and I also found some dusty but charming oil paintings of wildlife by native artists. We brought these back with us, as well as some rich Tanzanian coffee and the strongest black tea I've ever tasted. Our most highly prized souvenir, however, remains the goatskin.

Back at the parish, it took more than one showing on a big-screen TV to satisfy the curiosity of parishioners about our trip. Joachim and I greatly enjoyed taking them on a video safari. Life slowly returned to normal. Plans for rebuilding All Saints continued to develop, with never-ending modifications. We had to go back to the drawing board twice as the result of two extraordinary gifts, both out of the blue. From my work on DCLAAE, I knew parishioners sometimes clamor for stained glass windows, or for the 'churchy' sound of a pipe organ. I also knew the Diocese would not approve 'bells and whistles' like these where money was tight, so neither were in our budget. Then lightning struck – twice. It became apparent that a Higher

Power wanted the new church to have stained glass windows *and* a pipe organ, and found a way to make it happen.

Breaking ground for the new All Saints in 2002.

First, Joe Mazza, a much-loved founding member of the parish, died, leaving a substantial portion of his estate to All Saints – several hundred thousand dollars. Rather than apply the entire gift to the cost of construction, I thought it only fitting to acquire something we could not otherwise afford in his memory. I consulted my friend Harry Bumpus and found Wayne Warren, a parish musician, who knew how to build pipe organs. In a shuttered Presbyterian church in Altoona, Pennsylvania, slated for demolition, Harry located a venerable classical instrument made by Moller – almost a hundred years old – that with twenty-four ranks of pipes would be perfect for All Saints. I signed a contract for it over the internet, and Wayne flew up north to disassemble and label its thousands of pipes one at a time, as well as its console, wind chests, and other internal mechanisms. The organ filled an entire moving van. Like a line of ants, curious parishioners off-loaded this precious cargo, putting it into storage for over a year until the major dust of construction had settled. Finally, every single piece was carefully transported to a protected staging area in the nearly completed building, where Wayne began the tedious task of reassembly over the next few months.

Every church that has ever been built has some amazing stories to tell, like this one. From my perspective, how this pipe organ came to be at All Saints was a minor miracle and a labor of love from start to finish. Love always finds a way. Although unable to be completed in time for the dedication of the new church, this majestic instrument – as striking in appearance as tonal quality – was ransomed and rebuilt for about eighty thousand dollars – considerably less than the cost of a comparable electronic substitute. What happened next came as even more of a surprise.

A phone call from a member of the parish, Nermine Rubin, alerted me to the availability of some stained glass windows that her parents, Egyptian-born Dr. Nagui and Desiree Khouzam, had commissioned for a church near Orlando. The message didn't make sense to me at first, and when you're building a church, people want to give you all sorts of things you don't really want, so you have to be careful what you agree to accept. Nermine explained to me that as a last resort, her parents had to have the windows removed from the church to protect them, because they had begun to be damaged by vines being allowed to grow up the side of the building. The pastor would not respond to the pleas of the donors to cut back the vines, nor did he make it easy for them to do what they felt they had to do. I'm not sure even this convinced me, but after talking to the architect, Will Alexander, the two of us agreed to go to Orlando and take a look. Off we went to meet Nermine's parents. What we found at the church was truly a shock.

At the parish we were directed to a metal shed at the back of the property where the groundskeeping equipment was housed. Slick with an oily residue from the gasoline fumes, leaning up against steel shelves on a gritty concrete floor, stood row upon row of stained glass panels – each two feet by two feet. Tucked among the lawnmowers and weed whackers, we counted one hundred thirty-two of them, stacked up against each other on a slant, bending under their own weight. A few pieces of glass had already cracked. Neither Will nor I could believe our eyes.

Two stained glass windows in All Saints' daily Mass chapel.

My dad had made stained glass panels for years. Besides the glass being fragile, I knew that the thin lines of lead holding the pieces together are only so strong and have to be handled carefully. What we didn't yet fully understand was that here were six life-size scenes depicting events in the history of salvation – from the Annunciation and Nativity through the Last Supper, Crucifixion, Resurrection, and Pentecost. In two others, Jesus was teaching in the Temple at Jerusalem and changing water into wine at Cana. All eight had been exquisitely detailed, painstakingly designed, painted, fired, and assembled by Sister Diane Couture and her team of professional artists at the Sisters of St. Joseph Architectural Stained Glass Studio in St. Augustine. I estimated the value of the treasure we were looking at in the dust at a quarter-million dollars. Needless to say, we accepted.

The Khouzams weren't finished with their gift yet. They arranged for the stained glass panels to be gotten out of harm's way, properly crated, and shipped to All Saints the very next day. When the time came for them to be installed, they brought Sister Diane and her team in to do the work themselves. It was perfect. This amazing true story – how the walls of All Saints turned into windows – is another minor miracle only Love could have wrought.

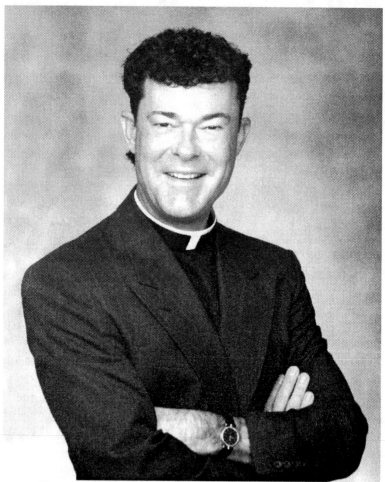

Happy at the prospect of building a permanent church.

XIX   IN THE FAST LANE

Right after Christmas, Mike and I took a chance and drove out to Denver in my Firebird. We were going to fly standby on United, but blizzards had already forced Chicago's O'Hare and even Denver's new airport to shut down more than once that winter. The snow started falling when we hit Missouri. As we drove through the night, it got heavier, swirling around like crazy. I stayed behind a semi, keeping its tail lights in view just to know where the road was. By the time we got to Kansas City, it was dawn, and we hit some ice. That brought the early morning rush hour to a crawl. But soon we were cruising again, across the plains and snow-covered Rockies all the way to Moab, a sleepy Utah town in the heart of red rock country.

As more and more people discovered the awesome sandstone arches and canyonlands nearby, Moab had begun waking up. Fortunately for us, a relatively heavy snowfall on Christmas day turned the usually bone-dry desert into a winter wonderland. Seeing ice on the Colorado River was hardly what we expected, but hiking in the pure cold air under a clear blue sky felt great. Even with wide tires on my car, for a tense moment we felt it start sliding off the dirt road on the way up to Fisher Towers. I had unknowingly stopped on some ice. Seeing so many familiar landmarks dusted with snow glistening in the sun – Corona Arch, Butch Cassidy Arch, and the spectacular warp in the earth's crust known as the Waterpocket Fold – was a photographer's dream. Jack Frost had done his best to etch Negro Bill Canyon and Morning Glory Arch in monochrome. With ice crystals clinging to freeze-dried weeds and grasses, nature had painted a wintry still life breathtaking in beauty. At Bryce Canyon we trekked through snowdrifts hip-deep in places, looking down on a fairyland of snow-capped pink sandstone pinnacles. After all that excitement, Mike and I quietly observed the dawn of 2001, not to mention the new millennium – or its first anniversary, depending on your point of view – in Hurricane, Utah.

I've always loved classical music, so over the years I've enjoyed going to see the Florida Symphony Orchestra perform at Ruth Eckerd Hall in Clearwater. Other than for Cuban food, I rarely go to Tampa, but I finally got to the Performing Arts Center to watch *Phantom of the Opera,* to see Simon and Garfunkel in concert at the Times Forum, and to view the graphic 'Bodies' exhibition at the Museum of Science and Industry. Though not a sports fan, I've watched the Tampa Bay Lightning play hockey at the Ice Palace, an NCAA basketball tournament at the Forum, the Rays play the Red Sox at Tropicana Field, and even a monster truck rally at Raymond James Stadium. Mike and I have enjoyed camping at some of Florida's outstanding state parks – on the fine white sand beaches of St. George Island, along the alligator-choked Myakka River, and even on Bahia Honda Key. We both love fresh seafood. Whenever passing through the Panhandle, we stock up on 'bulldozers' – Florida lobster cousins – in Panacea. We can't drive the Gulf Coast without stopping for 'kitty' fish fillets, or pass through Louisiana without munching on some 'mudbugs' – crawfish tails. There isn't much we wouldn't do for stone crabs, oysters on the half shell, or whole soft-shell blue crabs – more of our favorites. Life without seafood would be grim.

Mike, Dad, and I acting silly at dinner.

Ever ready to explore new venues, in May of 2001 Mike and I traveled to Poland where my nephew Joshua was teaching English at the university level in the small city of Kielce. From Warsaw we took a train south to his tiny apartment, not much larger than an office cubicle, in a building left over from the Communist era. After surveying the countryside from Chęciny's medieval castle perched high on a hill, we grabbed some Polish sausage and ducked into the first couple of churches we were to visit. For Mike and me, Poland became all about the churches – not because everyone's Catholic or we're priests, but because of all the eye candy. The cathedrals of western Europe are spectacular in their own right, but they pale compared to these splendiferously overdecorated monuments to Polish piety. In a single building, disharmonious architectural styles – Visigoth, Victorian, Roman, Rococo, Byzantine, and Baroque – are layered in a manner that is strangely appealing. With so much competition for attention, the overall effect is nearly indescribable, slightly overwhelming the senses. Akin to great museums of art, Polish churches are so cluttered as to be barely functional for worship – a liturgical consultant's worst nightmare. The floors are uneven, paved with the stone-cold crypts of obscure princes and overstuffed prelates. Replete with lofty colonnaded baldacchinos, gilded reredos, crow's-nest pulpits, grandiose paintings, shiny marble statuary, electrified crystal chandeliers, vaulted ceilings, frescoed domes, and filigreed woodwork, their ebullient beauty is no less than striking.

In Kielce, we met Kasia, later to become Joshua's wife, and his friend Father Alexander, a diocesan seminary professor, who hauled us around whenever Joshua couldn't. It was springtime in Krakow, a city wrapped in legend where time flows differently, and where more robed priests and habited nuns roam the streets than in Vatican City. Under the mantle of its native son, Pope John Paul II, the Catholic Church in Poland seems to have been caught in a time warp as well. Nevertheless, my antiquated stereotypes of eastern European life were quickly swept away in this excitingly lively Old World city. The Royal Castle at Wawel, complete with its own cathedral, captivated us. Fronting on the main market square filled with pigeons reminiscent of St. Mark's in Venice, St. Mary's red-bricked Basilica produced its famed trumpeter in the window of its bell tower at the top of the hour. Never had I seen anything like the intricately carved wooden altarpiece over the main altar, opening wide its massive doors to reveal stunning gilded icons. Outside, electric streetcars and horse-drawn carriages rumbled over the cobbles. We sipped non-alcoholic Zywiec beer at an open-air café on the square, where mimes posed as statues and artists painted. Sweetly serenaded by a strolling violinist on the street, we were dazzled by the fleet fingers of an accordionist playing Bach. After ascending the grand staircase of our modest hotel beneath vaulted stained glass windows, we looked out over a flowerbox of red geraniums at white tulips and blue spruce.

My misconceptions about Polish food vanished quickly, too. I savored all the roast duck, borscht, and goulash I could get, and even the smoked cheese at Zakopane. Two things Poles love are fresh flowers and grilled sausage, never hard to find. Speaking fluent Polish, Joshua hired a driver to take Mike and me out to the infamous Nazi concentration camp at Auschwitz. Words cannot adequately describe how deeply moving this experience was for both of us. How any human being can deny the reality of the Holocaust is beyond me. We listened intently as the Jewish woman who guided us described in glowing terms the heroism of Maximilian Kolbe, a priest who was canonized a saint in 1982 for saving the life of a stranger, the father of a family, by giving up his own. Father Alexander also took Mike and me past his boyhood home in the country. With great emotion, he recalled for us how Jews fleeing the Nazis knocked on his door and how his parents gave them as much bread as they could carry. Their bodies were found shot to death down the road the next day. His story brought tears to our eyes as well as his own.

With Josh, we boarded a train south to the resort town of Zakopane in the rugged mountainous region of Poland bordering Slovakia. The alpine scenery here was no less spectacular than in the Rockies. We took several hikes through forests filled with gushing stone-filled streams, one all the way to the exposed top of the highest mountain. Assaulted by an icy wind, we looked down in all directions – as through from the top of the world – on smoky dark-green valleys dusted with patches of snow. Like a scene from *The Sound of Music*, we found ourselves on the shore of a lake against a backdrop of stunning glaciated cliffs. We could have been on Mount Evans or at Lake Louise. Zakopane is also where I saw a horse 'putting on the feedbag' for the first time.

Poles have great determination. After taking us by the ruins of a medieval castle and through the countryside to see several churches – not as gaudy but as lovely as those in the city – Father Alexander was determined that Mike and I should get a close-up view of the Black Madonna, the centuries-old miraculous jewel-encrusted painting at the former fortress of Jasna Gora, now a world-famous Marian shrine in Czestochowa. Beyond the usual crowds drawn to this site, tens of thousands of Poles were present for a special event, making it difficult for the three of us to stay together. I don't like big crowds and usually stay away from them. Even the enormous basilica here is dwarfed by the massive bell tower attached to it. Looking down from its heights, I could see this was the biggest crowd I'd ever been in. Most pilgrims to Czestochowa have to be content with a glimpse of the highly-prized icon from a distance, through the gilded gates separating the nave of the basilica from the chapel where the Black Madonna hangs. Besides that, a half-dozen bishops were concelebrating Mass in the chapel.

Father Alexander was not to be deterred. Obviously knowing his way around, he led us through the crowd into the sacristy to a closed door. In an act of unabashed clerical bravado, he opened the door and stepped right into the sanctuary of the chapel where the bishops were standing at attention during the reading of the Gospel. Mike and I thought we might be struck by lightning, but we were too afraid *not* to follow Father Alexander across the sanctuary – in front of the entire assembly as though no one were there – behind the altar where the hallowed image of Madonna and Child is suspended. We could have reached out and touched her. Few living souls can ever claim that. Mike and I did our best to look innocent and inconspicuous, but I'm afraid the video cameras in our hands gave us away. Having reverenced the icon profusely, we had no choice but to depart as obtrusively as we had arrived.

Josh was as excited as we were to visit the Czech Republic next door to Poland. So we boarded an overnight train to Prague, another marvelously scenic Old World city steeped in antiquity and mystery. Here too, the many churches – those magnificent Gothic structures standing for centuries – held great fascination for us. Rising majestically above a skyline punctuated with minarets, stone spires, crenelated fortresses, squat square towers, and storied bridges, what the churches of Prague lack in gleam they make up for in elegance. Their narrow, buttressed naves, slightly less cluttered with statuary and stonework than their Polish cousins, are paved with the tombs of kings and lined with the shrines of saints.

With so many ancient monuments illuminated at night, Prague becomes a romantic storybook of lights. Descending the longest escalator in the world into the medieval bowels of the city, we learned how to ride the subterranean rails to the places we wanted to go. We couldn't leave Prague without going to see the home church of the legendary statue of the Infant Jesus and his regal wardrobe, both showcased in glass. Then we wandered the stone streets, passing under ancient archways, climbing every turreted tower, and sipping Clausthaler – a Czech non-alcoholic brew – alongside the Vlatva River. To sample a slice of life in the country, we hopped on an aged electric train to Kutna Hora, a quiet medieval town in the hilly heart of Bohemia dwarfed by a gargantuan cathedral, a relic of the

Middle Ages. A study in stonework, this aging, unadorned edifice stood as a symbol of life in the past.

Back in Warsaw – drab and modern by comparison to Krakow and Prague – we took in a concert in Lazienki Park, brimming with spring flowers. After climbing to the top of the Palace of Culture and Science for a panoramic view of the city, we visited the Chopin Memorial and the site of the Warsaw Ghetto Uprising during World War II. With enough souvenirs to sink a ship – Ukrainian nesting dolls and Polish painted wooden plates inlaid with brass, amber jewelry, blue Czech lead crystal and ceramics, a set of watercolors from Wawel and an oil from Prague – Mike and I winged our way westward. Flying with credit card miles on Alitalia, we didn't mind the overnight layover in Milan, nor the authentic northern Italian cuisine we enjoyed for dinner.

Just as for a married couple, a priest's silver jubilee is always a big deal. I joined Mike and a group of his parishioners on a Caribbean cruise celebrating his twenty-fifth anniversary in 1999. By 2001, I had spent half my ordained years at All Saints, so when my jubilee rolled around in May, the whole parish joined in the celebration. My first pastor, Bishop Larkin, came out of retirement to join Bishop Lynch and dozens of priests at two festive liturgies featuring a harpist, hand bells, duets with Dad on piano and organ and my friend Zsuzsanna on cello, and Mike playing guitar – just as he did at my First Mass. My godmother Kate came all the way from Denver, and my classmate Vince, ordained with me at the Cathedral twenty-five years before, joined me as well. A week later I gave the homily at Vince's jubilee in Sarasota. Hundreds of guests enjoyed a delectable buffet afterward, catered outdoors under the tall pines. Sharing this auspicious occasion with so many family and friends was another great joy of my life.

So why did I become a priest? That's the question everyone always asks. The way I answer it hasn't changed. I became a priest because I was born into a family of faith. I witnessed the lifelong love of my father and mother for the Church and for each other. I loved the priests and sisters I knew from my youth. I had the support of my family and friends. But I became a priest, not because of these things or because I wanted to, but because God wanted me to. I was chosen for God's own reasons. My vocation, therefore, is God's gift to the Church as well as mine – a mysterious coupling of human and divine. Ultimately, the reason is Love. Circumstances differ, but the cause, for every priest, remains the same.

In July, 2001, my family was saddened by the death of my mother's aunt, Sister Mary Louann, in Toledo. A nun for an incredible seventy-five years, her parents – my great grandparents – came from Alsace-Lorraine on the border of Germany and France. Mom and I drove up to Ohio for her funeral Mass, which I had the honor of celebrating at the Provincial House of the Sisters of Notre Dame. If that woman isn't a saint, none of us even stand a chance. She prayed for me every day of my life, even before I was born. I have no doubt that's another reason I became a priest and I'm still here.

Every now and then something happens that puts you on your way to a place you've only dreamed of going. About the last place on earth I ever thought I'd get to, Tahiti is one of those places. When an advertisement came tucked in with my credit card bill – a charter flight from Los Angeles and a week-long Polynesian cruise for under a thousand dollars – I thought it was too good to be true. But it was true, and I'm glad I didn't waste any time booking Mike and me on one of Renaissance Cruise Lines' brand new ships carrying less than seven hundred passengers. It's a good thing I did. Timing proved to be everything in this case – in more ways than one. Due to the uncertainty of flying to Los Angeles on standby, we allowed an extra day to get to L.A. from Tampa and to get back. It's a good thing we did that, too. After a walk around Hollywood and a couple of pizzas, we were on our way to Papeete in the morning. It was September 5, 2001.

Because Mike and I wanted to be on and in the water snorkeling much of the time, we didn't take our cameras.

We bought some decent equipment – rubber masks and fins made in France, not the plastic stuff sold in Florida. The South Pacific is like no place else on earth. On each of the six islands we visited, high jagged volcanic peaks and pinnacles rise dramatically from the center, dissolving into ridges forming bright green valleys. Clear, calm, turquoise lagoons, silver threads of falling water, lush tropical vegetation, and exotic flowering plants abound. Outside Papeete, the capital of Tahiti, the ports we visited on Moorea, Bora Bora, Huahine, Raiatea, and Taha'a were unspoiled and uncrowded.

On one island, we took a boat into the interior up a river lined with hibiscus and birds-of-paradise, past lava caves, fern-filled grottoes, trickling waterfalls, coconut palm plantations, banana forests, and melon farms. On a visit to a pearl farm, we watched a highly-prized black pearl being harvested from a rare black-lipped pearl oyster. It takes many months for a lustrous coating to be secreted over an implanted spherical nucleus to form a single pearl. For Mom I bought a necklace, and for myself a pendant in the shape of a fishhook, made from the iridescent lining of one of these 'retired' pearl-bearing oysters. On another island, we bought a dozen dried vanilla beans to bring home, observing the lengthy process by which this pure, expensive flavoring is made. Ten years later, I'm still making vanilla with these beans, simply by letting them sit a few months in a bottle of rum. On yet another island, we watched long swatches of cotton being dipped by hand into various colors of dye to make *pareos* – sarongs, the native dress.

As gorgeous as the islands of French Polynesia are, an even more fantastic world of unparalleled beauty lies beneath the surface of the ocean – one Mike and I explored with great delight. For a couple of dollars, we hired a local man with a boat to take us to the best beaches for snorkeling and drop us off. Unlike Florida, the water is deep right offshore, and one is instantly transported to an undersea wonderland that defies description. An incredible array of neon-colored tropical fish surrounded us in the warm clear water, nibbling on spectacular gardens of brilliantly-hued coral, watching us warily, taking refuge in the gently swaying sea grass. Out of the tug of the current, giant manta rays cruised in the blue depths below. Sea creatures great and small presented themselves on all sides. Admiration and curiosity kept us going for hours. The effect on us was mesmerizing. Sometime we didn't quite know what we were looking at or what was looking at us. This was the open ocean after all. Once, something moving beneath a rock turned out to be a pair of gaping jaws on a gigantic moray eel, as big as we were. Getting out of there in a hurry was the closest I've ever come to walking on water.

Our ship had arrived at the island of Bora Bora very early on the morning of September 11. Along with everyone else, Mike and I were still asleep in our stateroom when we heard the captain's voice – as though he were standing right there – stating solemnly that something had happened in the United States. The halting video loop of a fireball over Manhattan broke the rest of the news. The bizarre images incessantly being replayed were incomprehensible. In our rudely awakened state, it all seemed like a dream.

The captain came back on to say all telephone calls to the United States would be free. There were a lot of New Yorkers onboard, anxious to confirm the safety of their loved ones. There were suddenly no strangers on our ship. So far from home, and unable to return for the moment, we were all in the same boat – for an extra day, it turned out. Renaissance Cruise Lines bore the cost. September 11 pushed them over the edge. They went out of business two weeks later.

For anyone intent on taking out more Americans, a cruise ship anywhere in the world was a sitting duck. The Cruise Line put armed patrols in the lifeboats and began circling the ship. No one knew what to expect but no one wanted to take any chances. The strangest feeling came from realizing that all flights to and from the States were grounded. I didn't know it at the time, but by coincidence, my parents were also stranded – in Frankfurt, Germany, on their way home from visiting their grandson in Poland.

The ship organized an impromptu prayer service later in the day. We went. So did everyone else. There are no atheists in the foxholes, and there weren't any on the ship on September 11. People began to let their guard down. After all, they were still on vacation. Mike and I found a Catholic church on Bora Bora. We wanted to go in and say a prayer but – true to form – it was locked. The shops, however, were open, and we found the souvenir we prize most highly, though ever a reminder of that fateful day – a lifelike replica of a tropical fish, standing on its pectoral fins, fashioned entirely from native shell inlaid with mother-of-pearl.

The strangest twist to this international odyssey was yet to come. Mike and I knew there would be disruptions in air travel across the country for days when we arrived in Los Angeles. What we didn't expect was to walk right off our chartered flight from Tahiti right on to our originally scheduled connecting flight home – as though we'd planned it that way to begin with. It's still hard to believe. But sometimes, the magic works.

One of the waterfalls along the Columbia River Gorge in Oregon.

XX   SURGING AHEAD

In the wake of September 11, hundreds of our Protestant and Jewish neighbors joined us at All Saints on Thanksgiving for an interfaith prayer service. The focus was on the power of hope to overcome fear. With high hopes for the future, and at least a little apprehension, the parish was now preparing to build. On All Saints' Day, I blessed the ever-expanding Garden of Life Memorial Mosaic, well on its way to completion in the narthex. Then the entire wall was removed and put in storage during construction.   A considerable amount of demolition had to take place first. Daily Mass would still be celebrated in the nursery, and the parish office would remain open, though working in it would be noisy and messy. The biggest logistical problem would be finding a suitable location for parishioners to gather for Mass on the weekend.

One of the ideas we considered was going 'under the Big Top' – setting up a huge tent over part of the parking lot for the nine long months that construction was expected to take. It might have worked but it would have cost more than anyone thought.   Neighboring congregations put out the welcome mat when we asked to 'borrow' their houses of worship for Sunday services, but no one could accommodate us on Saturday evening. We couldn't afford to lose a third of the parish, so that effort fell apart.   Finally, we made arrangements to use Curlew Creek Elementary School, just a couple of blocks from the parish site, for the duration. Leasing this space would be costly, but it was comfortable, convenient, and reliable. We knew we would lose some people for the time being. Parishes always do, whenever the service they provide is disrupted. We also knew people would come back, and that hundreds of new parishioners would flock to All Saints once the gorgeous new space for worship was completed. In the wake of church-related scandals, and in the midst of a sagging economy and a war, attendance and support did wane somewhat during construction. But the commitment of the majority of parishioners remained firm. The true spirit of All Saints was undimmed.

I wanted the crucifix for the new church to be unlike any other, and I knew the artist who could accomplish this. Jorge Posada, a master wood-carver, was commissioned to sculpt a life-size figure of Jesus, reaching down from the cross with one arm extended, holding a gilded dove – representing Jesus' gift of his Spirit, the gift of his peace, being handed over to the Church for the salvation of the world. I am proud of the fact that, along with the stained glass windows and the pipe organ at All Saints, the crucifix – *Christ Our Peace* – is a true work of art. Like the Church itself, it is both traditional and contemporary, instantly capturing the attention of every person who enters All Saints.

Excitement over what was about to take place at the parish was building as 2002 began. The parish mission conducted by the legendary Dominican Val LaFrance fed right into it. With his inimitable, dramatic style, Father Val – just hitting his stride at eighty years of age – had a full house, and he nearly brought the house down. Once more, members of our neighboring congregations joined parishioners for a six-week interfaith study of the great religions of the world. Events like these are what break the monotony of routine parish life, attract new members, and get people involved in something for the first time. The faith formation of children is important, but parishes that don't offer adults imaginative opportunities to learn and grow as well cannot expect much beyond the status quo. Our longstanding, mutually supportive relationship with Guardian Angels School proved useful. Arrangements were easily made for All Saints' children to attend religious education sessions at Guardian Angels while construction was going on.

We were all sad to see Father Msaki, with his studies completed at last, return to Tanzania permanently in March. I was alone in the parish once more, but not for long. We quickly welcomed another African priest, Gabriel Msipu Phiri from Zambia, with open arms for the summer.

It was springtime in the Rockies when my brother Mark got married in a stone chapel high up in the mountains in April. Mike and I, my folks, my two sisters and my niece all made it out to Denver for the happy occasion. We had a great time acting silly together as families do when they come together at times like these.

Mike and I headed to Alaska for the second time in late May of 2002. From the heavy snow blanketing the mountains across Turnagain Arm and the chunks of ice still clogging Portage Lake, it was clear summer had not yet arrived. On a hike through a forest of spruce with our friend Rick, we came to a cliff overlooking a raging river. Mustering our courage, we managed to pull ourselves across it in a wire cart suspended from a cable high overhead. Then we traveled east through the Matanuska Valley to explore the interior of Wrangell-Saint Elias National Park, relatively unknown but America's largest. After spending the night in a solitary log cabin deep in the woods, we got to the tiny settlement of McCarthy and the abandoned copper mine at Kennicott. Under a clear blue sky we hiked out onto Root Glacier, surrounded by the spectacular peaks of the Wrangells – the highest in North America. Along sixty bumpy, muddy miles back to civilization, breathtaking panoramas were created by gathering storm clouds reflected on the glassy surface of pristine lakes. A moose running at full tilt across the road startled us, only to be followed seconds later by three grizzlies chasing it, one after another. This was wild Alaska at its best.

Crossing the Kenai Peninsula, we took the coastal road along Cook Inlet all the way down to Homer. Returning to Seward, we entered a world of otters and eagles, seals and whales, sea birds and calving glaciers, plying the chilly waters of Kenai Fjords National Park. A few moose, caribou, and spring flowers made an appearance as we rode an old school bus through the vast unspoiled reaches of Denali National Park. But a heavy cloud cover concealed all but the lower reaches of Mt. McKinley, as is often the case. Wet weather prevailed on this trip, but the splendor of Alaska manifested itself once more, whetting our appetite to return to this wondrous land yet again.

A few weeks later Mike and I revisited four of our favorite national parks out West. Though there was less snow than in years past, a splendid array of summer wildflowers decorated the glacial valleys and sparkling lakes of the Rockies. Purple-blue wild irises have always been my favorite. Sitting under quaking aspen beside a swift mountain stream watching marmots scurry across lichen-splotched boulders never grows old for me. We also watched moose, some with huge antlers, munch on underwater weeds, and herds of elk, still shedding their winter coats, graze with their dappled calves. Leaving his new wife Pat for a day, Mark came up from Denver to join us on a hike to picture-perfect Mills Lake, still ringed by patches of snow. In the Tetons, Mike and I ascended three thousand feet through a verdant alpine valley to reach semi-frozen Surprise and Amphitheatre Lakes. After trudging through slushy snow the last mile to an elevation of ten thousand feet, we finally caught our breath, only to have it taken away at the sight of these two crystal jewels.

The Tetons are one of the most striking mountain ranges in the world. At Schwabacher's Landing on the Snake River in Jackson Hole, we discovered an ideal spot for photographing them in all their glory, especially at dawn, along with their reflection on the glassy surface of a still pond. Exploring nearby, we followed a long muddy road to little-known Granite Hot Springs, a perfect place to relax in a natural setting. We also found our way to the source of the Green River, a major tributary of the Colorado, at scenic Green River Lakes with Square Top Mountain in the rugged Wind River Range looming in the distance. Just like the national parks, our national forests hold many such treasures for the seeker.

With their steaming cauldrons, bubbling mud pots, and hissing fumaroles, the polychromatic geyser basins of Yellowstone never fail to fascinate. Old Faithful was right on schedule, but a freak hail storm out of a clear sky took us by surprise. A lone wolf with her pack of pups passed hurriedly in the distance, while we watched bison tiptoeing over the thin crust of earth separating them from pools of boiling water beneath the surface. Among feathered friends, Mike and I sighted ptarmigan and yellow-bellied sapsucker woodpeckers. We took time to study a skulking coyote, a lumbering black bear, jumping white-tailed deer, sure-footed mountain goats, and the fastest land animal in North America – with those endearing little antlers shaped like a can opener – the pronghorn antelope. Water plunged mightily over the lava rock at Tower Falls and roared relentlessly through the amazingly colorful 'Grand Canyon' of the Yellowstone River. Sulfurous warm water flowed gently over the brilliantly hued limestone hills and delicate calcium terraces of Mammoth Hot Springs, delighting the eye if not the nose.

Formed in 1959 when an earthquake dammed the Madison River, Quake Lake lies at the southern tip of Montana where Wyoming and Idaho meet. Slogging along the shore as though we were the last two people on earth, Mike and I picked up an armful of driftwood to bring home. Later I coated it with a thick, clear, high-gloss epoxy finish, to preserve the beautiful shape and tone of the wood in its natural state. Just inside Idaho, we discovered yet another treasure in an out-of-the-way place – magnificent Mesa Falls hiding in plain sight in Targhee National Forest. Finally we made it to St. Mary Lake, long a favorite place, set so serenely in such mountain majesty on the east side of Glacier National Park, our final destination. It was windy as usual at Many Glacier, where we climbed up to a cold, blue-tinted Iceberg Lake, still thawing in July. Along the Going-to-the Sun Road, we stopped to admire slender Bird Woman Falls, fed by snowfields high above, plunging five hundred feet into a lush glacial valley. No trip to Glacier would be complete without a hike to Avalanche Lake, encircled by a wall of snowbound mountains brimming with waterfalls cascading from their heights. One more glorious day – at Waterton Lakes, Glacier's sister park across the Canadian border – put the finishing touch on another unforgettable Rocky Mountain adventure.

After cutting through the last red tape, All Saints finally broke ground on September 1, 2002. Another giant step was being taken in accomplishing the mission of the parish from its foundation – building up the kingdom of God on earth. My sister Julie and I had carefully created a circular sand painting of a cross and crown, the parish logo, in multiple colors. After a prayer for success was offered up, the representative dignitaries ceremoniously dug into it with spray-painted gold shovels. The next eleven months were going to be the busiest of my life, but help was on the way. Another priest arrived from Tanzania, but a victim of culture shock, he stayed at All Saints less than a year, returning to Africa a short time later. It was another two months before demolition actually got underway, right after the parish celebrated its fifteenth anniversary the first weekend of November. We decided to go out with a bang and a nod to tradition by hosting one last roller skating party in the emptied-out parish center the night before. Trying to show off in front of the kids, I got a bang on the head as well, though it didn't knock any more sense into me. Construction and our temporary relocation to Curlew Creek Elementary stretched for nine long months. Parishioners flocked to several carefully guided tours of the construction site, so they could see the progress slowly being made.

One of the best things that happened to me and to All Saints through these years was getting to know J.C. Zavalnak. If we're lucky, life sends a few good friends our way – some for many years, others for just a few. In his late twenties, J.C. was a tall, good-looking young man with an extraordinary talent for working with young people. We needed a new youth minister at the parish, and Guardian Angels School needed a science teacher. He fit the bill for both. Kids, teenagers, and parents loved him. Since we had no place to celebrate Holy Week services during construction, J.C. worked with our teens to stage two presentations of the 'living' Stations of the Cross outdoors on Good Friday,

2003.   People were moved to tears.   The youth group
organized a bike rally and picnic on the Pinellas Trail in
May.   Dozens of parishioners walked, rode, and skated their
way through Palm Harbor, raising ten thousand dollars for
youth ministry and the new church being built.   Mike and I,
and our architect Will Alexander, were among them.   J.C.
got more teenagers involved in the life of the parish than
ever before.   I joined the youth group on two trips, one to
Tomahawk Lodge where J.C. and I paddled kayaks and the
kids floated down the Rainbow River on inner tubes, and the
other to Six Flags and Stone Mountain in Atlanta.   I don't
think I've ever had more fun as an adult than on these two
occasions.

With experience in the building trades, J.C. was indispensable in helping me monitor progress throughout
construction and in planning for the management of the new
facilities.   We both enjoyed working closely together and we
became good friends.   While neither of us was looking for a
relationship resembling that between a father and a son,
something like that developed between us.   J.C. was also
drawn to Mike, and the three of us had a lot of fun going
places and doing things together.   One of the best things that
has happened to Mike and me as a result of our friendship
over the years is that most of his friends have become friends
of mine, and vice versa.   J.C. left All Saints a few months
after I did.

Precisely because I am not married, friendship is that
much more important to me as a priest.   Often elusive, it is
all the more precious when found.   Mike is my best friend, in
a category by himself.   I have other good friends among the
clergy, but more of my friends are lay people, not priests.
Most of them are people I knew as parishioners or people I
worked with.   Of course there are risks involved in
befriending parishioners and co-workers.   For that matter,
there are risks in befriending other priests.   Like everyone
else, priests occasionally experience failures in personal
relationships.   That's just part of life.   It can get messy, and
it's always painful when friendships end, especially between

co-workers or between parishioners and their priest. It has happened to me and to every priest I know. On the other hand, I've never known a priest who didn't have at least one personal relationship with someone on the parish staff, or in the parish, or both. What is more natural than wanting to spend time with people you like? Who else is a priest supposed to befriend than the people he sees every day or every week? Where else is he to go to find friends?

Priests are not looking for friends 'with benefits' – at least they're not supposed to be. We need close personal relationships with other males, not just other priests, and with females. While priests are only human, it is reasonable to assume that the Church only ordains candidates found to be mature. A person who has attained maturity can be expected and must be trusted to respect boundaries. Human nature being what it is, there are always going to be people incapable of minding their own business. Some people find themselves compelled to say something about everything a priest says and does – usually to as many people as possible. A priest's personal relationships, his choice of friends, is always a favorite topic.

At one time or another, every priest I know has been an innocent victim of wagging tongues in this regard. Not only is this always hurtful, it can be devastating. Over the years, some have been suspicious of the nature of my relationship with Mike. At least one person on the staff at All Saints was suspicious of the nature of my relationship with J.C. Saying too much about this led to an unfortunate resignation. You can't 'put the toothpaste back in the tube.' People are going to do and say what they're going to. But jealousy and morbid curiosity lead people to say and do strange things – especially with regard to priests. Nothing in the course of my ministry has been more hurtful to me than this. Nothing is more detrimental to a priest's vocation than the unwarranted, unthinking things people say – especially about the company priests keep.

Another friend from whom I learned a great deal, not only about building but about life and greatness, was Will

Alexander. Will was the architect I worked with for five years planning and accomplishing the rebuilding of All Saints. Ironically, the first time I met Will years earlier, I didn't like him. But the better I got to know him, the more I came to respect him, and eventually to love him. In his life and in his life's work, he displayed a brilliant intensity and passion. At a low point in my life, he was there to hold me up. Though not Catholic, Will had great respect for the many priests for whom he worked selflessly and untiringly, as he did for me at All Saints. Will was that rare human being who always made you feel better by the time you left than when you arrived. His pursuit of excellence was relentless. I know I'm a better person for having known him. I admire so much the courage, gentleness, humility, style, good humor, and grace he displayed in life. Will died in 2006. He was my friend, and I miss him. I will always be proud that his name, along with mine, is engraved in bronze on the wall of All Saints.

The Emerys are friends of mine, too. Longtime members of All Saints, Ken, Mary Ellen, and their daughter Grace have always opened their hearts and their homes to me, both in Florida and in Michigan. Just thinking of all the good times we've shared makes me happy – skiing at Boyne Mountain and Nub's Nob, sledding down the driveway, going to Tahquamenon Falls and Petoskey, frying perch and broiling whitefish, jumping on the trampoline, kayaking on Lake Michigan and picking up stones along the shore. We've been there for each other during some tough times. The Emerys proudly display two of my paintings on their walls. Even when we haven't seen each other for months, it's like old home week when we do. More than friends, they're family to me. A priest becomes part of many families over the years, but only a few become friends like these.

One more person who has brought joy to my life, in the least amount of time, is Vicki Wells-Bedard. Though she's now back home in Michigan, Vicki directed Diocesan communications for several years. I've never bonded so quickly with anyone as with this remarkably gifted woman who for her whole life has found one way after another to serve the Church. I met my match in her quick wit. That two responsible adults can act so silly and enjoy it so much has been a gift we have shared. Vicki believed in me enough to get me to do a live interview on local television when the Pope died. Now she is slowly losing ground to a rare type of dementia. I want her to know I believe in her just as much. She is my friend.

These are snapshots of a few people who hold a special place in my heart. Every priest should be so lucky as to have friends like these. Part of the satisfaction of pastoring a parish as long as I did at All Saints is that you get to see families grow and become friends right before your very eyes. This happens all the more when people band together to start a new parish and over time grow together to become a true parish family. This is what happened – and I'd like to think I helped make it happen – at All Saints. It was a joy for me to watch, as I did many times in sixteen years, parishioners working together – transporting the organ in a thousand pieces from storage to the parish site, cleaning the dusty pipework and scrubbing hundreds of church chairs, assembling benches and planters for the new courtyards, and dozens of other tasks in preparation for the dedication of their new church.

While staying on top of construction was a grueling task, I did get away twice. I joined Mike on another parish cruise after Thanksgiving, visiting the largely unspoiled island of Dominica, Barbados with its decidedly British flavor, Isla Margarita off the tip of Venezuela, and its Dutch neighbor, Curacao. After Christmas, J.C. joined Mike and me on our third Northwest World Vacation to Singapore. The five days we spent there, even with the long flights coming and going, were an unbeatable deal and just plain fun. This island nation off the southern tip of the Malay Peninsula is unique in all the world. Though densely populated and as cosmopolitan as you can get, Singapore is covered from head to toe in lush tropical greenery. It's hot and humid all the time, and everyone speaks English. Our hotel was draped in orchids. After paying our respects at elegant Hindu and Buddhist temples, we visited factories producing pewter and fashioning jade into figurines. Out of curiosity, we discarded our sandals and donned robes to enter a mosque in the Islamic quarter of Singapore. We ducked into a non-descript eatery to try some Arab cuisine, including mutton, which proved quite tasty. That's the kind of place I like to eat. Fancy restaurants make me nervous. I'm not into paying big bucks for food that's often mediocre. Holes-in-the-wall are often much better.

My mouth is still burning from the chili-laden lunch we had in 'Little India,' another distinct ethnic neighborhood found in Singapore. There we found some dusty but finely inlaid panels of wood depicting scenes of rural life in India. Set in a rainforest, Singapore's zoo was fabulous. We enjoyed the diversity of its flora and fauna not only by day but on a night safari to view nocturnal animals under the stars. My favorites were the giant fruit bats, eliminating mangos and papayas almost as fast as they devoured them, hanging upside down all the while. Singapore's vertical skyline literally shimmers at night, especially from a bum boat on the Singapore River. The national symbol, a lion's head, can be seen everywhere, on everything. We got our passports stamped again on a day trip to Malaysia where we sampled life along the coast where people call floating houses home. After watching archer fish take aim and spit a stream of water at prey with remarkable accuracy, Mike and I bought some underwater scenes on hand-painted batik fabric, successively wax-dyed in brilliant colors. Against our advice, J.C. bought a lifelike clay iguana mounted on a tree root too big to pack. After managing to get it through security, he charmed the flight attendants into stowing it for him on all three flights home.

The highlight of this trip was our visit to Singapore's playground, Sentosa Island, via cable car on New Year's Day, 2003. A resort on a par with Epcot and on a scale to match, Sentosa boasts an entire underwater world, among other things. After walking through this spectacular aquarium, J.C. and I dodged water bullets and splashed our way through a block-long wave pool in the shape of a Chinese dragon, before Mike joined us on the beach for a swim in the warm waters of Singapore Strait. On the horizon freighters were headed into the massive port of this extraordinarily entertaining Asian city-state. The first day of the new year ended with an incredible laser light show, projected onto a dazzling array of dancing fountains, shooting skyward to the throbbing pulse of ear-splitting music. A wild taxi ride made it a night – and a trip – the three of us will never forget.

Getting ready to explore a narrow slot canyon in Utah.

XXI   FINISHING THE RACE

It was Saturday night, August 2, 2003.   As the sun was setting, it was starting to rain.   Rather than gathering in the courtyard as planned, hundreds of people huddled in the great hall.   A hush came over the crowd as those involved in the building of the new church ceremoniously 'handed it over' to the bishop, who in turn invited the people to enter for the first time singing for joy.   The ancient rite of dedication, begun in darkness with candles, incense, and an elaborate anointing of the altar with holy oil, proceeded flawlessly into the night.   Bishop Lynch, who hated the old All Saints but fell in love with the new, was in his glory.   So was I.   Only on the day I was ordained did I experience as much affirmation – from priests and bishop, family and friends, but especially from my parishioners.   I beamed with pride.   The point I made in my remarks that night was the same one I'd been making for sixteen years.   As magnificent as the new space for worship was, 'church' is not a place but a people – not the building where people gather, but those who by gathering become 'church.'   The house we build is for God's people, and when we gather, God is home.

Any building project of this scope and duration takes a toll on those closest to it.   This was my second time around, so I was the wiser for it, but there were times I didn't manage the stress very well.   There was infighting among parish staff who for almost a year had been massively inconvenienced, having to work under the adverse conditions created by construction.   Everything was new, and the same old ways of doing things wouldn't work any more.   No one adjusts easily to change.   Having been preoccupied with construction for so many months, I was about worn out, my patience was short, and my mood at times not endearing.   To some extent, all this was to be expected.   The guests had left, the party was over, the full heat and humidity of summer had descended, and my vacation was still weeks away.

No one was expecting what happened at the next staff meeting. Everyone was taken aback when a usually congenial member of the staff launched a verbal attack on J.C. J.C. had a lot to learn, but he was also gifted. I was determined that his gifts not be lost to the Church altogether. When I defended J.C. – as I would have defended any staff member under attack by another – the attack was turned on me. The person rose, shouting contemptuously, finally resigning and storming out. That was a show-stopper for sure. No one said a word. The person with the anger management problem in that room was not me.

We can all only take so much. We all have our bad days. The staff member could have apologized, even later on, and we could have worked things out. Everyone would have understood and gone on with their business. Sadly, that's not what happened. Not content with berating the two of us, the person foolishly began saying that children were not safe at All Saints. While most people did little more than raise an eyebrow at this bizarre and baseless suggestion, the incident gave the parish a black eye and left a bad taste in everyone's mouth. With anxiety still lingering over scandals in the Church, the mere suggestion of an unsafe environment was appalling. I saw this rant, like the poison pen letters sent to parishioners in the early years, as an attack on the Church itself.

The pastor is always the one who gets to clean up messes like this. Believe it or not, things like this happen in every parish, at least once in a while. Every pastor could write a book on the antics of some staff members. I know I could. I'd seen grandstanding before, but the grandiosity and jealousy in play here really surprised me. I consulted the powers that be about how best to handle the situation and took their advice. Some inconvenience resulted, but the crisis passed. However, within a week or so, I arrived at a decision I knew would alter the course of my life, though I had no idea how much it would eventually do so. I realized the time for me to leave All Saints had come.

In the course of sixteen years, I had fully accomplished the task I was originally given to do – rather admirably, if I say so myself. The parish would benefit from new leadership, and I needed a new challenge. Bishop Lynch and I had already talked about parishes I might be suited for when the time came. He had expressed the hope that I would leave All Saints "at the top of my game." I had hoped to stay a little longer, but with the new facilities up and running, I instinctively knew the time had come. I didn't need anyone to prompt me. I made my decision. I went to see the bishop, and I let him know. He didn't disagree. We discussed who might replace me. I offered to replace Callist Nyambo at St. Joseph in St. Pete.

Before I left on vacation, I wrote a column for the parish bulletin – something I did almost every week – breaking the news to the parish. In the pre-blog era, this was an effective way for a pastor to communicate and maintain a friendly, informal rapport with his parishioners. My column was to be opened by the parish secretary at the appointed time while I was away. This was tough for me to do, but it had to be done. I don't like doing things in secret, but it worked like a charm. Being away, I avoided at least a few people coming in gnashing their teeth. Everything was set in motion for what would be my last weekend at the parish and my farewell reception. After sixteen years, a sense of relief was already setting in. It was a *fait accompli*. I thought I would soon be appointed pastor of another parish.

With construction over and something new to look forward to when I returned, I was ready for vacation. Mike and I were thrilled that J.C. would be coming with us this year. For years, bringing young people along and introducing them to the wonders of our national parks and the beauty of nature had been a source of joy for Mike and me. In a way, I think it kept us young. Even now, Mike and I still act like kids from time to time. Watching J.C. get excited at places he was seeing for the first time made us both happy and rejuvenated us once more. Our first stop, as usual, was to visit my brother in Denver, his wife Pat, and their two teenage girls, Helen and Nancy. The whole gang of us splurged on going out to eat at *The Fort* – a famous restaurant in the foothills specializing in wild game. We enjoyed acting silly and had great fun devouring such delicacies as buffalo tongue, buffalo fillet, buffalo ribs, stuffed quail, venison sausage, and Rocky Mountain oysters.

After driving up into the thin air at the top of fourteen thousand-foot Mt. Evans, we headed west across the Rockies to Arches, one of the national parks we love most. It didn't take J.C. long to go off trail and find a way through the maze of red sandstone. Somehow he managed to climb above Landscape Arch – the longest, thinnest strand of rock in the world suspended like a rope bridge – and look down on it. Since the area beneath the arch had been closed off, gaining this new vantage point was a welcome discovery. Watching J.C. scamper effortlessly up slickrock walls with his long limbs, Mike and I couldn't help but notice a resemblance to Spiderman – one of J.C.'s comic superheroes, and perhaps an alter-ego. Ravens and jackrabbits watched with curiosity as we bumped and bounced our way along the salt-encrusted floor of the desert outside Moab. It's always a nerve-racking experience climbing from the White Rim up onto the high mesa in Canyonlands National Park known as Island in the Sky. The switchbacks of the Shafer Trail are unbelievably narrow and steep. Not for the faint of heart, this favorite road trip of mine requires caution but always yields high adventure.

It was September. This time of year thunderstorms carried from the Pacific by monsoon winds bring welcome moisture to the arid desert regions of the Southwest. Billowing clouds and distant slashes of lightning create stunning celestial displays and brilliant rainbows. But sudden storms also bring life-threatening flash floods. We were nearly caught in one that set a record, bringing a year's annual rainfall in one afternoon. Raindrops falling on our heads turned first into a downpour, then a veritable deluge. Hiking through Natural Bridges National Monument in remote southeastern Utah, we witnessed nature's awesome raw power at work. From all sides water began rushing through notches in the slanted sandstone walls, cascading down slickrock into bone-dry washes, turning them into raging, red rivers of mud. We nearly became part of a massive mudslide ourselves. The dirt road out to Muley Point – a splendid lookout over the fantastically carved plateau eleven hundred feet below – was too muddy to attempt, so we began our descent on the gravel Moqui Dugway. Something made me look over the edge. I could see that the switchbacks below had disappeared. The road down was gone. From the onslaught of heavy mud-laden rain, the steep grades carved into the rock ledge had collapsed. We were able to back up in the nick of time, avoiding what would have been certain disaster. Having to make a detour of a hundred miles to get back to our campground was a small price to pay for our lives.

On a hike out to Corona Arch, impressive by its sheer girth, J.C.'s penchant for finding a way to the top of every rock led him and Mike up the back side of the arch to stand on its top. I stayed below with the cameras. Contrary to what its name implies, slickrock is not slippery. But climbing up is easier than getting down. Unable to avoid looking down, Mike was as frightened as I'd ever seen him, creeping along like a crab, trying not to fall forward. I held my breath as J.C., who had had less trouble, talked Mike down the rest of the way. In this fascinating landscape of strange sandstone shapes, we discovered a few arches we'd never seen before, tucked in hidden-away places off the trail.

After an up-close view of the generators inside the hydroelectric plant at Glen Canyon Dam, we took J.C. to the north rim of the Grand Canyon – all the way down to Roaring Springs deep inside, as well as all the way out to Toroweap for the most stunning view of all. In Zion National Park, we kept a firm hold on the chains along the extremely narrow ledge – with a sheer drop-off of a thousand feet on each side – leading up to Angels Landing. After hiking miles through the Narrows, we relaxed in the secluded emerald pools that Mike and I had discovered four years before. We tripped to Tuacahn one night for a rousing outdoor performance of *The Unsinkable Molly Brown.* From the bottom of Bryce Canyon, we stared up at the towering pink 'trees' of its great stone forest. Traveling the Burr Trail along the rare and incredibly colorful landform known as the Waterpocket Fold, we successfully navigated Escalante's crisscrossed canyons to reach Capitol Reef. We were surprised to find that autumn had arrived, at least in the higher elevations. Frost had already clothed the aspens in red and yellow, orange and gold. We were about to discover natural beauty of even greater magnitude in Cathedral Valley, the most scenic backcountry area I've even seen in the United States.

Driving through this stark desert terrain in the north-east corner of Capitol Reef is slow going, requiring a high-clearance vehicle that can ford the Fremont River at exactly the right point. Numerous sandstone monoliths, shaped by erosion over centuries into great cathedral-like temples of rock, stand as silent sentries guarding a landscape of solitary beauty, with vistas unrivaled anywhere. Here the desert hills, composed of bentonite and painted with a rainbow of hues, sparkle with gypsum crystals in the sun. Cathedral Valley was a priceless find. If I ever have to pick a single favorite place, or my favorite trip, this will be it.

Back in the saddle at All Saints for the final time, my last hurrah went beautifully. What little I hadn't already removed from my office, I quietly packed away. I dreaded packing up the whole house I had lived in for so long, but I started in on that, too. My parents stood with me for more than a few tearful goodbyes on my final Sunday. I left the parish with the same words of Pope John XXIII that I had quoted so often: "We are not on earth to guard a museum. We are here to cultivate a flourishing garden of life."

I've never doubted the love and support of the vast majority of my parishioners across those sixteen years. In fact, they kept me going with constant reminders of how much I meant to them. I remember a great many of their names and faces to this day, for they were a part of my life for a long time. God put them in my hands. I only dropped a few. I hope they've forgotten by now. Those who hurt me, I've let go. I've learned that life's too short to live any other way, if you want God to wipe your slate clean at the end.

Of course, there were a few people who couldn't wait for me to leave. I knew who they were. Years ago someone keyed my car. That wasn't a very nice thing to do, but after a while, familiarity does tend to breed contempt. It happens in every parish. If people wait long enough, they'll get their wish. In my case, it just took a really long time. I'm not one of those priests who always wears a 'happy face' and goes around flashing a big smile and glad-handing everybody he sees. That's fine, but it's just not me. Without my ever saying a word, people sometimes assume I'm mad or in a bad mood simply because I have a serious expression on my face. They're usually mistaken. Once in a while I am angry or irritable – like everyone else – but more often I'm just thinking about something, and inattentive as a result. I have on occasion frightened people by letting my anger show. For that I am sorry. I sometimes overreact. I have to watch that. Just like my father, I tend to display all my emotions flagrantly. Other than in jest, no one has ever had to ask, "Tell us how you really feel, Greg."

A few former employees claim that I was less than a benevolent dictator or a hard taskmaster. They're entitled to their opinion. People almost always blame their boss when they quit their job, even though they have other reasons. The way the system works, even if someone else handles personnel matters in the parish, pastors still wear the hat that says 'Boss.' Some say I drove people out of the parish whenever my disposition was less than sunny. Some I'm sure I did. Every pastor does. It goes with the territory. People wrote letters complaining about things I did that they didn't like. They do that in every parish, too. In my opinion, those letters get more attention than they deserve.

No matter what a pastor says or does, someone is going to complain about it. Some things are hard to say, but they still need to be said. Some things are hard to do, but they still need to be done. Being a pastor is not a popularity contest, and the most popular pastors are not necessarily the best. Some are afraid to say or do anything that might rock the boat, so they say and do very little or nothing at all. That wasn't my problem, and that's not leadership in my book. A parish doesn't get started and built without a pastor with clear vision willing to take some risks.

As I recall, there were nearly a thousand registered and supporting families at All Saints when I left in 2003. In my estimation, that's quite an accomplishment, considering that I started from scratch. There were no massive defections as a result of anything I ever said or did. But, being the pastor, I was often blamed for the things other people said and did. Critics need to remember how quick people are to leave a parish – or the Church itself – these days, and how slow they are to stay. A lot of people just 'go shopping' until they get what they want – a baptism, a wedding, their child in Catholic school, for example. They only do as much as they're told they have to do, showing up at church for a few weeks and putting an envelope in the collection. Once they have what they came for, we don't see them any more. Their commitment vanishes. People also need to focus more on the message, and less on the messenger. Messengers come and go, but the message remains.

I didn't keep a foot in the door when I left All Saints. I'm sure my successor appreciated that. Leaving was hard enough. That would only have made it more difficult on everyone. Other than picking up mail for a few weeks, my visits to All Saints have purposely been few. What was most difficult for me was leaving behind both the place I worked and the place I lived at the same time. Leaving either one is traumatic. Leaving both at once is ridiculously hard, but that's what priests go through every time they move. After sixteen years, I felt the loss deeply for some time. On the other hand, I was excited at the prospect of pastoring a new parish before long. I assumed that was still the plan. I knew it might be a while, since the summer, when most appointments take effect, had passed. I had the condo on the beach to stay at in the meantime. Everything would be fine.

Early in 2000, I invited Bishop Lynch to make All Saints one of the first parishes in the Diocese he would visit in an official capacity. He did, interviewing staff, council members, and parishioners at large. His report back to me could not have been more positive and affirming. Over the next four years, we had several cordial conversations, but something seemed to be altering his perception of me. I continued to believe that I would be given another parish when the time came for me to leave All Saints.

In April of 2004, six months after I did leave All Saints, we reached an impasse. When the bishop, who had come to believe I had a severe anger management problem, asked me to undergo a clinical psychological evaluation, I was dumbfounded. I respectfully declined, pointing out that I had 'been there and done that' twenty years ago when I spent four months at the House of Affirmation. I had been on a therapeutic journey ever since, spending hundreds of hours in counseling since 1984, with a great deal of positive growth to show for it.

We haven't discussed the matter since. Several years ago I applied for the pastorate of St. John Parish on St. Pete Beach. I did not receive a response, and I have not applied for a parish since. I was offered the position of Director of Cemeteries a year ago. When I realized that I would have to run a business full-time and no longer be able to do most of the parish work I love, I respectfully declined. I could have done the job, but my heart would not have been in it.

I will soon mark thirty-five years as a priest of the Diocese of St. Petersburg. I am in good standing, but without an official assignment for seven years. I retain the status and the salary of a pastor, for which I am grateful. At sixty, I'm ten years shy of the age for retirement. People say I look younger than I am, yet they ask if I'm retired because they see me doing what retired priests do – helping out in parishes. I am far from retired. What retired priests do for an hour or two a week, I now do full-time, or whenever and wherever I am needed. I've discovered that people – even other priests – have a penchant for identifying every priest with a particular parish. In my case, that no longer applies. When they ask "Where are you from, Father?" I just say "Here." When they ask "What parish?" I just say "This one." If they persist, I say "St. Elsewhere." They've never heard of that one, so they usually just smile and walk away. People don't know what to make of a priest who works throughout the Diocese rather than just in one parish.

In other words, I've had to reinvent myself, as it were. It hasn't been easy, but after seven years, it seems to be working. Having a sense of humor helps a lot. That's always been my saving grace. I couldn't have written this book without it. I have to admit that, at first, I was in shock. It seemed like a bad dream that couldn't be true. It felt like my whole life was suddenly grinding to a halt. I didn't know what to do. I went through the whole range of emotions. I felt misunderstood, misjudged, and wronged. As time went on, I felt as though I was being put out to pasture or on the scrap heap. No one made me feel this way, but these were my feelings. I struggled for years to overcome them. By living one day at a time, I learned to dismantle the wall I put up until, finally, I let the last of these feelings go.

I've never fully understood why this turn of events took place in my life. In this life, I doubt I ever will. That I have failed at times in the sight of God and other human beings I am sure. My life is an open book. Every priest has his strengths and weaknesses. At this point in my life, I know mine well. I have no use for false humility. I believe myself to be as fit and capable as any priest I know, and more so than some.

Why haven't I been appointed a pastor again? Every priest I know has asked me that question. My friends and family wonder. People come up and ask me in every parish I go to. I really don't have an answer. I believe God does, and he hasn't revealed it to me. If God wanted me to be a pastor again, I would be. God always gets what he wants, but I don't. That's life. That's the way it is because I am not God, though I'd like to be – just for one day. It's taken me years to come to this realization. Intelligent people can be rather thick-headed at times. My own thoughts and feelings got in the way. For one thing, I fell into the trap of believing I was *entitled* to another parish. In the seminary I learned that church law says something to the effect that once a priest has been a pastor, he's entitled to a parish of equal or greater dignity. I thought I deserved it, I'd earned it, so why wasn't it being handed over to me on a silver platter? I had a right to another parish. I also *expected* the bishop to give me another parish, so when he didn't, I resented this for years. I expended all that psychic energy for nothing. I put the blame on him. I forgot that expectations are merely resentments in training. They never do a body good. Going around expecting things only leads to disappointment when you don't get them. I took it too personally. That was my second mistake.

The third irrational belief I held was that the only way I could ever be happy was by being pastor of a parish again. After all, I was one for sixteen years. There were times when I wasn't very happy being one, but that didn't matter. It didn't occur to me then, but in a sense, what I was saying was that just being a priest wasn't good enough for me. I would never consciously think that or say it, but I was obsessed with remaining a pastor. I thought I simply had to manage a parish. I knew how to run one, so that's what I had to do. Looking back on this now, I can also see a control issue here. Finally, my need to please authority figures – in this case, the bishop – kicked in. It was obvious that he wasn't pleased with me. I had to try harder, I thought, until he was. I could not be happy until he was happy with me. I love the succinct definition of 'compulsion' – it's an irresistible act.

A gentle and compassionate Franciscan priest by the name of Jim Jones helped me find my way out of this self-defeating thinking. For several years I sought spiritual direction from him. I knew Jim was the right person to talk to when we discovered we were both ordained on the same day in the same year. I began feeling better about myself and my situation. He led me to a deeper understanding of the intensely personal nature of my vocation. He helped me to realize that I had nothing to prove to anyone. As a pastor for all those years, I had done most everything a priest can do, and more. Realizing how much I had accomplished, I arrived at a place of greater self-acceptance and inner peace – just what I needed. I'd like to think that a little of Jim's wisdom and holiness rubbed off on me.

Clearly my bishop views me differently than I do. I'm hardly the only priest who has ever had a difference of opinion with his bishop. It wasn't easy to hear the things he said to me, but I've taken them to heart. I'm well aware of my need to manage anger and stress more effectively. A.A. has helped me with that. I know how much progress I've made over the past twenty-seven years. That's how long I've been in recovery. I know that my family, longtime friends, and counselors all recognize this. I've successfully maintained sobriety going on nineteen years. My heartfelt desire is to continue on this track to the best of my ability. I'm doing that, one day at a time. I take issue with anyone who depicts me as some kind of ogre, or believes that I am out of control.

People used to think priests and bishops were faultless and knew everything. Some bishops and priests thought so, too, and a few act like they still do. We know better now. Bishops cannot possibly know all of their priests personally, unless they all write a book like this. You may be surprised that, at this point, I have come to see the wisdom of my bishop's decision not to appoint me pastor of another parish. In other words, I have accepted it, and with acceptance comes peace. Were it any other way, I would not have half the serenity or effectiveness I now possess. I am grateful to Bishop Lynch. More than ever, I enjoy doing what I'm doing. It's what I was ordained to do, and I do it well. That's good enough for me.

XXII   OFF-ROAD ADVENTURE

People say life begins at forty, or fifty, or something like that. My new life began at fifty-three. Moving into the condo on Sand Key was a chore, but it didn't take long for me to settle in to what were already familiar surroundings. Of course, I needed to part with some things I had accumulated by living in the same house for sixteen years. Getting used to the slow-moving traffic on the beach also took a while. A quieter, more pleasant place to live, however, would have been hard to find. The Gulf of Mexico was right across the street. It wasn't long before I landed on the board of directors of the condo association as treasurer. What I learned in this capacity came in handy later.

At a clergy conference in the fall of 2003, the bishop suggested that I announce my availability to assist parishes. The moment I did so, I became one popular guy. Everybody and their brother started calling me, beginning with St. Timothy in Northdale, the newest church in the Diocese designed by my friend Will. More and more parishes asked me to help, primarily for Mass, confessions, penance services, and funerals. For the most part I was doing the same things I'd always been doing as a priest, but in constantly changing places rather than just one. This has pretty much been the story of my life for the past seven years. I've assisted at more than thirty different parishes, doing everything from signing checks, to providing emergency coverage, to preaching on stewardship, to reforming the ushers, to giving days of recollection, to teaching RCIA, to conducting a holy hour, to visiting the hospital, to anointing the dying, to baptizing children, to witnessing marriages. The only thing that has changed is that the boundaries of my 'parish' have expanded greatly to embrace the Diocese itself. I chose to become a diocesan priest, and I have never been one more than I am now.

Without having to shoulder the burden of administration or a fixed schedule of services at one parish, I am free to meet the needs of multiple parishes as they arise. This has required flexibility on my part and an ability to observe the local custom, so to speak, rather than my own ingrained way of doing things. Going with the flow is now almost second nature to me. Though it's not the way I naturally tend to be, it didn't prove to be that hard at all. I actually enjoy it now. I find it makes life much easier when you go with the flow whenever you can.

Preaching has become one of the things I enjoy most and look forward to every single day when I celebrate Mass. You can really tell a lot about a priest from the way he preaches. You can tell whether he really believes what he's saying or not. You can tell whether he dreads preaching or relishes it. Some priests are better at connecting with their hearers than others. You can imagine how difficult it is for those who come from another culture or whose first language is not English. Some priests seem altogether unaware that they are supposed to preach on the Scriptures. For a few, preaching is sheer drudgery, an onerous task, equally burdensome for those subjected to it. I was taught that the purpose of a homily is to teach but also to entertain. Apparently, I do this fairly well. People comment constantly. When they tell me they enjoyed my homily, I tell them I did, too. Why shouldn't a homily be able to be enjoyed? Apparently this doesn't happen all the time.

Of course a priest has to know the people to whom he's preaching. If he doesn't know what their lives are really like, he doesn't stand a chance. Most newly ordained priests tend to be rather dull in their preaching. They also tend to be rather dogmatic, especially these days. A lot of preaching tends to be more theological than spiritual, and more intellectual than sensate. One of the biggest favors someone did for me as a young priest – I think it was a nun – was to tell me I sounded like 'a stuffed shirt.' I'm sure she was right, though my feelings were hurt at the time. For a long time I had a bad habit of nursing hurt feelings and storing up resentments rather than swallowing my pride and letting hurtful things go. I am now the wiser. Age and experience have taught me that. Life is too short for anything else.

Getting to the right church at the right time on the right day has gone well so far. Getting to Mass on time is obviously a problem for some people, usually the same ones, especially during the week. Though I don't wear a watch, if I did, I could actually set it by the time of their arrival. They may be late, but at least they're consistent. These people are not going to change. They are creatures of bad habit. Then there are those who look at their watches with practiced disdain when the priest doesn't show up on the altar at the exact minute Mass is scheduled to begin. They need to get a life. If anyone ever says to me, "Father, you're late," I just ask, "Why, has Mass started without me?" Sacristy clocks do not rule the world, and it's a good thing they don't.

I have to drive a lot more than I used to, but having lived here most of my life gives me an advantage in knowing how to get around and how long it should take to get from one place to another. The only parishes I've ever failed to get to on time are the beach parishes – St. John, St. Jerome, St. Brendan – when traffic is backed up hopelessly or the roads are closed for a bike or foot race. On weekends, I usually have to go from one church to another, sometimes to a third, and occasionally even to a fourth. But there is so much less stress in my life now that I can handle this with ease. I'm a much friendlier driver than I used to be, although I still grumble from time to time at the number of unnecessary traffic lights and their ridiculous length. On a good day, having a sense of humor helps. I also do a lot of praying behind the wheel. When the price of gas was edging toward four dollars a gallon a few years ago, I got rid of my less-than-fuel-efficient Trans Am for a much thriftier though not-as-much-fun-to-drive Kia. By shedding four cylinders and two hundred horsepower I really didn't need, I gained about ten miles per gallon. Like my life, my style of driving has changed.

It's no secret that I like a change of scenery now and then – as often as possible, in fact. I think that's one reason

I've taken to my new job so well. It's nice to be welcomed by friendly greetings and smiling faces everywhere I go, every single day. One parish – St. Elizabeth Ann Seton in Citrus Springs – even puts my name on their marquis when I'm due to show up. People greeted me at All Saints every day for sixteen years, but this feels different. Somehow I am perceived as special. Now and then, I feel as though I bring comic relief. I find a little clowning around in the sacristy puts people at ease. As an outsider, parishioners view me with curiosity. I'm something of a novelty, so they pay attention to me. They seem to listen to what I have to say because they haven't gotten used to hearing it. I try to use this to good advantage. I find it easy to win people over simply by being my best good-natured self.

I love my job now more than ever. Being a priest, especially on Sunday morning, brings out the best in me, and I hope in everyone else. The unique opportunity I have to touch thousands of different people's hearts every single week – far more than I could reach in a single parish – constantly amazes and challenges me. I find that people have great respect and love for their parish priests. I do everything I can to reinforce this. I never take sides. I refrain from judgment, and make only positive statements. My hope is that each local church has somehow been built up by my being there, and that I have done a good enough job to be invited back. That doesn't seem to be a problem.

I also have time to minister to people that priests confined to parishes rarely can. From time to time I conduct Sunday afternoon vespers at several large retirement residences, such as Lake Seminole Square where Dad lives. Hundreds of older folks – Protestant as well as Catholic – who find it difficult to get out to church gather to worship at these services each week. They are genuinely thrilled to have a Catholic priest lead them. I am also on call for chapel and graveside services at several area funeral homes, when parishes cannot provide a priest, but families – from out of town or with no parish affiliation – still want a Catholic priest to conduct a service. They, too, are always grateful.

I couldn't miss a birthday party for my friend, Liz Kessler, in May of 2004, marking the beginning of the second century of her life. This dear woman prayed for me every day since I buried her husband Paul from St. Jude thirty years ago. That's probably one reason I'm still going. She made it to a hundred and six.

June of 2004 found Mike and me heading north-westward again, this time with J.C. and his girlfriend Michelle, whose parents Mike and I both knew from St. Thomas. After stopping to visit my brother and his family once more, we were greeted with a spectacular array of summer wildflowers in Grand Teton National Park. While there wasn't much snow left on the jagged peaks, we saw more moose munching on willow branches in the marshes than ever before, as well as marmots sounding their territorial alarm at our approach, and a few roving bears. Hiking seven miles in and several thousand feet up to the head of Death Canyon – despite its somber name, one of the most scenic spots in the Tetons with breathtaking views – we did find snow covering the upper reaches of the rocky slopes. For a day, J.C. and Michelle were able to experience some of Yellowstone's wonders as well – its thundering waterfalls and painted canyon, steaming sulfurous aqua pools, bubbling cauldrons of mud, and herds of bison.

Then it was on to rock-strewn meadows filled with glorious yellow glacier lilies in Montana's Glacier National Park. Ascending the trail to semi-frozen Ptarmigan Lake, we watched in amazement as a herd of mountain goats brought their kids down a rocky ledge to play on snowy patches – literally kicking up their heels, leaping and jumping straight up in the air, cavorting like children splashing water – a spectacle we'd never seen before or since. We also came close to some usually elusive Rocky Mountain sheep with their trademark curved horns. Mike and I set out on one of the toughest but most rewarding high-altitude adventures we've ever had, climbing first through a spruce forest, then scrambling above tree line along deep red rock walls and ledges, up and over the shoulder of Matahpi Peak through

Siyeh Pass, zigzagging down across snowfields (occasionally sliding on our butts to save time), and finally descending through alpine meadows along a cascading creek plunging into Sun Rift Gorge. We came about as close to the top of the world as you can get – like a scene from *The Sound of Music*. Emerging from a late afternoon thunderstorm in the distance, the sun smiled on us with a rainbow. It was windy and cold at the summit, but worth every step up and down it took to get there.

Crossing the Canadian border to spend a day at Waterton Lakes in Alberta was uneventful. But much to our surprise, our reception when we headed north to spend a week in Banff and Jasper was less than friendly. We were rudely ordered to pull over by Canadian customs officials while the car and camper were searched and we were interrogated. All our passports were in order and there was nothing illegal in our possession. The offensive treatment we received was uncalled for. As a result, when we were finally allowed to proceed, we promptly turned around and headed for home, cutting our trip short. J.C. and Michelle were not enjoying each other's company, and Mike and I had already visited the Canadian Rockies more than once. It was a long and quiet ride back to Florida. We enjoyed some good times and spectacular scenery on this trip, despite the fact that it came to a premature end. No trip is ever perfect.

In October, I set off on my own for a couple of weeks, something I don't usually enjoy but needed to do for myself. There are no seasons to speak of in Florida, and I had time to visit a few familiar places at a beautiful time of year. I flew to Denver where I spent a peaceful fall day with my brother Mark and his wife Pat strolling through the red rocks of Roxborough State Park, with its great slabs of stone jutting skyward amidst champagne-colored aspens. The crisp fresh air grew colder as I gained altitude driving west across the Rockies. High up in the forests of southwestern Utah, I bundled up to hike along the rim of Cedar Breaks National Monument, a miniature Bryce Canyon where rocky orange fingers reached up to grasp the icy blue air. Even the barren desert scenery around Lake Mead was brightened by jumbles of multicolored rock spewed from ancient volcanoes. Finally, the snowy Sierra Nevadas rose up, signaling my arrival in California, the road beneath me twisting and turning more wildly with each mountain mile.

I had forgotten how lovely the marble flowstone formations were that graced Crystal Cave deep inside Sequoia National Park, and the grandeur of the groves of giant cedars in Kings Canyon. While the rivers still ran, by this time of year the great waterfalls of Yosemite were tired trickles, hardly able to reach the boulders at their base. The air was thick with smoke, making the massive walls of gray granite that hemmed in the Valley look even more ominous. Roadside painters tried to capture serene stretches of the Merced River, lined with bushes tinged with autumn gold. Winter was on the way. A ghostly haze hung over Yosemite's trampled meadows, now devoid of tourists. Though shrouded, its proud peaks and bold domes still inspired awe.

Dad and my sister Beth at Calvary Cemetery.

One of the other things I did the first year or so I was out of the parish was to serve as a chaplain for Celebrity Cruise Lines. At that time Celebrity tried to have a Catholic priest onboard every cruise. In addition to celebrating Mass every day – usually in a cocktail lounge or cabaret – I conducted a Protestant service on Sunday, a renewal of marriage vows for couples celebrating anniversaries, and a Mass for the crew below decks, usually late at night. For the cruise director, Mass is just another activity to list in the daily schedule of events. But for some reason, Catholics seem to value the opportunity to attend Mass at sea even more than they do on land. Perhaps it was the novelty and familiarity of going to Mass on a ship that attracted so many people, but they flocked to this 'activity' in droves. The unifying power of the Mass was even more apparent as people coming from parishes with diverse customs from all over the country and the world participated almost effortlessly in unison. I had no trouble at all recruiting individuals to serve, read, and help with communion. This proved to be an exciting, new, and wonderful experience of Church, not only for them, but for me. People openly expressed their gratitude for my being there. Other than when a priest is onboard, Catholic crew members rarely have a chance to go to Mass for months at a time. On Celebrity's ships, most of them come from the island of Goa off India's coast. They were especially grateful for the opportunity for Reconciliation and exceptionally devout.

Since each ship is responsible for providing what the chaplain needs, some were better than others, but I was able to make do with whatever was available. I enjoyed the challenge in any case. On six cruises, I spent a total of fifty-six days at sea, enjoying myself like any other guest when I wasn't working. In addition to the usual ports of call, I got to less-visited nooks and crannies in the Caribbean – Panama, Honduras, St. Kitts, Costa Rica, St. Maarten, Aruba, the Dominican Republic, and Grenada. Best of all, I got to bring a guest on each cruise for free. Mike and J.C. each came with me twice. I brought Dad along for his eighty-fifth birthday, and Sojan Punnakkattu Joseph, Mike's parochial vicar from Kerala, India. After getting some expert advice, I bought myself an expensive present – a large diamond – in St. Thomas, center of the diamond trade in North America. Interestingly, like any loose gemstones, unset diamonds are considered a 'rock' by U.S. Customs. They must be declared but are not subject to tax. I had an eighteen-karat gold setting made for my 'rock' when I got home. I have few other valuable possessions.

A priest is supposed to make a retreat each year. For the first time in 2004, I took part in a week that has renewed my spirit every year since, sponsored by Guest House at the Franciscan Center in Tampa. The fellowship I have found with the priests who come to this gathering from all across the country is greater than I have found anywhere else. Guest House is the primary residential treatment center for priests and religious men and women who seek to recover from alcoholism and other addictive disorders. While I did not spend time at Guest House when I attained sobriety, I admire greatly the priests I've come to know intimately who did. Bob Martin is the exceptional counselor who continues to guide our recovery during this week each year. Mike and I are proud to count Bob and his wife Michel among our friends. Speaking with a wisdom that comes from his own experience in recovery, Bob's understanding of God, the Catholic Church, and priesthood never ceases to amaze me. Having made the recovery of priests and religious his life's work, he is a great gift and blessing to the Church, as well as to me personally and thousands of others he has helped to heal. Each year now, I look forward to this week more than any other.

As 2005 began, it occurred to Mike and me that if we were going to share a home in retirement, we would need more space than we had in our condo on the beach. With real estate prices hitting an all-time high and people selling quickly – including my parents, who had just sold their condo for top dollar almost overnight – we decided to put our condo on the market. Since I was living there, we needed to start looking for something more suitable right away, so that I could move as soon as we sold. We found a more spacious town home with an enclosed two-car garage not far from the Bay on the other side of Clearwater. We both loved it, so expecting a quick sale at the beach, we borrowed money from our parents as a short-term loan. The location was ideal, and so was the timing, we thought. We would sell at the top of the market and make a hefty profit. That was our plan, but like most plans, it failed to work as we had hoped. There's not much point in saying it would have, had we acted a month or two sooner.

Using two different realtors, we had two different contracts written over the next two years, both of which fell through at the last minute. Meanwhile, we closed on the town home, and I moved in in October, while the condo sat empty. But paying property taxes and monthly fees on two places at once nearly killed us financially. The gridlock in real estate sales and the unprecedented drop in property values had already begun. Mike and I never wanted to be landlords, but using a local agency, we quickly succeeded in leasing the condo. We were able to begin paying our parents back a little each year, something we had planned to do right away and all at once. Property values at the beach are still dreadful and sales almost nonexistent. We are still leasing and getting hit with assessments from time to time. Such is life. Things will get better. They always do. Well, they *almost* always do, once God stops laughing.

My niece Laura and her friend Bryan rode out to Salida, Colorado, with Mike and me in June of 2005. While we set up the Hi-Lo, they set up camp with my brother and his wife beside a stream in San Isabel National Forest. Mother Nature provided the entertainment. A water ouzel, a determined little bird, put on quite a show for us, repeatedly diving underwater looking for food, bobbing up and down, and flitting back and forth to its nest under a rock ledge overhanging the stream. An experienced backpacker, Mark led us under a turquoise sky on a five-mile hike that was a bit much for our first day out – starting at an altitude of nearly eight thousand feet and climbing three thousand feet further up to Hayden Pass in the snow-streaked Sangre de Cristo Mountains, carpeted in every shade of early summer green. The next day, the six of us ran the raging white water of the Arkansas River through the infamous Royal Gorge, not once but twice, and not without peril. My sister-in-law Pat was thrown out of the raft, just before the most severe rapid. While dangerous, this is not an uncommon occurrence. That's why everyone wears life jackets and helmets. Our guide, a professional, had rehearsed us for this very possibility. After watching helplessly at first, we all made it through the drop. Then, while he steered the raft, we managed to pull Pat back in to safety. Because of where this happened, a professional photographer on shore captured this little drama on film. The photos, and the expressions on our faces, are priceless. Despite this harrowing experience, every one of us wanted to run the river again as planned, so we did – this time without incident.

With a chill in the morning air, Mike and I headed once more to the Black Canyon where we navigated hairpin curves on the steep gravel road to the rapidly coursing Gunnison River at its bottom. Walking along its banks we attracted a couple of ticks – small bloodsucking arachnids that can transmit disease when they attach themselves to passersby. We routinely check for these nasty little hitchhikers, so this wasn't a problem. On my fifty-fifth birthday, we set eyes for the first time on the unique mushroom-shaped pinnacles of smooth rock known as hoodoos in remote Goblin Valley, near Capitol Reef National Park in south central Utah. Surrounded by walls of eroded cliffs resembling a lunar landscape, a veritable army of these bizarre chocolate-colored formations stands silently at attention, as though frozen in time on the desert floor. Sadly, we learned of the death of longtime family friend and former Diocesan attorney, John DiVito. I tried to get a call out to his son Joe, but cell phone service in this neck of the woods is tentative at best.

My nephew and niece, Joshua and Laura Welsh.

Armed with information from the internet, Mike and I had decided to try our hand at a new exploit on this trip – canyoneering. To begin with, we would explore some of the slot canyons of the great San Rafael Swell. A giant wave in the earth's crust pushed up millions of years ago, the sandstone, shale, and limestone of this part of the Colorado Plateau was carved by water into an immense maze of colorful valleys, canyons, gorges, mesas, and buttes. Foreboding to some, such a landscape invariably invites discovery by others. Without the threat of flash floods from monsoonal rains in late summer, we walked up a dry wash into Little Wild Horse Canyon where for the remainder of the day we trudged, climbed, jumped, and slithered our way deeper into the belly of the Swell until coming out on the other side. Returning by way of Bell Canyon, we had to turn sideways to negotiate some passages, squeezing between narrow, pockmarked walls. The next day we took on Crack Canyon. Not knowing quite what to expect always makes for high adventure. With a narrow slice of blue sky ever present overhead, we made our way for miles through these constantly twisting, often challenging corridors of slanted rock. Without seeing another human being all day, in some of the most remote places on earth, Mike and I seem to find great fun.

The desert in the vicinity bloomed with the juicy pink fruit of prickly pear cactus and a surprising variety of flowering bushes. The sharply pointed spires of Cathedral Valley took aim at the sky as we dared to enter this stunningly scenic expanse of desert again. We stopped to pay our respects at two magnificent mute monoliths – the twin Temples of the Sun and Moon, their gypsum crystals glistening in the noonday sun. The temperature soared as we drove deeper into the barren desert surrounding Lake Powell, where water levels were at record low. We saw marinas that had been left high and dry and long-submerged canyons that were now above water. On the way to the splendidly isolated Needles District of Canyonlands National Park, everyone stops to examine the prolific collection of petroglyphs – human hand and foot prints, hunters on horseback with bows and arrows, squirrels, goats, rams, snakes, and antelope – carved into Newspaper Rock.

After stopping to photograph aptly-named Wooden Shoe Arch, we embarked on one of the most dramatic hikes in the national park system – an exhausting eleven-mile loop through a relatively flat grassy area surrounded by amazing rock formations known as Chesler Park. Here hundreds of red sandstone 'needles' jut out of the ground. Weirdly-shaped spires supporting delicately balanced rocks give the appearance of a futuristic city. Elsewhere the trail drops down into narrow cracks between massive sandstone slabs. Coming upon an enormous cavern in the maze of rocks, we were suddenly awed at the sight of hundreds of cairns – small piles of stones picked up and stacked on top of one another, created individually by those who had passed this way before us. Cairns are usually set up a distance apart to mark the way. Seeing so many together gave us goose bumps. This felt like a sacred place. A sense of peace came over us. We felt a spiritual presence. We had made a remarkable discovery in an unexpected place.

Despite the notoriety of this hike, our only companions were a few jackrabbits, lizards, and horned toads. Here and there a roadrunner sped across in front of us as we passed between weathered mesas in the Valley of the Gods and overlooked the 'goosenecks' of the San Juan River. We could see the ruins of ancient dwellings on the floor of Canyon de Chelly. Crossing the Painted Desert, we admired the rainbow of colors to be found in logs and slices of trees turned to stone in Petrified Forest National Park. We stopped at El Morro National Monument, where for four hundred years, conquistadors and kings, priests and pioneers – many of whom carved their names onto the massive sandstone wall – came to drink from a cold spring in the desert. El Malpais, a little-known national monument of volcanic origin, attracted our attention. Seemingly lifeless, this vast and arid lava wasteland surprised us with caves frequented by bats and lined with ice, sink holes, craters, cinder cones, and a great natural arch. Finding an even more remote and less visited destination wasn't easy, but Mike and I managed to. Tucked away inside America's first designated wilderness area, we found Gila Cliff Dwellings National Monument, surrounded by pristine forest, to be an all but undiscovered gem.

Other treasures awaited our discovery in New Mexico. Based on a suggestion in National Geographic's *Adventure* magazine, we explored a few *arroyos* – dry creek beds – near San Antonio, hiking up a few of these rocky gulches despite the intense heat, just for the sake of discovering what might be there. Crossing a vast expanse of desert, we came across a startling sight known as the Very Large Array – a complex of twenty-seven gigantic antennas forming a single instrument for observing the planets, stars, galaxies, and black holes. Stretching for miles, the National Radio Astronomy Observatory can be seen from space. While searching for extra-terrestrial intelligence is not its purpose, it has been used as a backdrop in countless science fiction movies. If it turns out we are not alone, it seems the folks who run this place will be the first to know. We also toured the National Solar Observatory on Sacramento Peak where Mike and I escaped the heat and learned more about the sun in one hour than we did in our entire lives. Carl Sagan would have been proud. Putting on jeans and jackets in the desert seemed strange but it kept us warm crawling through the illuminated subterranean scenery of Carlsbad Caverns. As though on cue, looking like wisps of smoke, nearly a million Mexican free-tail bats spiraled out of the cave's mouth at dusk.

A little red square on a map with an intriguing name in the middle of nowhere always piques my curiosity, and has led to some amazing discoveries. One was Sitting Bull Falls, a veritable oasis in the midst of the Chihuahuan desert. Reclining in a cool spring-fed pool carved out of rock when it's a hundred degrees outside is one of life's simple pleasures. Just to the south, we entered Guadalupe Mountains National Park in the big arm of west Texas, a peaceful place of quiet beauty seldom visited due to its remoteness. Leaving the creosote bushes on the salt flats of the desert behind, we encountered an amazing diversity of flora and fauna exploring McKittrick Canyon – distinctive juniper trees with bark resembling an alligator's hide, madrone trees with their unique paper-thin peeling red bark, deciduous trees like oak and maple more often found up north, and even aspen, pine and fir at higher elevations. Towering stalks of brilliant yellow flowers from century plants dotted the hillsides. A rainbow-colored lizard crossed our path, and several rattlesnakes did us the favor of alerting us to their presence.

Big Bend National Park bordering Mexico in southwestern Texas was our last stop. The temperature of the air was the same as that of the hot springs we wallowed in on the edge of the Rio Grande – a hundred and five degrees. The stark beauty of Santa Elena Canyon struck us once more as walked along its sheer cliff walls. Nowhere does a fiery orange sun set more strikingly than over Big Bend's desert, silhouetting the outstretched arms of ocotillos reaching up from the earth against a pink and purple sky. As night fell, cooling breezes descended from the heights of the Chisos Mountains, bringing sweet relief from the heat.

The theft of Mike's video camera from the back seat – and the loss of the memories he had captured on film – put a damper on this southwestern odyssey. On the way home we asked a young man on the street in Chattanooga for directions to a tire store. He asked for a ride in exchange. We thought we were doing a good deed, but it was too late when we discovered what was missing.

My 'Aunt' Mildred and I feasting on Dungeness crab.

XXIII MAKING A GO OF IT

Every now and then life favors us with a pleasant surprise. One of mine has been getting to know Mildred Ramsdale, a parishioner of Mike's, and now one of our dearest friends. We've also become friends with her three kids – Wes, Kurt, and Terry – who are nearly our age. A remarkable woman, Mildred, a widow, is still a doting mother who defies every known stereotype of old age. Fit and trim, she is a whirlwind of activity, never worrying about herself but constantly looking after 'older' folks, and volunteering at St. Thomas Aquinas nearly seven days a week. She loves priests and treats us like kings. She enjoys life a great deal, finding her own fulfillment in taking care of others and putting their needs before her own. Though she'd be the last to admit it, she is one of the most unselfish, giving people I've ever met.

In addition to her big heart, Mildred has no fear and an amazing agility and stamina for a person her age. She shares Mike's and my love of the outdoors and adventure. She's gone camping all over the country, first with her family and later on her own. She still goes kayaking. In fact, she's joined Mike and me paddling upstream on the Rainbow and Silver Rivers, holding her own all the way. You don't meet many octogenarians like her.

So it was that I embarked on the first of my "Travels With My Aunt" to Utah at the end of 2005. Mildred and I took a chance, but we turned out to be perfect companions for each another on this outing – so much so that we went again, to the Pacific Northwest, in May of 2006, and once more, to Arizona, in November of 2007. Some may raise an eyebrow at a priest and an older woman traveling together, but frankly, we had such a good time we just don't care. Anyone who knows either of us knows we behaved with all due decorum. Just like Mike and I, Mildred and I are grateful that life favored the two of us with the opportunity to enjoy the never-ceasing wonders of America's national parks and each other's company at the same time.

After flying out to Denver after Christmas, we rented a four-wheel drive vehicle for some off-road adventure in the high desert, even though fine print in the rental agreement prohibits leaving the pavement, which is exactly what four-wheel drive is for. After getting to Moab, we rode out across the bumpy White Rim, often driving on bare rock, cautiously making our way up the steep switchbacks of the Shafer Trail to the mesa top – Canyonlands National Park's Island in the Sky. In the remote Needles district, we jolted our way along a rough sand track to a breathtaking overlook high above the Colorado River. Mildred and I discovered scenery in the backcountry around Moab that looked like it belonged on another planet, along the tortuous dirt roads leading out to Hurrah Pass and up the side of a sheer cliff to Gemini Bridges. These hard-to-find twin sandstone arches are split by a crack only a few feet wide in a canyon wall. It was cold but we kept warm hiking out to massive Corona Arch, then up to Delicate Arch and past Landscape Arch with the snow-capped LaSal Mountains ever on the horizon. Ice lined the banks of the Colorado, but despite the frigid night air, the outdoor hot tub at the motel felt great.

While it was too cold to slog through the Narrows in Zion National Park, Mildred and I did climb a thousand feet up Angels Landing for a spectacular view of Zion Canyon's full length. Since pulling oneself up holding on to chains along a steep ledge of loose rock was required to make it the rest of the way to the top, I went on alone. This was the only time I advised Mildred not to go with me. As I told her, I didn't want to have to call her kids to tell them their mother fell off a cliff. This time, prudence did prove to be the better part of valor. From Zion, we headed south out of St. George on an overcast New Year's Day to Toroweap, leaving civilization eighty dusty miles behind. The view of raging rapids on the Colorado River three thousand feet below this isolated vantage point on the north rim of the Grand Canyon – here less than a mile across – simply stuns the senses. A winter fairyland awaited us at Bryce Canyon, where hundreds of pink pinnacles poked skyward from a glistening blanket of freshly-fallen snow. Our eyes feasted on a rainbow of color passing through the canyons of the Escalante along the Burr Trail, the 'back door' into Capitol Reef National Park, set aflame by a fiery sunset. Under an azure morning sky, we marveled at patches of frost and the sharp shadows cast by spires of rock across the desert floor in the remote reaches of Cathedral Valley. There we paused to 'worship' at the twin Temples of the Sun and Moon, majestic sandstone monoliths, before braving an army of eroded chocolate phantoms in Goblin Valley. Finally, like the trooper she is, Mildred threaded her way right beside me through miles of serpentine passages beneath tall stone walls inside Little Wild Horse Canyon – retracing Mike's and my steps through this 'slot' in the San Rafael Swell the previous summer. Not a bad ten days for an old lady and a priest.

Six months later, the two of us were at it again. This time my now eighty-year-old 'aunt' and I flew to Portland, Oregon in May. Our quick spring trip to the Northwest began and ended along the famously scenic gorge of the mighty Columbia River, where we hiked to half a dozen thunderous waterfalls, all flowing at full tilt. At Eugene, we discovered a true botanical treasure – a breathtakingly beautiful rhododendron garden in full bloom, situated in a forest on a hill in the middle of the city. The brilliance of these enormous flowers gave my first digital camera quite a workout and provided the inspiration for several paintings. Then, at eight thousand feet, we were amazed to find warm temperatures and sunny skies over Crater Lake, a uniquely wondrous place. This deepest lake in the United States, with the bluest water on earth, lies inside a caldera, an enormous volcanic crater, entirely encircled by cliffs that were still deeply buried in snow.

Heading to the coast, we began our seaside journey northward along the Pacific, stopping to take photos at every ocean vista, walking through moss-laden rainforests, marveling at stately ancient redwoods, climbing down to beaches piled high with storm-tossed driftwood, and ascending the spiral staircases in still-working whitewashed lighthouses. We couldn't resist the hypnotic pull of restless surf crashing onto waiting rocks, or the din of minions of seabirds nesting on offshore sanctuaries. Sand dunes along the coast were awash with the buttery yellow blossoms of blooming bushes as far as the eye could see. Chill billows of fog rolling off the ocean gave the rusty wrought iron and peeling paint of the harbor light at Bandon a distinctly ghostly aura.

In a hot tub at the motel in Coos Bay, Mildred and I struck up a conversation with a couple of commercial fisherman that yielded the location of the best seafood on the Oregon coast – a 'shack' outside Newport. It was so good I've been back twice since. There's nothing quite like halibut or prawns fresh from the Pacific. After giving our regards to Haystack Rock off Cannon Beach further up the coast, we made it all the way to the remote, soggy north-western corner of the U.S. mainland and the temperate fern-clad rainforests, primeval in appearance, of Olympic National Park. The early morning silence and almost mirror-like surface of the ocean at Ruby Beach came as a shock, but the elements of nature in this unnaturally still place conspired to provide scenes of flawless beauty. Snow still adorned the Olympic peaks as well as the loftier slopes of the Northern Cascades to the east, largely concealed beneath winter's thick white mantle. Descending through the wilds of central Washington, Mildred and I climbed one last 'mountain' – Beacon Rock, a granite monolith looming eight hundred feet over the Columbia River. We celebrated appropriately, feasting on fresh Dungeness crabs.

A year and a half later, in November of 2007, we headed off on one more adventure to Phoenix, where Mildred's son Kurt lives. I figure Mildred being my 'aunt' makes Kurt my 'cousin' along with his brother Wes, who came to visit while we were there. In our ridiculously tiny rental car, the two of us put-putted to Montezuma Castle – one of a number of lesser known national monuments in the

Southwest that preserve ancestral Puebloan cliff dwellings – and Montezuma Well, a spring-fed limestone sinkhole. The Little Colorado River Gorge was our next stop on the way to the south rim of the Grand Canyon, so much less crowded this time of year than during the summer months. Mike and I used to tell the kids we took with us years ago that *this* was the Grand Canyon. Not knowing any better, they believed it until they laid eyes for the first time on the real thing. The 'real thing' never looked better than in the crisp, clear, cool air of fall under a warm sun. We spent a peaceful day exploring the silent ruins of Wupatki, Sunset Crater, and Walnut Canyon near Flagstaff and hiking through lovely Red Rock State Park near Sedona.

Back in Phoenix, Mildred and I ventured with Wes and Kurt out into the desert, to Boyce Thompson Arboretum – a magnificent botanical garden featuring every type of plant known to grow in the desert regions of the world. The three of us guys briefly escaped the heat of the city by climbing twelve hundred feet up appropriately named Camelback Mountain. Mildred and I took off for Tucson to see the famous cacti in Saguaro National Park, then the stark Sonoran desert scenery of Organ Pipe Cactus National Monument on the Mexican border. Our final exploit took us up into the canyons of the craggy and colorful Superstition Mountains, steeped in legend, east of Phoenix. With that last best dose of Arizona finery engraved in our memories, we flew back to the flatlands of Florida

As on our two previous jaunts getting back to nature, Mildred and I covered a lot of ground in a short space of time. We both enjoyed every minute we spent doing so and consider the experience a privilege. Age, and for that matter, gender is irrelevant when you're having fun. Like all the trips I've taken with Mike, these "Travels With My Aunt" have added joy to my life. How lucky I am to have a friend like Mildred Ramsdale.

Anyone who goes to Mass on a regular basis knows that priests working in Florida today come from all over the globe. Quite a few arrive on loan from dioceses and religious congregations in Kerala – a state in southwestern India where Catholicism thrives – including Mike's former parochial vicar, Sojan Joseph. As we got to know Sojan for the fine priest and good friend he is, Mike and I decided to take him up on his offer to visit his homeland, just as we had joined my associate, Joachim, in Tanzania five years before. It took a year of strategic planning, and quite a few frequent flyer miles, to make that happen, but in August of 2005, Mike and I did.

Sojan met us at the airport in Kochi (Cochin) on the Arabian Sea where the familiar heat and humidity of the tropics greeted us. Kerala is famous for its abundance of coconut palms. Natives drink the milk from coconuts like water, with vendors on every corner ready to hack one open with a machete. We saw forests filled with huge teakwood trees and stands of bamboo. Locals are skittish, especially at night, of elephants known to lurk therein. In the highlands, we saw troupes of cavorting monkeys and tea plantations on the hillsides. Kerala also has endless beaches with palm trees swaying in the wind, lush tropical foliage and flowering plants like hibiscus, and a lot of backwater where cormorants were a familiar sight. We spent a day exploring canals, resort-lined lakes, even an island, observing life on the water from the water – natives in houseboats, in stilt houses, pushing their small craft with poles, weaving rope from coconut fibers, mending fishnets, and raking mussels into their dugouts. We stayed overnight looking out on a rice paddy, and another night on a river in the middle of tapioca fields and rubber plantations. The traditional ayurvedic massage Sojan arranged for Mike and me had to be our most exotic venture. Having your entire body rubbed with oil by a stranger without speaking a word for half an hour was a pleasurable if strange experience not soon forgotten.

While the women in Kerala wear colorful saris, most men wear the traditional long white cotton garment wrapped around their waist, often tucked up at the knees, called a mundu. It's hot, so for the most part, everyone wears flip-flops. Of course this makes having to kick your shoes off every time you go in a temple, a mosque, or a church quick and easy. Priests celebrate Mass barefoot.

As you might expect, every city in India we visited was teeming with people and traffic. It's noisy, and you have to watch your step walking alongside a sea of bicycles, mopeds, three-wheeled scooters, subcompacts, trucks and buses. Sojan took us to visit his old seminary as well as places he had worked as a priest. His friends graciously took turns putting the three of us up and serving us delicious meals. Ranging from bland to spicy, Indian fare admittedly took some getting used to. Almost everything is served with rice, often seasoned with leaves. We were also wined and dined at the homes and farms of Sojan's siblings all over Kerala, where we saw black pepper, yams, tarot, turmeric, pineapple, plantains, cocoa beans, cashews, papayas, ginger, and rubber plants growing, as well as a crop of palm trees that produce a medicinal nut. In some places people still plow with a team of water buffaloes and sow seeds by hand. Indians love pure gold jewelry. Sojan took us to his brother's jewelry store, where Mike and I, like kids in a candy store, were simply dazzled. His mother Maria gifted us both with gold rings embedded with a single elephant hair forming a black band – our most precious souvenir.

The pronounced change in language and customs we encountered crossing into Karnataka, Kerala's northern neighboring state, made it seem like we were entering another country. Our destination was the ancient city of Mysore, home to an utterly decadent royal palace and glitzy temple complex. After touring the palace we started shopping in earnest, with Sojan in tow as 'negotiator' of all sales. He saved us a fortune in rupees. Seeing him with two tourists, vendors assumed he was a hired guide. Already aggrieved at the hard bargain he drove, they reluctantly offered him the customary kickback on whatever we bought. This gave us some good laughs. Mike was taken with two exquisitely detailed carvings of inlaid wood – a deer sipping from a stream and the Last Supper – so we had them shipped home successfully. We also nearly bought out a silk bazaar featuring an incredible array of sequined wall hangings and bed and table covers, each more gorgeous than the last. Somewhere on this once-in-a-lifetime trip we found an even more irresistible treasure, a jeweled rug, hand-stitched with hundred of semi-precious stones – jade, tiger's eye, topaz, garnets, and turquoise – sewn into ornate floral patterns fringed with gold thread. Rounding out our treasure trove were statues of three Hindu deities to serve as lesser household gods: a rosewood Krishna, a brass Kali, and a copper Ganesh.

A sudden downpour did nothing to dampen our enjoyment of the synchronized water ballet that lit up the night at lovely Brindavan Gardens. Row upon row of lush green terraces and manicured flower beds perforated with channels of coursing water were illuminated by a rainbow of lasers and spotlights playing on dancing fountains. After all that shopping I was hungry, and a bag of deep-fried chili peppers did the trick – much to Mike's and Sojan's amazement. We spent the most time in snarled traffic crossing the city of Bangalore in order to get to Bannerghatta National Park, an immense zoological preserve where Mike and I came nose to nose with two snow leopard cubs nearly as big as we were – *inside* their cage. Unbeknownst to us, Sojan slipped their keeper a few rupees to give us a thrill that nearly caused our hearts to stop. Straddling these rare big cats, Mike and I petted them, hoping they'd been well-fed. Not seeming to mind the intrusion, they were playful enough. I probably won't be doing this again any time soon, though. We enjoyed meeting Sojan's sister, Sister Joyce, who runs a huge Catholic school in Bangalore, as she rode up to greet us on a motorcycle. We already had something in common. Needless to say, the nuns took good care of us.

Finally, the three of us flew to the sprawling city of Hyderabad in Andhra Pradesh, where cultural differences were again noticeable, in part due to the large Muslim population. Here we wandered through a Disneyesque lakeside park, the NTR Gardens. Trying not to stare, we were taken aback a bit by the dozens of women wearing burqas, covered in black from head to toe, some with only a slit for their eyes to peer through. It's disconcerting to see these images on the news, but even more so in person. We toured a large mosque where, wearing shorts, we had to wrap a black cloth around our legs. We were also pressed to make a donation – something I've never experienced visiting a Catholic church anywhere in the world. Advising us to keep a low profile due to some anti-American sentiment, Sojan took us to Charminar, an elegant medieval monument of massive proportions with four towering minarets represent-ing the four pillars of Islam. This majestic open-aired architectural wonder features imposing arches, a central dome, an arcaded balcony, and delicate stuccowork, not to mention a great view of the city in all directions from the top. It's not quite the Taj Mahal, which is still on my bucket list, but it's probably as close as I'll get.

From Hyderabad, Mike and I flew home, but not without incident. After we got on the plane, it just sat there, for at least an hour, without moving. Being trapped on a plane going nowhere is an awful feeling, not to mention a waste of time. Consequently, we were late arriving at the domestic terminal in Mumbai and it was dark. We still had to retrieve our treasure-laden luggage and drag it up onto the bus that would transfer us to the international terminal several miles away. The bus driver drove like a demon. Apparently airport personnel were aware of our fate – or accustomed to it – as they grabbed our bags and waved us through as we made a mad dash for the gate. This 'midnight marathon' was not the end of it. Everyone glared at us for having held up the plane's departure. We weren't able to land in Amsterdam due to fog, so we landed in Germany, where two more hours were wasted standing in line waiting to be rebooked. The only thing KLM did was hand out bottled water – not a good idea for people having to wait that long in line. Retrieving our luggage yet again after landing somewhere in the United States, we were slightly more alert than zombies but in one piece. After enduring customs, we made our final connection not into Tampa but Orlando, still a two-hour drive away from home. Now I know why the Pope always kissed the ground when he got off a plane. Indeed, aerial antics add to the adventure of traveling to distant places – this time to a land of a billion people where sacred cows really do wander down the street undisturbed.

J.C. and I at dinner on a Celebrity cruise ship.

The following year Mike and I got to enjoy the change of seasons, barely observable in Florida, not once but twice. Gladly leaving late summer's oppressive heat and humidity behind, we flew on an internet special from Orlando to Anchorage. Our friend Rick first took us an hour north up into heavenly Archangel Valley near Hatcher Pass, already ablaze with autumn hues. Like a scene out of *The Wizard of Oz*, the three of us hiked along merrily on a lush carpet of kaleidoscopic color, grazing on blueberries and digitally harvesting fields of white-tufted 'Arctic cotton' grass. Here, on the last day of August, 2006, we wore jackets. On the horizon we watched distant peaks of the Alaska Range take on salmon shades of alpenglow as the darkness of fall's lengthening night descended.

A photographer's paradise the first two weeks of September, Alaska has few main roads to travel, but any turnoff yields boundless opportunities for exploration. Stalks of crimson fireweed and amber grass floated in a sea of magenta shrubs and rusty bushes bearing red-orange berries. Stately stands of blue-gray spruce and golden groves of aspen conspired to create reflections of halting beauty in the still waters of prolific ponds. Majestic mountainscapes were even mirrored in puddles and potholes. A gastronomic adventure awaited us in the town of Talkeetna, where we were pleasantly surprised by the taste of fiddleback fern. Its still-furled tips sautéed in garlic butter proved tender tidbits. Nothing quite describes, from a hundred miles away, the sight of Mt. McKinley's overarching great white form rising into the cobalt firmament. Lady Beauty is everywhere to be found, but Alaska may well be the land of her birth.

Spilling out of unseen ice fields, melting glaciers send milky rivers of silt running to the sea, carelessly stripping logs of their bark, strewing them like toothpicks on gravel bars that part their hurried waters. Under a crystal blue sky, we bounced along by bus through Denali National Park's interior, all the way to Wonder Lake, past vistas that left us breathless. Freezing temperatures that night left us sleepless inside an unheated tent, poorly protected from the numbing cold. That discouraged further efforts on our part to avoid steep tariffs on scarce lodging. Perfect weather accompanied our day-long trek across the most photogenic stretch of dirt road in the country, the hundred-mile Denali 'highway.' Kettle lakes, ringed round with spruce and pocked with raised clumps of grass called tussocks, sparkled in the sunlight. Thousands of these depressions in the earth were formed by icebergs left behind by glaciers moving across the Alaskan tundra. As the ice melted, they slowly filled with water to become lakes. Approaching the border of Canada's wild Yukon Territory, we passed through a tiny outpost with the curious name of Chicken. I've wanted to visit the Yukon ever since watching Sergeant Preston as a child when television shows were still in black and white. In contrast to the unpleasant ordeal Mike and I experienced the last time we tried to enter Canada, this was a snap.

Long-abandoned hilltop boulders splotched with black and tan and pale green lichens dotted our route across the aptly named Top of the World highway. We passed through technicolored highlands contoured ages ago by great moving mountains of ice. A solitary grizzly determinedly sauntered past. We ferried across the Klondike River at Jack London's Dawson City, scenically situated at its confluence with the mighty Yukon. Completing our circle through the Yukon Territory, we found ourselves surrounded by sweeping panoramas in Canada's Kluane National Park. Excitedly we headed toward the beckoning summits of Wrangell-Saint Elias for our second foray into America's largest national park. This time we ventured fifty miles into the interior to the tiny town of Nabesna. A veritable rainbow of frosted ferns, blanched leaves, stiffened sedge, overhanging branches, and moss-covered rocks lined the gurgling purple brook that wound its way through pristine forest. The massive Matanuska Glacier stretched its glistening toe down into the long valley stretching out ahead of us, pointing the way home.

Finally, from Eagle River Mike and I headed south to the small town of Hope, the solitary settlement on the southern shore of Turnagain Arm. Originally thought to be a river, this body of water was so named because the English explorer Captain Cook had to keep turning his ship around while searching unsuccessfully for the Northwest Passage. At Hope we learned the hard way not to walk on the beach – a deep layer of glacial silt that immediately sucked us in up to our knees. A brilliant sunset over the water made up for this faux-pas. From Whittier, we set out on a waterborne excursion to the northwestern reaches of Prince William Sound, observing colonies of harbor seals resting on the rocks, and leopard seals lounging on ice floes. The crack of a 'calving' iceberg resounded like cannon fire from time to time, releasing a small tidal wave that rippled across the ice-choked surface of the frigid water – one of a dozen spectacles making this, our third Alaskan adventure, every bit as remarkable as the first two.

Between India and Alaska, you'd think Mike and I had had enough flying for one year. But with a week of vacation left, we were at it again three weeks later, winging our way toward Grand Teton National Park in Wyoming. It was the second week of October, 2006. Winter was right around the corner. Using award travel, the easiest place to get to was Idaho Falls. From there we drove up and around through Yellowstone, so much less crowded in the fall – chilly, but as steamy and colorful as ever. Yellowstone all but shuts down with the first snowfall. That happened a day or two later.

Heavy clouds hung over us most of the time, making the few still-leafy aspens on the hillsides pop out all the more, like orange dots. Mike and I did some heavy duty hiking on this trip, but later we rested our weary bones in Granite Hot Springs, a natural thermal pool exuding a faint odor of sulfur, hidden in the woods an hour's drive away. After walking six miles into Paintbrush Canyon and several thousand feet up to Holly Lake, with the fresh scent of pine in the air, it smelled like Christmas. We climbed even higher, though not as far, to wintry Surprise and Amphitheatre Lakes. These glacial bodies of water are surrounded by sharp peaks and subalpine meadows, absent wildflowers but strewn with lichen-encrusted rocks and dusted with patches of frost. They take on an otherworldly appearance at this time of year. To the lone observer, the long shadows and slightly muted colors of autumn possess a tranquil beauty all their own. Only the faint trickle of streams, the honk of itinerant geese, and the far-off trumpeting of rutting elk interrupted the blissful silence.

Overnight it snowed, heavily enough to make Jackson Hole look like another place, as though God had dumped a bag of powdered sugar on the peaks. Unaccustomed to being in the car before dawn to catch the sunrise on the Tetons across a pond, Mike and I, still half- asleep, were startled by a solitary buffalo galloping across the plain that nearly careened into us. More crisp than before, even the air seemed tantalized by the mountains' newly-donned white coat. A ptarmigan joined us on the trail, cleverly cloaked by nature's soggy patchwork of pine needles and fallen leaves on the snow-bitten ground. Finally the sun began to pierce the morning mist, revealing a picture-perfect winter wonderland as we ascended through the forest to the heights. The heavy falling snow had stripped the aspens of their remaining leaves, pale yellow at best, unveiling their white-barked bodies and leaving their denuded branches pointing empty skyward. By the next day, however, except on the peaks, the snow disappeared as quickly as it had come.

A gloriously sunny morning on our last day propelled Mike and me to go the distance – an ascent of three thousand feet over ten miles one-way – to Marion Lake, our longest hike ever. At an elevation of ten thousand feet, our destination – at the very top of the Tetons – lay at the head of majestic Granite Canyon. As usual, we passed only a couple of people all day, and it was windy and cold when we finally arrived and ate the apples and granola bars we'd carried. Getting all the way back down before dark didn't appear to be a problem. It was always faster and easier coming down than going up, though harder on the knees. I tend to trip over more rocks than Mike does, but sturdy hiking boots kept us from doing any damage to ourselves. Neither of us had difficulty breathing in the thin air. But we were not anticipating the problem we were about to encounter.

Our friend Rick had just given me a book to read on bear attacks in Alaska. I'd just finished reading it on the plane, in fact – scary stuff. This was Wyoming. Bears were getting ready to go to sleep for the winter, and we hadn't even seen one on this trip. That changed quickly. Amid the lengthening shadows still a couple of miles from the trailhead, *four* bears materialized at once – a mother with her three cubs – a dangerous situation. I don't know if I was more scared or less scared as a result of reading that book, but I was scared. Mike on the other hand seemed content videotaping the ursine family steadily moving toward us on the trail. It took a minute to persuade him that we needed to take evasive action at once, but I finally prevailed upon him.

So, speaking softly – imploring the bears in dulcet tones not to eat us – we slowly backed away in an attempt to disappear into the thicket along the stream that cut through the bottom of the deep valley we were in. No cell phone signal, of course.

Anxiously clawing our way through the willows and scrambling across the rocks, we got scratched and wet and cold, but we made it to the other side. Hoping the bears would lose our scent, we tried to put as much distance between us as possible. Making headway through the scrub where no trail exists is slow. Between the dense vegetation and the rapidly descending darkness, my heart was still pounding as we finally crossed back over downstream, hoping the coast would be clear. It was. We had not become dinner after all. We couldn't wait to get back to civilization. By the dim beam of a flashlight we hurried the last couple of miles, finally collapsing into the safety of the car, exhausted but relieved.

Priests and friends forever.

XXIV   KEEPING UP THE PACE

In November, Bishop Larkin – my first pastor, mentor, and friend – died. He was a great believer in the power of stewardship, as I've always been, attempting to practice sacrificial giving in my life as well as challenging my parishioners to do the same, with considerable success. For that reason, I was pleased to accept Mike's invitation to preach on stewardship at his parish, St. Thomas Aquinas in New Port Richey, at the beginning of Advent. Stewardship takes time to grow, but even in these troubled economic times, St. Thomas is doing well. After the holidays Mike and I took our kayaks and his Hi-Lo down to the Everglades for a few days as 2007 began. In February we spent a week in Hawaii, taking advantage of a package deal I found online for a bargain basement price. This time we just relaxed and went to the beach – like everyone else who goes to Hawaii. Not even bringing cameras, we took bus rides around Honolulu and walked a great deal, all the way from Diamond Head back to Waikiki, along the waterfront searching for seafood, and scouting the length of the beach each morning for the best breakfast special. Though small, we found the Aquarium fascinating, as well as a couple of pieces of jade jewelry and a couple of Hawaiian shirts. Another pleasant surprise was being treated to native island music, song, and dance at Sunday Mass.

Of course, life can't be all fun and games and going places. My work assisting parishes always comes first. I've found the trick is traveling smart – efficiently – by doing your homework and planning carefully well in advance. Things don't always go as planned, but that's the best way to make the most of your time and money. For me, getting away frequently is more gratifying than staying a long time. As a rule, the farther away you're going, the longer you should stay. Anyone can become a better travel planner with practice, and these days, the internet is an indispensable tool.

'Writing your own ticket' usually saves time and money. Anticipation is half the fun.

Another small way I found to serve a group of people I had an affinity with was as chaplain for CALIX, a little-known Catholic organization for people affiliated with Alcoholics Anonymous – whether members, spouses or relative of members, or persons otherwise affected by alcohol abuse. Effectively 'in recovery' one way or another, everyone drawn to CALIX benefits from the mutual support gained by sharing the Eucharist and meeting together monthly. CALIX – the Latin word for chalice – continues to flourish under the auspices of St. Jerome Parish on Indian Rocks Beach. In all honesty, most participants are recovering Catholics to some degree as well, having become inactive or disillusioned with the Church at some point. CALIX's only end is to foster personal spiritual growth. That in turn comes from choosing to view life in such a way that the good always outweighs the bad.

For five months in 2007, I was called back to active duty, so to speak. Bishop Lynch asked me to take care of St. James Parish in Pasco County – just a few miles north of Mike's parish – for an unspecified period of time. An hour's drive from home, St. James was a little too far to commute, so I had to close up shop as it were in Clearwater, at least for the time being. I was concerned that for the first time in twenty years, I'd be sharing a house with another priest, but I rarely saw him and we got along fine, so it was never a problem. However briefly, I somewhat ironically reprised the very role I had struggled so long to give up, that of pastor – technically 'administrator,' but still the guy in charge. I wasn't supposed to make any big changes, and I didn't. But thrown into this role, one instantly inherits the politics that go with making any decision at all.

Coming from another diocese, my predecessor had only been administrator of St. James for eight months before his departure without much explanation. During that time, he had changed a great deal, mostly in an attempt to take the parish back in time to what he perceived as the golden age of the Church. There seems to be a lot of that going on these days, particularly with younger members of the clergy. That did not particularly endear him to the parishioners, now wondering what would happen next. Though he vowed to return, he never did, though no one knew that at the time.

Though only a short distance from Pinellas, until I lived and worked in Pasco County, I never realized how different it is. As bad as the traffic on U.S. 19 in Pinellas is, it's worse in Pasco. In general, life in Pinellas is tame by comparison to Pasco. For one thing, a great many of Pasco's residents come from New York and are of Italian descent. However, contrary to the stereotype of New Yorkers as uncaring people, I found the parishioners of St. James to be affectionate and gregarious. They certainly took a liking to me. So did the parish staff, except for three who made it clear they were loyal to my predecessor – as though I had anything to do with his absence. Painfully awaiting his return, they made it clear they had no use for me. I guess they needed to feel they were in charge, so for the most part, I let them.

Like all the parishes in Pasco, St. James has a lot of funerals. From the moment the parish was notified of a death, every grieving family received personalized attention from Anna Hart, herself a widow and a woman of great compassion. No one was more devoted to St. James than Anna, a knowledgeable leader in the liturgical life of the parish as well. Ministry to the bereaved is a critical component of pastoral ministry. Every pastor prays for a person in their parish as sensitive and capable as Anna. Today I count Anna, a Brit by birth with a disposition as intense as my own, and her husband Andre, a biking Dutchman, among my friends.

While I was at St. James, something bizarre happened that I know I'll never forget. It wasn't funny at the time, but it got Holy Week off to a bang and made all the papers. After the procession into church on Palm Sunday, the microphone outside was still live. Teenagers hanging out in the parking lot stealthily grabbed the open mike and started shouting rap lyrics into it, complete with expletives. Their voices boomed through the church. Taken by surprise and shocked at what they were hearing, parishioners couldn't do much but grin and bear it. New Yorkers are pretty tough and even the old ladies in church had probably heard worse. I've learned that the best thing for a presider to do when there's a disturbance is nothing. If I had reacted wildly, so would everyone else and we'd have had a panic. The disruption didn't last long anyhow, as a group of men in the church took off chasing the kids through the neighborhood and uttering some unholy words of their own, I'm told. One of them fell and broke his ankle. The cops noticed the commotion and gave chase of their own. With the kids in custody, I was put in the position of having to decide what to do. I just didn't have the heart to press charges. I myself got June off for good behavior.

I can honestly say I enjoyed my time at St. James and did my best despite the awkwardness of the situation I was given. I became quite popular simply by letting things go back to the way they were before my predecessor started changing them. The bishop asked me if I would be willing to stay, but by mid-summer he appointed another priest pastor – the fourth the parish had had in thirteen months. I also enjoyed every minute I spent at Bishop Larkin, the struggling interparochial school adjacent to St. James with the most lovable principal in the world – Sr. Regina Ozuzu from Nigeria. Celebrating Mass for graduation was a proud moment for me as well as for the kids.

Hoping to get the jump on the hordes of tourists that descend on California's national parks each summer, Mike and I headed straight for California. If you love narrow winding roads endlessly twisting up and down, the Sierra Nevadas are the place to find them. After touring Crystal Cave, which has an unusual iron gate shaped like a spider web at its entrance, in Sequoia National Park, we hugged the side of one cliff after another to get out to Mineral King. At road's end, we began climbing through a picturesque alpine valley filled with elk, along a rocky stream still rushing with the spring thaw. We finally reached Monarch Lake, a turquoise jewel set in a rocky glacial bowl called a cirque, completely surrounded by snow-capped peaks. Such incredible natural beauty never grows old and is always a feast for the eyes. Strangely, Mike's Yukon sputtered on the way back to the campground. Careful observation under the hood revealed the telltale signs of hungry marmots that had gnawed insulation and spark plug wires, causing only minor damage. Groves of giant sequoias are scattered throughout the Sierras, as well as thunderous waterfalls like Grizzly and Roaring River in adjacent Kings Canyon National Park, a place as grandiose as its name. Several banded snakes eyed us hiking along a splashing stream to an unusual canyon where falling waters pooled in pure white marble rock.

These scenic wonders were only the prelude to the splendors hidden in Yosemite Valley – among earth's most precious natural treasures. Even the high and mighty would be humbled hiking along such massive walls of rock so close to rivers of freefalling water crashing onto boulders. The tranquil sight of Yosemite's sheer peaks and smooth domes at sunset is beyond compare. Mike and I survived the daring climb through cold, blowing mist to the brink of mighty Nevada Falls. Timidly we stepped out onto the bald promontory of Glacier Point, surveying a dozen cataracts carving the wooded slopes beneath.

Splashed with lupines, foxglove, and tiger lilies, the northern California coast boasts a rainbow of wildflowers in late spring. Churning chasms, crashing breakers, and spouting horns spewing showers of sea foam all invite closer inspection. An array of miniscule marine life – mussels, starfish, anemones, and sea urchins – teems at a slower pace in secluded tidepools. Patches of orange poppies and purple irises poke through the verdant coastal cloak. Waves of white cow parsnip wash right up against the pounding surf. Miles of beached boulders and shipwrecked rocks stretch out like great greystone whales on the horizon. These led us toward taller trees – the silent redwood sentries guarding California's coastal forest ranges. Rare Roosevelt elk roam by the sea, near a sheltered canyon with emerald green walls of ferns fifty feet high.

The quaint antique lighthouses sprinkled along the Oregon coast no longer signal ships, but manned by volunteers, their beacons still sweep land and sea. Driftwood-littered beaches and offshore sea stacks, remnants of long-eroded headlands, also beckon the curious. The weather at Crater Lake was a mixed bag containing sun, clouds, snow, rain, and fog – in other words, the usual. A spin on a jet boat up the thrashing Rogue River into Hellgate Canyon provided a wild ride, tempered by the soundless subterranean splendor of Oregon Caves National Monument. Arboretums abound along the coast as well as opportunities to savor fresh seafood. Mike and I took a moment to sit in the crotch of a Pacific coast landmark, the enormous Sitka spruce at Cape Meares known as the Octopus Tree. We heard the snort of stellar sea lions lounging at the base of nearby cliffs. Finally we came upon an expanse of grassy sand dunes decorating the coast, and a sphagnum moss bog filled with carnivorous plants.

Mount Hood towered resplendently over the lush valley of the mighty Columbia River where Mike and I hiked to some of the photogenic waterfalls idyllically situated along the gorge. From the Washington side, we climbed Beacon Rock and toured the Bonneville Dam and a textile factory, before visiting the peaceful forested grounds of the Grotto, a Marian shrine in Portland, and the world-famous rose gardens downtown. With the sweet scent and dazzling display of roses in bloom freshly imprinted on our senses, we bid farewell to the City of Roses to begin the familiar cross-country trek home.

This trip provided with me with the inspiration for several new paintings. I was pleased to exhibit my work for the first time in November of 2007 along with other area artists at a show sponsored by St. Thomas in New Port Richey. I feel welcome at a lot of parishes, but since leaving All Saints, St. Thomas is the one where I feel most at home. Certainly part of the reason is that the pastor is my best friend, but I'm also proud to have guided the parish a few years ago in making modifications to their worship space. Few parishes enjoy the quality of liturgy and music that St. Thomas does today. Amazed and thrilled at having sold a dozen paintings on my first attempt, I thought it only fair to give a portion of the proceeds back to the parish.

Before the end of the year, Mike and I got away for a week on a Caribbean cruise out of Tampa. We find this a great, relatively inexpensive way to relax in our own backyard, as it were – one we try to take advantage of nearly every year.

Light of Christ Parish near my home in Clearwater is fortunate to have Jacob Monteleone, a gregarious, down-home Cajun, as pastor. Having become something of a fixture there over the past few years, I was honored to accept his invitation to give a parish mission during Holy Week in March of 2008. Traditionally, missionary priests went around attempting to scare sinners into repentance by any means possible – the more dramatic, the better. That's not me. People respond to my preaching because it's down to earth. So the theme I chose was simply 'Following Jesus Today.' In other words, what does it take to be a disciple in the twenty-first century? My answer to that is that it doesn't take more of the same old-time religion. It takes authentic spirituality – trust and letting go. That's what I talked about, as well as gratitude and happiness. Talking about sin is useless without giving examples of grace. Conversion is the work of a lifetime, an ongoing process. The response was enthusiastic. The parish was energized. I was humbled. I'm thrilled at having the opportunity to give this three-day series of talks again in March, 2011, at St. Michael the Archangel Parish in Hudson.

At the end of May, Mike and I set off on perhaps our most intrepid outdoor adventure to date – exploring a vast, spectacularly colorful area of southern Utah designated as Grand Staircase-Escalante National Monument in 1996. We had ventured through this desolate region before, but never into its heart to observe the throbbing life of the desert up close. Now we wanted to navigate its very arteries – the slot canyons hidden along Hole-In-The-Rock Road, named for a natural crevice in the sheer cliff overlooking Lake Powell at its end. The 'road' itself is sixty brutal miles of burning hot sand and tire-gouging gravel, but it's the only way to access some of the most extraordinarily beautiful and secret places on earth. For the most part, trails here are not marked and precise information is difficult to come by. This makes the challenge of finding these mysterious vaulted sandstone corridors an even more compelling proposition. But we succeeded, negotiating Peekaboo Canyon's rather short length and broad arched passageways without too much effort. Foreboding as its name implies, Spooky Canyon – about as tight and narrow in places as a human being can squeeze through – proved more difficult, causing Mike and me to wonder whether we were going to make it through or not, and what we would do if we couldn't. Neither of us is claustrophobic, but the only thing that got us to the other end was being able to see the sky above. Having twisted my body into every known configuration and then some, conquering Spooky Canyon was probably the greatest physical contest of my life thus far.

Standing on the amazing sandstone 'Wave.'

The quirky, eroded rock formations in Devil's Garden were impressive. We were pleasantly surprised not to have to wade through the hip-deep water we expected to find in Tunnel Canyon. After meandering an hour through a scorching desert full of rattlesnakes, never knowing for sure whether we were going in the right direction or not, the beauty we found inside Zebra Canyon was truly otherworldly. Ascending a hill of sand between narrowing stone walls conducted us through an inconspicuous portal in the rock. Suddenly we found ourselves climbing great steps of sand into the cathedral-like chambers of the canyon, its slightly slanted vertical walls of striated stone buttressed against the sky. Celestial golden light shone from above. Striped with strands of white, Zebra Canyon's undulating walls of mauve and tan are smooth, except where embedded with heavy iron nuggets. Privileged few ever behold the beauty of this secret, sacred place. A feeling of awe, like being in church, came over us.

Hiking through a bizarre landscape littered by boulders spewed forth as volcanic bombs, Mike and I arrived at secluded Upper Calf Creek Falls where – moistened by a thin strand of water flowing from a spring-fed pool – the desert blooms prolifically. Only a few inches of rain fall here each year, leaving the shallow waters of the Escalante River to sustain life in these arid canyonlands. Slogging our way along, Mike and I came upon several stone arches and a natural bridge concealed within the stained orange cliffs lining the stream. Then, on the way to the north rim of the Grand Canyon, we cooled off at Bryce Canyon, where a solitary patch of snow still clung to the side of a slope. That night we made camp amid the pines at Jacob Lake.

Coming back up the Kaibab Trail after a daylong descent into the Grand Canyon's glorious depths, we spotted heavy gray clouds gathering. It was the fourth of June. Within an hour, a freak snowstorm dropped the temperature to freezing. Quickly coating the forest with white, the blizzard also felled a tree across the road, temporarily immobilizing us. Somehow the fragile yellow blossoms on the cliffrose bushes managed not to wilt. Heartier pink cactus flowers poked their way through the snow. Mike and I made our way back slowly through the slush. The forest roads were still slippery with mud the next day, but we managed to reach some obscure overlooks of the Grand Canyon seldom visited by anyone but squirrels. A panorama of land and sky stretched out beneath us for a hundred miles at Crazy Jug Point. From Toroweap, too, we stared down at the ageless Colorado, rushing violently three thousand feet below. Upstream we watched the river rolling more calmly through Marble Canyon and around Horseshoe Bend. From Lake Powell, Mike and I climbed a treacherous dirt road miles up the side of the Kaiparowits Plateau, a massive eroded landform that features some of the most brilliantly colored cliffs and sandstone formations in the world. The vistas of Lake Powell from this desolate high desert plain were like scenes on another planet.

We could not leave this land of cottonwood-lined washes and vermillion cliffs without a foray into the mother of all slot canyons, Buckskin Gulch, the longest and deepest in the world. Getting to the trailhead required a painfully long, slow ride on a badly rutted gravel road with the descriptive name of House Rock Valley. Threading our way like ants through tight Wire Pass down into the narrow, curving canyon of the mostly dry Paria River literally paved with rocks, Mike and I were awestruck staring up hundreds of feet at the base of sheer orange sandstone walls, glowing as if red-hot in the noon-day sun. Few places in our travels have made a deeper impression on us than this, but an even more extraordinary phenomenon – one that has never been equaled – awaited our discovery the next day.

This happened not by accident but only as a result of winning one of ten highly-coveted permits in a lottery conducted online months in advance by the Bureau of Land Management. Had the hiking gods not smiled upon us, Mike and I would never have gotten to visit the 'Wave' that day or any other. With detailed instructions and topographic map in hand, we set out across three unmarked miles of rugged, blazing desert to find it. After being blasted by occasional bursts of wind-whipped sand, we set our eyes at last upon our destination – the Holy Grail of hikers and photographers alike. Arguably the most fantastic rock formation in the world, the 'Wave' is set like a hidden gem on a slope in the spectacular Coyote Buttes straddling the Utah-Arizona border. An incredible sandstone swirl in the earth formed over millions of years, the 'Wave' took shape as ancient sand dunes were compacted and calcified by natural forces, then sculpted into smooth, undulating forms by the erosive action of wind and rain. The hard-packed layers of maroon, pink, white, yellow, and amber sand have tiny fragile ridges that require treading carefully. Setting foot on the 'Wave' was a once-in-a-lifetime thrill. But Mike and I feel privileged to have witnessed the breathtaking beauty of this whole amazing land – a place called Escalante.

Dwarfed by giant waves of desert sand frozen by time.

Work, of course, was waiting for both of us when we got back from vacation. Mike O'Brien followed Mike Lydon as pastor of St. Justin Martyr in Largo. All three of us grew up in the same neighborhood and parish in St. Petersburg, St. Jude, the Andrews and O'Briens just a couple of blocks apart. Having put up the same multi-purpose building in Spring Hill as Mike Lydon had at St. Justin and I had at All Saints twenty years before, Mike O'Brien asked for my help – knowing of my work on the Diocesan Commission for Liturgical Art, Architecture, and Environment and my familiarity with St. Justin. The parish wanted to refresh their home with a 'facelift' – a low-budget non-structural renovation of their worship space for their twentieth anniversary. Happy to take up the challenge, I put on my liturgical consultant's hat. After listening to the ideas of parishioners and conferring with both Mikes, by July I came up with a detailed proposal and design I felt would meet their budget and their needs. The new configuration for St. Justin was a rather daring reversal of the current orientation of their worship space – one that had always seemed backward to the three of us. Everyone liked it, and St. Justin engaged an architect and contractor to build it. If I say so myself, the finished product not only looks great, but it works very well. Of course it wouldn't be much good if it didn't. The parishioners of St. Justin are proud of their renewed worship space, and so am I.

Mom and Dad sold their condominium overlooking the Intracoastal Waterway across from St. Pete Beach in the summer of 2005 and moved to their new home at Lake Seminole Square – a large retirement center not far away where assisted living would be available if and when they needed it. With friendly neighbors and staff, their main meal provided each day, and an array of opportunities for healthy living and recreation, they took to it like ducks to water. Dad's ninetieth birthday was approaching in October of 2008, so Mom, my sisters, and I set about planning a great celebration. Brendan Muldoon was kind enough to let us have the party at St. Jerome. Beth and Julie sent out invitations and conjured up a terrific menu, music-themed decorations, and the requisite birthday cake. My brother Mark flew in a couple of days before to help get everything set up, along with in-laws, nieces, nephews, and family friends like Mike. I put a slide show of Dad's life together – from baby pictures through World War II to organ concerts – and Mike entertained on the guitar. Rather than use a caterer, we ourselves wined and dined at least a hundred guests in style – some our family had known since coming to Florida more than forty years ago – including some wonderful priests.

An elegant affair, Dad's party was a classy celebration of life and a labor of love. A family friend played the harp during a second celebration two days later – on a smaller scale but just as lovely – with Mom and Dad's friends at Lake Seminole Square. With all six members of the family present, we recalled a great many memories of our lives together over the years, making this time all the more precious. After all, life is short. We never know how much time we have left. We knew that Mom, going on eighty-four, wouldn't have long. Our world had been rocked only a few weeks earlier by the discovery that she had cancer. By now everyone knew. Heaven was already being besieged with prayers for her. Rather than let this unwanted news put a damper on Dad's party, without a word it became for everyone a celebration of Mom's life as well as Dad's, and of their life of sixty years together. No one could see the feeding tube Mom knew she would need that was under her dress. The beautiful smile on her face at Dad's party never waned. She started chemo and radiation the very next day.

My sister Julie and I at Mom's wake.

XXV   GOING THE DISTANCE

Mom died less than ten months later, in July of 2009. The type of cancer she had – esophageal – is fairly rare and was fairly advanced by the time it was found, primarily as a result of the difficulty she was having swallowing. Her kidneys were already failing and dialysis was looming. It was just her time to go, and her courage in accepting the fact that her days on earth were drawing down remains an inspiration to us all. I'm convinced her own great faith and the love of her family is what made it possible for her to know when it was time to let go. Life will never be the same for me or for any of us kids, and least of all for Dad. He's enjoying life reasonably well at ninety-two, but it's not as much fun without Mom. Mom did the only thing she could do with Dad – leave him with us. She left us with each other.

Despite the success of her treatment, watching Mom lose weight and much of her strength over those months was an unwelcome reminder that none of us are going to live forever, at least not in this world. Because she was alright with that, we were able to be, even though it went against our natural instinct to want to hold on. That I believe was her greatest gift to us, yet one so typical for her – to be more concerned for those she would leave behind than for herself. But that is what a mother's love is all about, and it never ends, even with death. That's what's so brilliant about having Mary, the mother of Jesus, as the mother of priests and the mother of the Church. God knows we need her. Immortalized in Michelangelo's *Pieta*, the image of Mary seated, slightly slumped with grief, cradling the body of her dead Son, our great High Priest, in her arms says it all. She gave us Jesus, but before they gave Jesus back to her, Jesus gave her to us. That classic image speaks volumes to me about God's love for the world and everyone in it, and about my mother's love for me. It's all one mystery Mom understands perfectly by now.

Even during these difficult months, there were redemptive moments, especially for my youngest sister Beth, who along with Dad displayed uncommon valor in overseeing Mom's constant care, and who has now become the 'little Mother' in overseeing Dad's well-being. Two weeks before Mom's death, the extended family gathered to celebrate her and Dad's sixtieth wedding anniversary. With everyone present, I celebrated a Mass of thanksgiving in the newly-refurbished worship space at St. Justin. In her wheelchair, surrounded by so much love – human and divine – Mom was in her element and in her glory, and the strength of her spirit shone.

Hospice provided compassionate support and advice to Beth as well as Mom and Dad during the last few weeks of Mom's life. They always do. Providentially, after Sunday Mass the day before she died, I brought Mom Viaticum – 'food for the journey' – in the form of Holy Communion. Dad and I had no way of knowing it would be but hours before her communion with her Maker would be complete. The call that she was nearing death came Monday morning as I was celebrating Mass at Light of Christ. Being at my mother's side as she peacefully breathed her last has been the most poignant moment of my life thus far – as sacred as it was painful. That scene – Dad, Julie and her family, Beth and I gathered round Mom at home in her favorite chair, holding on until it was time to let go – is indelibly etched in my mind. Mike arrived moments later. As we walked with Mom's body down the long hall to the hearse, he gently recited the touching prayers for one who has just died.

Knowing the day would be coming, I had prepared a visual tribute to Mom, a slide show of her life, for her wake. Hundreds of friends came to the funeral home where Mom's body, white-beaded rosary in hand, was laid out in her favorite blue dress, with a couple of tissues tucked up her sleeve at the last minute by my madcap sisters. Difficult as it was, I celebrated Mom's funeral Mass and gave the homily at Blessed Sacrament Church in Seminole. Every member of my family took part in the liturgy, and a dozen priests joined me at the altar. Well-crafted music accompanied by organ and harp lifted our spirits, including the now famous *Gloria* Dad composed forty years ago, and a song of farewell lovingly sung by Mike. By his presence and with his own kind words, Bishop Lynch touched the hearts of all present and perhaps healed a few. I can't imagine what Dad was feeling as we took Mom's body to Calvary Cemetery. She would be the first to find rest in the crypt they bought there years before. They hadn't planned it that way, but then life rarely goes as planned. Mike had buried his dad only two months before, and in a reversal of roles, I had helped his family through their ordeal. For years, Mike and I had talked about having to deal with the death of our parents, wondering who would be the first to go. Now, in two months, two were gone.

Life goes on, however, and it's a good thing it does. Even if Mike and I had known we were going to lose two of our parents in such short order, sitting around waiting for them to die wouldn't have helped them or us. Life is for the living. In November of 2008, ten years after our first trip, the two of us went back to Thailand for a week. We still had a bank of air miles to use up, and Northwest was offering a big discount on vacation packages to Asia. It may sound strange, but having enjoyed ourselves so much on our first trip to Bangkok in May of 1998, we stayed at the same hotel and revisited the same exotic places – the glittering Grand Palace, the chaotic 'Floating Market' at Damnoen Saduak, and the tranquil ruins of Ayutthaya. We spent a couple of days just riding up and down the dirty Chao Phraya River in longboats, taking in the bawdy sights, the clanging sounds, and the tantalizing smells of the city – walking like ants amid the crush of its twelve million youthful inhabitants, and visiting every temple and market, every shadowy shop and boisterous bazaar in our path. Though not as steamy and stagnant as before, a pall of polluted air still hung over Bangkok, muting the sun's glow on the parapets of its gilded pagodas.

The glitz and glamour of Thailand becomes even more apparent at night, never more so than during the annual 'festival of lights' – Loy Krathong – Mike and I were fortunate to witness. Under the light of a full moon, we walked blocks through Bangkok's open-air fresh flower market, immersed in an endless stream of human traffic along a wall of vendors' stalls bursting with a riot of colors. On this night millions of Thais take to the streets with their homemade floats – made from banana leaves and palm branches, decorated with flowers, candles, sparklers, incense sticks, and coins – to set them adrift on the nearest body of water. Bangkok itself is interlaced with hundred of *khlongs* or canals all flowing into the Chao Phraya. Originally intended to appease the water gods, today Loy Krathong is largely an excuse to have fun. It was great fun for us to watch people flocking shoulder to shoulder in earnest to the water's edge to launch their luminescent floral offerings. Even in the street where most of it is consumed, Thai food is to die for, but Mike and I drew the line at deep-fried grasshoppers and grubs. The vroom of bumboats, brooding buddhas, dragons and garudas, the scent of orchids and the taste of spice make Bangkok one of my favorite places, one I hope I'll see again.

Another new year dawned. It was now 2009. Mike and I took a week to revisit another familiar place, the canyonlands we know so well in Utah. The drive across the Rockies from Denver in January always depends on the weather, but clear skies made it go without a hitch. To be sure, it was cold. There was ice on the Colorado River and on the steep switchbacks we would have to negotiate to get down onto the White Rim. Even with four-wheel drive, however, making the descent under these conditions was too risky. Though there was precious little left to eat in the desert, bighorn sheep were grazing on the gnarled stumps of juniper bushes. The brittle black branches of willows beside dried-up washes stood out against patches of dirty white frost on the shaded ground. Clusters of tall dead grass and frozen weeds stood motionless on the desert's crusty floor. Long shadows played on crevices in the slickrock, concealing great arches in plain sight. Then, as if by magic, fresh snow fell like flour through heaven's sieve, reviving the thirsty desert, fashioning from its barrenness even greater beauty.

In Utah's wild backcountry, the earth bares her soul as nowhere else. Every shade of color ingrained in her carpet of sand, etched in her great stone bluffs, and hidden in her canyon depths reveals another facet of her ageless being. I find that peering into her inmost recesses unearths the secrets of her heart, and my own. Perhaps that's why Mike and I keep coming back.

Ready to ride my red 2009 Kawasaki Ninja.

Every now and then something happens that you don't expect. *Consumer Reports* routinely reviews certain models of new cars as well as other products. For the first time in years, the issue I was reading had a review of two small motorcycles. One was Kawasaki's 250cc Ninja. I rarely have such a strong reaction to an ad, but it was love at first sight. After keeping our 1982 Honda SilverWings for twenty-one years, Mike and I had been bikeless for the past seven. I had no idea how he would react, but I don't remember him putting up much resistance. At first I thought two guys our age might look silly riding 'crotch rockets,' as bikes like these that make teenage boys drool are commonly called. Then I thought, "If it's fun, who cares?"

My hopes were almost dashed when the first dealer we went to acted as though he could care less. The next one was more solicitous, and we were sold. Like most cars sold in the United States, most motorcycles are ridiculously overpowered. Getting nearly sixty miles to a gallon of gas, these are just right. They purr along nicely without making a lot of noise. Bikes aren't cheap, and while it was a stretch, we could actually afford to pay for these. Mine is red and Mike's is blue. Yes, I wear a full-faced helmet. In the traffic around here, I'd be crazy not to. I ride my Ninja to church whenever I can, which is almost all the time in Florida. Some people are amazed to see a priest walking into church with a helmet in hand. They'll get over it. They always do. Mike and I had forgotten just how much fun riding can be. I'm glad we finally remembered. Life is short enough as it is.

In June of 2009, shortly after Mike's father died and shortly before my mother's death, we spent three weeks revisiting some of our old haunts in Colorado. It was unseasonably cold and wet the whole time. Thunderstorms swept with majestic fury across proud blue skies, conjuring fantastic shapes and shadows in the clouds. Walking along the crest of the great sand dunes nestled in south central Colorado, it felt as though we had been transported to the Sahara, except for the weird juxtaposition of the snowy Sangre de Cristo peaks looming on all sides – like the strange juxtaposition of death to life, so close together yet so far apart. Watered by the nascent Rio Grande, the emerald plains of Alamosa wore an ultraviolet mantle of wild iris checked with lacy white cow parsnip, to the delight of the camera's eye. Unable to stay on top of rocks worn smooth by the ever-rushing waters, Mike and I splashed our way up a frigid silver stream gushing from a cave with ice-lined walls to a waterfall that left us shivering. Having a second pair of (dry) hiking boots at the ready saved the day.

Pale pink and orange and yellow cactus flowers punctuated the dusty cliffs of Mesa Verde, once inhabited by Native Americans. Protected by their sword-shaped leaves, stalks of ivory yucca flowers swayed in the breeze that blew across the jagged depths of the Black Canyon, carved by the relentless slicing of the Gunnison River through ancient metamorphic rock. Clinging to a sheer cliff face, Bridal Veil Falls watered Telluride's lush alpine valley, clothing its hills in spring green. Split-rail fences zigzagged across boulder-strewn fields sprinkled with powder blue forget-me-nots and golden aster. Lavender lupine, cobalt larkspur, and scarlet phlox added their embroidery to the patchwork of fragile color at our feet. Strung along the lofty ridge of the Continental Divide from Grand Lake to Estes Park, the Rockies sparkled like a necklace of pearls, like whitecaps on a sea of dark green waves. Snow dusted the gravel slopes above the forest's reach by night, only to melt by day and trickle down to rolling streams. Along their banks antlered elk and moose sipped peacefully. Dippers flitted, blue jays played, and columbines labored to lift their drooping crowns toward the sun. Amid the cooler climes of Colorado's ice-laden lakes, lichen-splotched rock fields, jubilant creeks, and pine-scented woodlands, Mike and I found rest and refreshment for our souls yet again.

As September began, we used still more frequent flier miles and the last ten days of vacation on our fourth trek to Alaska. With our ever-eager friend Rick Newsham in Eagle River, we had no fear treading into Archangel Valley again, where the hillsides had been painted with every color on autumn's palette. As we headed north, Mt. McKinley proudly flung her great white head, fully uncovered, into a cerulean sky. Wearing a rainbow of camouflage, the tundra marched toward Denali's slopes. Rivers of rusty foliage alternated with waves of amber grass washing up against golden groves of aspen immersed in forests of dark green spruce. A thick spread of snowy icing pressed down upon maroon mountains. Chalky rivers tumbled in braids down gravel valleys. After a grilled feast of halibut, salmon, and cod in Fairbanks, Rick and Mike and I bedded down beneath the stars in our trusty tent, unfazed by the freezing temperatures outside. Clean-burning catalytic heaters and air mattresses did the trick. Never have I seen a more glorious sunset filling a cloudless sky with glowing bands of sky-blue pink and gold late into the starry night.

Venturing even deeper into Alaska's sparsely populated interior, we entered new territory, exploring a land of picture-perfect lakes north of Fairbanks. Every shade of blue in the sky, every glimmer of green and spark of gold in the trees along their banks found flawless reflection on their mirror-like surface. A hundred miles west, we came to the quaint outpost of Manley Hot Springs at road's end without setting eyes on a single soul – except the soul of the Great Land itself. The vast Alaska Range – unparalleled in North America in its height and breadth – came into view as we traveled the length of the Denali Highway once more, stopping to photograph every distant glacier and silt-laden stream frothing with milky snowmelt. Along the way we were struck by the sight of an entire mountainside, already splayed with autumn's colors, stained by copper, nickel, platinum, and gold with a rainbow of metallic hues. Alpenglow descended softy on the mountains at dusk, slowly turning their snow-white peaks to pale pink points of light.

Rick's son Michael joined us on a hike seemingly to the top of the world overlooking Portage Glacier on the Kenai Peninsula. On the way we endured a nasty swarm of gnats. Finally, dwarfed by our proximity to the massive river of ice, we could see every detail in the huge swirls of compacted ice studding the glacier's surface and in the well-defined moraine – a dark ridge of rocky debris like a spine down the middle – as though we were only feet away. The brilliant waxy red leaves and berries of tundra plants at our feet caused us to tread lightly. Along Turnagain Arm at sunset, we happened to be in the right place at the right time to witness a rare natural phenomenon – the leading edge of an incoming high tide, a tidal bore. Mike and I had witnessed this unusual occurrence, like a miniature tidal wave, once before in 1978 on the Bay of Fundy in Canada. Even more of a coincidence is the fact that our friend Rick, a teenager at the time, was with us then, too. In this awesome land of the midnight sun, we watched as pink-edged clouds in a purple sky were set ablaze with a fiery orange glow.

The weather almost always deteriorates as one approaches the coast in Alaska, but even in cold drizzle and fog we were able to walk right up to the chunky blue slabs of creeping ice on the toe of Exit Glacier near Seward. Threads of butterscotch, tangerine, and gold were woven into the verdant velvet carpet covering the hillsides of the great glacier-spawned Matanuska River Valley. The high and mighty summits of the Wrangells – more massive and taller than the Rockies – rose up around us, their pure white caps of snow brighter than the sky itself, as they drew us deeper into their majestic domain along the road to Nabesna. In the morning light, no less than spectacular reflections appeared on the windless faces of the crystalline lakes at the mountains' feet. Made skittish by hunters swarming over the open range, a few reticent moose, some well-camouflaged ptarmigan, and a dashing auburn fox made the briefest of appearances. Deep inside Wrangell-Saint Elias National Park, we wandered again through the abandoned copper mine at Kennicott and along the crumpled edge of Root Glacier near the isolated settlement of McCarthy. Rain returned as we neared Valdez where even beneath gray skies, the soggy tundra reached down from Thompson Pass in all directions, a veritable kaleidoscope of color.

More than anywhere else in the world, the scenic splendor of Alaska has never ceased to pique Mike's and my curiosity or to capture our hearts. A few weeks before we caught up with Rick in Eagle River, however, I landed in Eagle River, Wisconsin for a few days. July of 2009 was the first time I'd driven back up north in eight years, passing through my old home town of Toledo on the way to visit and anoint my friend Vicki, suffering from frontotemporal dementia at her home near Lansing. After looking in on the Emerys at Harbor Springs on the shore of Lake Michigan, I zipped across the Upper Peninsula to join Mildred and her three adult children, staying on a chain of interconnected lakes in the heart of the 'Northwoods.' They had all rented jet skis, so I joined in the fun, even though it had been eighteen years since the last time I rode one. We had so much fun on these wicked water buggies that Mike joined us the following summer, as we tore up another chain of lakes in Minocqua, Wisconsin. On the way home, Mike and I spent a day with my brother and his family at their new home outside Chicago, with a quick hello to my buddy Tom Baker and his family in Indiana.

Family and friends have always been important to me, and my family has always been close. My bond with my siblings, and our bond with Dad, is closer than ever before. Just before Christmas in 2009, I joined my sister Julie and her husband Bill at their second home in Maggie Valley, North Carolina. It just so happened that the heaviest snowfall in sixteen years had just taken place, all but shutting down the town and making it impossible for us to drive up the mountain to get to their house. We had to lug everything a mile up the mountain, one cold, wet step at a time through knee-deep snow – and that was just the essentials, like groceries and winter clothes. We had to leave our cars parked in town for a couple of days, walking back down the mountain and back up again every time we needed to get something. Of course it was absolutely gorgeous, but trying to dig out from under a mountain of snow was hard work and more than we had bargained for. Under the circumstances, we were lucky to have heat and light, so we made the best of it. Much to our surprise, my nephew Joshua managed, barely, to drive up to the house with his family a few days later. The melting snow froze and turned to ice at night, making the steep one-lane mountain road even more treacherous. I had in fact slid off it previously on just one little patch of ice. How people put up with this sort of stuff all winter long up north I'll never know.

We picked up a 'flying saucer' and a sled in town that made hauling stuff up and down the mountain a little easier. It also made for a lot of fun flying down the long driveway without crashing into any trees. With my great niece Hanna and my sister's rambunctious dog, we all played in the snow as though we were still little kids. We had a ball building an anatomically correct snowwoman in the back yard. While I had to drive back to work on Christmas eve, these few days were the most fun and the whitest pre-Christmas I've had in years – though with Mom gone, the holidays would never be as merry for any of us as before.

The Andrews family at Dad's ninetieth birthday celebration.

XXVI   CHARTING MY COURSE

With my sister Beth turning fifty, and me turning sixty, two months apart in 2010, we decided to do something crazy to celebrate our landmark birthdays – even if everyone thought we were crazy for doing so. Together with Beth's two kids in college, Charlie and Carol Anne, we went skydiving for the first and probably only time. Believe it or not, this wasn't my idea, though no one had to twist my arm to get me to go along. It probably would never have happened except for the fact that my niece was going to school in Deland, halfway between Orlando and Daytona Beach, where she met the man who invented tandem skydiving. Mike and my brother-in-law Charlie Ford – neither of whom Beth or I could interest in our mad adventure – came along for moral support. While the four of us were airborne, the two of them kept each other company standing outside, looking up helplessly at the sky. Far from a fateful day, the fourth of March turned out to be unforgettably thrilling – at least for those of us who jumped out of a perfectly good airplane and paid good money to do so.

Actually, there were twelve people involved, thirteen if you count the pilot who flew us up to fourteen thousand feet before discharging his human cargo. Each of us had our own 'dive buddy' – the experienced skydiver to whom we were very firmly strapped – as well as our own personal photographer to video us on the way up and all the way down. These were not cheap thrills. The twelve of us filled a whole plane, so we got our own. It was clear and cold outside, about fifty degrees with a thirty mile-per-hour wind – at the altitude we jumped, more like thirty degrees, but we were too busy to notice. Our adrenaline was pumping. Just doing something like this with my youngest sister and my niece and nephew was exciting for me. Getting into our flight suits with all these people standing around making cute comments – our supporting cast, if you will – was hilarious. The only other things we put on were goggles and gloves.

Believe me, moving at a hundred and twenty miles per hour, you need them. I'm not talking about on the plane, I'm talking about my hundred and eighty-pound body falling through space. I looked like a blue banana.

Although the expression really doesn't apply, there's no foot-dragging on the way up to jump, so there's no opportunity to think about changing your mind once the plane has taken off. No one has to push you out of the plane. You're going down, that's all there is to it. Once the door is open and you're sitting on the edge with your feet dangling, there's no doubt where you're going – off into the wild blue yonder. At that point, it feels really good to be snugly harnessed to a 'professional' who literally 'has your back.' Besides, now you now know what it must feel like to be a Siamese twin. The only thing left to do is to sit back and enjoy the ride, and be content to leave the 'driving' to someone else.

To be human is to dream of flying. Fourteen thousand feet over Florida, I got as close to fulfilling that dream as I ever will. However briefly and perhaps awkwardly, I stretched out my 'wings' and soared like an eagle. It takes a little over a minute to free fall two miles. Because the experience is so unusual, it compares to nothing else. Your hair sticks straight up as though pulled by a magnet. With nothing underneath or around you, the view from a couple of miles above Florida looks like the view from the space shuttle – I could see the curvature of the earth, the east coast of Florida, and the Atlantic Ocean. There was no sound as I recall, and no sense of movement – at least not of falling. If anything, it felt like floating. With the perception of all my senses heightened, it felt as though everything was in slow motion. One minute seemed like ten. Deceleration, when the parachute opens, is fast but smooth, like passing through a time warp or breaking the sound barrier in reverse. All of a sudden there is sound again, and you float for another five minutes or so, like a bubble, the rest of the way to the ground. The parachute holding you up isn't dome-shaped like in old war movies. It's a broad, highly-maneuverable, wing-shaped sail that can land on a dime – in this case a small circle of sand. It looks just like you're in a plane coming in for landing. Even in a mighty stiff breeze, all four of us landed gently on our feet. Arm in arm, giddy with excitement, and wearing ear-to-ear smiles, we felt – and to the camera we looked – like a team of astronauts who just had their first ride in space. Why wouldn't we? We had done just that.

I can honestly say I felt no fear – a little anxiety a few days before, perhaps, but nothing approaching terror. That wouldn't have been much fun. Perhaps the fact that we were family helped. In any case, there is photographic evidence that the goofy smile on my face never left. Riding a motorcycle is fun, but it doesn't compare to jumping out of a plane. The beauty of tandem skydiving is that there's nothing you need to know or worry about having to do. My sister and I would do it again in a heartbeat, but the experience was so gratifying, the thrill so unique and memorable, once was enough. It was the thrill of a lifetime for me. It'll be hard to beat.

Several things about skydiving seem to apply to life in general. For one thing, I had to trust that the person I was attached to for my jump knew what he was doing. There are times we all have to trust other human beings. Trust is a sacred thing, but it's in short supply these days, with every alleged breach quickly seized upon by the media. People traditionally trust clergy – particularly priests – with deeply personal information, often confiding their inmost secrets, failures, weaknesses, and sins. The abuse of that trust in any way is despicable. It happens, but fortunately, most rarely. Whenever human beings are involved, human weakness enters in, failures occur, and pain results. Once trust is lost, it's hard but not impossible to restore. Be that as it may, it's sad when a person concludes that they can never trust anyone again. To achieve health and happiness in life, we need to trust – just as much as we need to hope, to love, and to be loved.

Another thing we need to be happy and healthy is to let go – as I needed to let go of the safety of the plane in order to experience the thrill of free fall. The tighter you're holding on to something or someone, the harder it is to let go. But life without letting go now and then is hardly worth living. That doesn't mean everyone should try skydiving – just that, in order to experience life fully, we need to take a few risks. We need to let down our guard and become vulnerable. We need to trust other human beings, but above all, we need to trust a Higher Power who cannot disappoint. The thing we need to let go of more than anything else is our own fear. Hate is a terrible thing, but the greatest enemy of love is fear, not hate. Fear and ignorance are what cause people to hate and hurt others. Letting go – of fear, of hurt, of the past, of anger – frees us. When people are free, they come alive. Letting go is the only way to be free to enjoy life as it was meant to be enjoyed by its Author.

Going places is a great way to let go of things that are bothering you. A change of scenery always does a body good. Mike and I finally used up the last of our award travel miles flying to Oregon for a week in May. Now that Mike was sixty-two, instead of buying another twelve-month pass for our national parks, for ten dollars he was able to get one admitting him and anyone with him for the rest of his life. For six days we treated ourselves to an incredibly diverse sampling of nature's gifts. After feasting on fresh halibut, we headed into the lush temperate rain forest of the Willamette Valley east of Salem. Once I learned that Silver Falls State Park in the foothills of the Cascades was the locale of a movie I had recently seen, I was determined to witness its spectacular scenery for myself. The eight-mile Trail of Ten Falls was cold and wet, but indescribably beautiful. Being able to walk up behind these stunning falls close enough to feel their thunder was a rare thrill.

We found out that spring is wet in Oregon. It rains about every fifteen minutes as showers blow past. Mike and I were constantly juggling ponchos, umbrellas, and cameras in an attempt to stay dry and warm – mostly in vain. We noticed that natives don't bother donning rain gear at all, they're so used to being spritzed constantly. We must have wiped water droplets off our lenses a hundred times. The wind on Marys Peak, the highest point in the Coast Range, was so severe even the birds were hunkered down in the grass. On display everywhere was a glorious array of wildflowers. Roses – for which Oregon is famous – had begun to bloom, and in Eugene, the giant rhododendrons in Hendricks Park were at their peak. It started snowing on the way up to Crater Lake, its bold blue depths in stark contrast to the pure white cliffs encircling its rim, still wearing winter's shroud. Reluctantly, the sun struggled to pierce the veil of overhanging clouds and roiling fog with its warming rays. An endless procession of showers drifted in from the Pacific, misting the emerald coast and moistening its sand.

Taking a leap of faith fourteen thousand feet over Florida.

From Cape Sebastian on the Pacific, we moved north. In a dense coastal forest at the end of a perilously narrow road out of Coos Bay, we discovered a fern-floored canyon shaded by giant maples and cedars concealing two priceless gems – Golden and Silver Falls. Otherwise hidden from all but God's gaze, each plunged ecstatically over sheer rock cliffs onto mossy boulders a hundred feet below. Back by the sea, purple-blue lupines and buttery yellow bushes decorated the dunes. A dozen stalwart lighthouses, once casting silver beams to storm-tossed ships, still stand along the coast. Offshore, cormorants and terns congregated in cliffside colonies. Giant swells lapped rows of rocks along the shore, momentarily swallowing them whole before regurgitating them wholesale. Far out on an irritated ocean, thunderstorms crept ominously along a gray-green horizon. Heavy blue-black clouds cast huge shadows over Mike and me as we walked along Cannon Beach past Haystack Rock. Near the top of the coast, we turned back to revisit the Columbia River gorge east of Portland – home to a dozen picturesque waterfalls, each set like a sparkling jewel in the rain forest's verdant crown, adorned with mossy rocks and delicate ferns.

My sixtieth birthday came and went uneventfully on June 12, 2010. I thought I might start falling apart, but nothing has happened so far. My two sisters took me to a Japanese steakhouse for dinner. We acted silly as siblings do, eating a lot and having fun. There's nothing more to tell. Because most priests take their vacation during the summer, it's always a busy time for me running around to parishes filling in for them. In September, Mike and I were ready to set off on yet another feature-length trek to the Northwest.

In just under four weeks, we covered eighty-five hundred miles in Mike's now-tired 2001 GMC Yukon XL, towing almost effortlessly his twenty-three-foot Hi-Lo camper. After years of practice, our division of labor is highly refined – I navigate and cook, he does everything else. We enjoy every minute of it, even arguing, because we end up doing everything together anyhow. It's a long haul from Florida to Glacier National Park on Montana's border with Canada – twenty-five hundred miles. Having made the trip several times over the years, we knew we could cover that ground in seventy-two hours. With reservations at a half-dozen campgrounds already made and a well-mapped itinerary, we had no worries. This time around we were spared even the slightest mechanical difficulty. Even with eight tires, not a single flat. I love it when that happens. The weather was another story.

The view across St. Mary Lake, in which solitary Wild Goose Island is seemingly suspended, is one of the finest mountain panoramas in the world – even when it's windy, rainy, and cold, as it was when we arrived. The world-famous Going-to-the-Sun Road across Glacier was still open but so torn up, even the little traffic this time of year moved at a snail's pace. Most of the breathtaking viewpoints were off-limits due to construction. Photography was a real challenge, but Mike and I were up to it. Despite gloomy, foggy conditions much of the time, whenever the sun shone, however briefly, we snapped away. Hiking was a little muddy, but the stellar vistas Glacier offers – of crashing waterfalls, misty mountains, and spruce-lined lakes – were worth every slippery step.

Technically, it was still summer, but the telltale rusty reds and orangey golds of autumn had already appeared. Then, as if by magic during the night, everything turned white. We woke up to thirty-five degrees and several inches of heavy snow that had turned Glacier into a winter wonderland. Every tree and bush was iced, every rock and cliff face flocked. It was still snowing. Unaccustomed to this type of scenery, Mike and I were enthralled. We drove up to Many Glacier, and pulling on stocking caps and gloves, headed off to Ptarmigan Lake – some four miles away and a third of a mile uphill. Imagine walking through cold, wet sand – that's hiking through snow. It's work, but nature's finest hour is when she dons her pure white mantle. Earth's colors seem to glow all the more.

Skies finally cleared, gradually revealing Glacier's purple mountain majesties and resplendent rocks and rills gloriously reflected on her silver-surfaced lakes. Singing in the rain – to alert any bears in the vicinity – we hiked along the stony shore of Two Medicine Lake to Twin Falls. The weather wasn't any better on the western slope of the Continental Divide. Nevertheless, we watched liquid turquoise tumble down a red rock gorge, slogging our way through a fragrant old-growth forest of cedar. The still, crystal waters of Avalanche Lake, hemmed in by glaciated stone walls dotted with hanging groves of aspen and laced with thin white ribbons of falling water, glistened in the sun's fleeting rays. Before leaving Montana, we explored the pristine wilderness of Flathead National Forest for the first time, inching our way up narrow rocky roads to the top of two peaks. The whole world, it seemed, lay in solemn stillness beneath us.

Crossing Idaho's panhandle, Mike and I meandered through the ripe apple orchards of Washington State to the 'Switzerland of North America' – the wild and rugged alpine terrain of the North Cascades. Creeping like the fog itself 'on cat's paws' along a narrow gravel shelf leading to Slate Peak, we pierced the clouds beneath heaven's great blue vault. At seventy-five hundred feet, we thrilled to glimpse Mt. Rainier's shining cloud-capped dome towering over lesser pinnacles a hundred miles away. As we approached her more closely, ferns began to cover the floor of the forest at her feet, and moss the rocks on her lower flanks. She, however, coyly refused to reveal her buxom upper reaches, preferring to conceal her voluptuous slopes in a tight-fitting sweater of cloud. Glaciers hidden in the folds of her garment spawned frigid rivers that rushed down great gravel veins in her lush green skin. A tortuous two-mile climb took Mike and me to the base of world-class Comet Falls, hurtling from the lip of a lofty hanging valley, plunging hundreds of feet through space in three staggered tiers. Unexpectedly, just as we were taking our leave, Mt. Rainier disclosed the full measure of her cloudless beauty to our disbelieving eyes, looming large on the pale blue horizon, glowing with dawn's early light.

Moving on to the jagged Sawtooth Range in the heart of Idaho, Mike and I set out six miles into the wilderness, past the mountains' startlingly perfect reflection in Pettit Lake to lovely Alice Lake sixteen hundred feet above it. Searching online for likely scenic destinations, I knew I had to find this tranquil body of water, ringed with golden grass and pastel bushes, nestled at the feet of El Capitan – a great high wall of stone angularly jutting skyward. That entire day we heard no sound but the chatter of squirrels, the rat-a-tat-tat of woodpeckers, and the squawk of birds on the wing. Next we revisited after many years the desolate volcanic landscape of Craters of the Moon National Monument – an apparent wasteland of treacherous black rock stretching for miles. But underground, the skin of ancient lava flows cooled to form long tubes as the molten mass moved on. Armed with lanterns and flashlights, we explored the cramped quarters of these pitch black caverns, exposing their ice-lined floors and walls to the camera's all-seeing eye.

A far cry from when we began this epic journey, the weather now was warm and the sky was clear and blue, making the Tetons just inside Wyoming even more enticing. Crowned with the golden glow of autumn, the mountains taunted a horde of photographers attempting to capture their ephemeral splendor. Gilded groves of white-barked aspen competed for attention with grazing moose and dappled does. A coyote on the prowl stalked a herd of skittish elk. Pebbled ponds were fringed with patches of pink thistles and pale purple asters. The sweet scent of sagebrush – and the sour scent of smoke – hung in a haze over Jackson Hole.

In the Tetons, Mike and I witnessed an extraordinary natural spectacle, unlike any we had observed before. As if the universe paused to take a breath, a seemingly unnatural stillness came over Jackson Lake – stretching absolutely motionless for miles, as if fashioned from solid aquamarine. Traffic ground to a halt at the sight – an entire range of mountains reflected flawlessly across the vast emerald blue surface of the lake, stilled by an unseen hand, as if frozen in time. A scene that caused jaws to drop, it was as unsettling as it was wondrous. It was Sunday. God was showing off.

The Grand Tetons reflected on the surface of Jackson Lake.

From the back side of the Tetons, we revisited an old haunt and discovered a new one. On the edge of Idaho, a scenic byway led us past potato farms to two of the last undisturbed waterfalls in the Northwest. Upper and Lower Mesa Falls, resplendent in their natural forest setting, kick up huge clouds of mist as their indigo waters plunge headlong into the Snake River's twisting gorge. Then, almost by accident, we crossed back into Wyoming again, coming to a dead end down a long dirt road in the least visited cranny of Yellowstone National Park. Commonly called Cascade Corner, this little-known region is so inaccessible, spectacular waterfalls hidden away in its depths are still being discovered. There under storm-laced skies we sauntered along the terraced, white-capped Bechler River, racing relentlessly downhill through virgin stands of alder and fir, climaxing in a tumultuous cascade over broad Cave Falls.

On the way home Mike and I spent one more day in the Black Hills of South Dakota, paying our respects to the dead Presidents at Mount Rushmore National Memorial. Coincidentally, it was one of these Presidents – Teddy Roosevelt – who established our final destination, nearby Jewel Cave, as a national monument in 1908. Filled with veins of marble and delicate, sparkling calcite crystals, Jewel Cave is the world's second longest. With one hundred fifty-two miles of passages at the moment, it's still being mapped and explored.

This brings us both – you and me – to the end of another amazing journey, and to the end of this book. There will always be more places to go. But every journey – and every book – must come to an end. Life's journey, however, is far from over. Even when it ends, the most wonderful adventure of all begins. I'm looking forward to taking that trip, but I'm not in any hurry. My life is still being mapped and explored. My story is still being written.

Look back to where you've been. Don't be afraid to explore your life and tell your story. Map out where you'd like to go. If you hear a little giggle now and then, it may just be that you, too, are making God laugh!

My sister Beth and her kids, Charlie and Carol Anne Ford.